Camp TV

CONSOLE-ING PASSIONS
Television and Cultural Power
Edited by Lynn Spigel

QUINLAN MILLER

Camp TV

Trans Gender Queer
Sitcom History

Duke University Press   Durham and London   2019

© 2019 Duke University Press
All rights reserved

Designed by Courtney Leigh Baker
Typeset in Garamond Premier Pro and Helvetica Neue
by Copperline Books

Library of Congress Cataloging-in-Publication Data
Names: Miller, Quinlan, [date] author.
Title: Camp TV : trans gender queer sitcom history / Quinlan Miller.
Description: Durham : Duke University Press, 2019. | Series: Console-ing passions |
Includes bibliographical references and index.
Identifiers: LCCN 2018037344 (print) | LCCN 2018044915 (ebook)
ISBN 9781478003397 (ebook)
ISBN 9781478001850 (hardcover)
ISBN 9781478003038 (pbk.)
Subjects: LCSH: Situation comedies (Television programs)—United States—History and criticism. | Television—Social aspects—United States—History—20th century. | Transgender people in popular culture—United States. | Gender nonconformity on television. | Gender identity on television. | Homosexuality and television—United States—History.
Classification: LCC PN1992.8.C66 (ebook) |
LCC PN1992.8.C66 M44 2019 (print) | DDC 791.456/53—dc23
LC record available at https://lccn.loc.gov/2018037344

COVER ART: (Top) *Hedda Hopper's Hollywood* © Pamandisam, LLC,
David Susskind Papers, Wisconsin Center for Film and Theater Research.
(Bottom) *Beverly Hillbillies*.

for ERICA

Contents

ix   Acknowledgments

1   Introduction. **Trans Gender Queer**
NEW TERMS FOR TV HISTORY

27   1. **Camp TV and Queer Gender**
SITCOM HISTORY

55   2. **Queer Gender and** *Bob Cummings*
HOLLYWOOD CAMP TV

88   3. **Marriage Schmarriage**
SEX AND THE SINGLE PERSON

131   4. **Trans Camp TV**
METHODS FOR *GIRL* HISTORY

155   Conclusion. **Around-the-Clock Queer Gender**
DIGITAL CAMP TV

165   Notes
197   Bibliography
211   Index

Acknowledgments

For inspiration and support in completing *Camp TV*, I thank everyone who told me they (or their parents) thought Bob Cummings was flamboyant on TV (or IRL) in the 1950s and 1960s; students and staff at the University of Oregon, where I began teaching in 2012, and at Northwestern in Qatar, where I taught from 2010–2012; workers at Education City, PLC (Prince Lucian Campbell) and McKenzie Halls, Duke University Press, United Academics, Arabica, Bard, Tandem, Yordprom, Local Sprouts, Last Stand, New Day Bakery, Espresso Roma, the Red Barn, Sam Bonds, Slightly, Perk, the Goat, the Duck Store, the Den, the Bates College library, Maine College of Art, the Portland Public Library, the University of Southern Maine library, University of Oregon libraries, UCLA libraries, the University of Southern California archives, the Paley Centers, the American Heritage Center, Brigham Young University special collections, Dartmouth College archives, Syracuse University special collections, the Peabody, the University of Georgia special collections, and the Writers Guild Archive library; the University of Oregon College of Arts and Sciences, the Qatar Foundation, the Sarah Pettit Fellowship, and the UCLA Film and Television Studies Visiting Researcher Stipend; Julie Tripp and Ker Cleary, Wendy Chapkis and Gabe Demaine, Sarah Holmes and Anna Schwartz, Natalie Phillips-Hamblett, Priscilla Layne, Marty Fink, Kate and Rebekah Rockwood, Angie Morrill, Anna deVries, Malic Amalya and Nathan Hill, Gabriele Hayden and Caitlin Mitchell, Jordache Ellapen and Jed Kuhn, Myron Beasley, Roger Mayo, Anthony Ruth, Shoniqua Roach, Chuck Kleinhans and Julia Lesage, Patricia Parcells and Christine Robins, Marilyn and Stretch Graton, Liz and Spencer Rand, Cy and Ron Barabas, Fran and Sandy Furman, Scott Miller, Chen Siwei, Vera Miller, Gary Miller, Kufners, Everses, Dorns, OSU's pop masculinities class, Jeff and Peggy Schanke, Herb and Dianne

Schanke, Helen Scattabo Schanke, Marge and Skip Miller, Jed Bell, David Leonard, Mimi White, Jim Schwoch, Nikki Dela Peña, Bianca Apps, Saeed Mohamed, Erin Libby, Arnold Marcelo, Mel Aquino, Christopher Hurless, Joe Khalil, Zachary Wright, Michelle Telafici, Rami Zein, Linda Toocaram, Muqeem and Minakshi Khan, Tim Wilkerson, Sonali Pahwa, Melissa Martinez and Kody Gerkin, Ann Woodworth, Sue Pak, Nikki Krysak, Robert Vance, Shakir Hussain, Hamid Naficy and Kelly Edwards, Allwyn Tellis, Wassan Al-Khudhairi and Orlando V. Thompson II, Sophia Al-Maria, Michelle Dezember, Margaret Rhee, Zach Cheney, Claire Graman, Diana Martinez, Dina Muhić, Steven Norton, Tyler McGuire, Ryleigh Nucilli, Danielle Seid, Dana Atrach, Sharifa Ahen, Scott MacDonald, Jerry Tartaglia, Raquel Gutiérrez, Gail De Kosnik, Jimmy Neal, Joe Medley, Lorrayne Carroll, Susan Feiner, Hugh English, Lydia Savage, Richard Grossinger, Lindy Hough, Oblio Stroyman, Aydian and Jenilee Dowling, Dorn McMahon, Melissa Johnson, Christopher Bartlett, Steve Rust, Arafaat Valiani, Chaim Vanek, Matt McLaughlin, Kurt Neugebauer, Debbie Williamson, John O'Malley, Rosalie Roberts, John Fernelius, Bill and Lynne Rossi, Harry and Connie Wonham, Mark Quigley, Tres Pyle, Paul Peppis, Libby Wadsworth, Corbett Upton, Mary Celeste Kearney, Michael Kackman, Chris Becker, Mena Mitrano, Racquel Gates, Meghan Sutherland, Devorah Heitner, Erik and Erin Larson, Beth and Veronica Corzo-Duchardt, Nargas Oskui, Linda Long, Lesli Larson, Sean Sharp, Sara Tripodi, Alisa Freedman, Julia Heffernan, Tina Gutierez-Schmich, Maure Smith-Benanti, Chicora Martin, Karma Chávez, Ryan Conrad, Jenifer Presto, Jeneé Wilde, Lisa Rogers, Lisa Shano, Lynda Frank, John Perry, Glen Tippin, Jyoti Kuhl, Rick Bouchard, Ron Unger, Jevon Peck, Doneka Scott, Kay Bailey, Michelle Wright, Audra Mahoney, Veratta Pegram-Floyd, Tim McGovney, Kevin May, Terry McQuilkin, Beth Magee, Julie Anderson, Josh Buetow, Liesl Johnson, David Yorgesen, Susan Meyers, Kathy Furrer, Karen McClain, Donna Laue, Marilyn Reid, Melissa Bowers, Lara Bovilsky, Liz Bohls, Anne Laskaya, Stephanie Clark, Heidi Kaufman, Stephanie LeMenager, Mark Whalan, Lee Rumbarger, Michael Hames-Garcia, Ellen Scott, Ernesto Javier Martínez, Lynn Fujiwara, David Vásquez, Karen Ford, Ben Saunders, Kathleen Karlyn, Jill Hartz, Richard Herskowitz, Mike and Keri Aronson, Carol Stabile, Kate Mondloch, Tara Fickle, Mike Allan, Colin Koopman, Dan Rosenberg, Justin Alves, Sergio Rigoletto, Gabriella Martínez, Daniel Steinhart, Masami Kawai, Dan Wojcik, Sharon Luk, Hank Alley, Shelley Stamp, Alfred L.

Martin Jr., Louise Bishop, Dianne Dugaw, Ralph Hofsaes, Michael Beluzzi, Courtney Rath, Martin Gostanian, Kathy Brown, Kole Oswald, Chris Finley, Courtney Leigh Baker, Jim Kleinhans, MECA, CSWS, Lillis, Lawrence, the EMU, Ryan Powell, Kara Keeling, Roxanne Samer, Elizabeth Peterson, Priscilla Yamin, Deborah Jaramillo, Jennifer Porst, Amy Sloper, Mary Huelsbeck, Jeffrey Jones, Ruta Abolins, Mary Miller, Mazie Bowen, Lucas Hatlin, Keith Burrell, James D'Arc, Sarah Wald and Caleb Connolly, Kirby Brown and Katherine Carvelli, Courtney and Peter Thorsson, Avinnash Tiwari, Betsy Wheeler and Jordan Shin, Lisa Gilman, Sangita Gopal, Mary Wood, Nick Davis, Ned Comstock, Hilary Swett, Mark Williams, Mark Quigley, Linda Mizejewski, Ethan Thompson, Lynn Spigel, Jeff Sconce, Rasha Al Sarraj, Sailor Winkelman, Ron Gregg, Priscilla Peña Ovalle, Sara Leone, Ken Wissoker, Elizabeth Ault, the two generous reviewers of this manuscript, and Erica Rand. I acknowledge the support of an Oregon Humanities Center subvention, and thank Scott Smiley for the index.

Introduction. Trans Gender Queer

NEW TERMS FOR TV HISTORY

Sitcoms of the 1950s and 1960s are littered with queer gender, gender involving stigma and negotiations of nonconformity. Yet the prevalent common sense, outside of camp sitcom fandom, has been that there isn't much to discuss in terms of queer sitcom history until the 1990s, when gay characters—white gay characters—become regularized, mainly in quality sitcoms directed at upscale markets, without any comparable influx of trans characters.[1] Transgender representation in particular is widely believed missing from mass media until recently and considered by some impossible prior to the emergence of the term *transgender*. Against this common sense, I argue that queer trans cultural production, namely genderqueer representation, was not at all absent and instead actually characterizes the pre-1970s output of the TV industry. Homogenous white middle-class families presumed cis, in other words thought antithetical to "trans," constitute the primary image associated with situation comedies. Gender-conforming families and suburban neighborhood ensembles occupy cultural memory as the overwhelming norm in the 1950s, but many series without a central married couple and kids were regularly pitched, piloted, and programmed.² Both these series and those that do provide a nuclear family and recurring domestic scene include queer gender.³ In the context of ridicule, queer gender emerged as a staple, a category of consumer product that is reliable by way of repeated reinvention, especially through sitcoms. Taking stock of the consistency of queer gender and the variety of ways in which queer gender manifested in sitcoms on the perceived cis side of 1950s television representation complicates ideas about trans difference and its queer possibilities in the past, as well as ideas about television, and what is possibly at play in TV production, understood as the production of television culture and TV texts. Archival objects preserving a record of texts, including episodes, personalities, brands, ensembles, stories, and ephemera, are a valuable source of queer gender expression transmitting trans history on a displaced wavelength.⁴

Sitcom history is not a history of progress toward positive representation. Sitcoms were a prime Hollywood export in the 1950s and 1960s, inseparable from US imperialism, sexism, and status quo race discrimination.⁵ Yet the roots of situation comedy camp are within black "dandyism," minstrel shows, mixed blackface performance, and other traditions emphasizing the overlap of Jewish and African Americans, or rather these and other diasporas commonly excluded from dominant conceptions of "American"-ness.⁶ I focus on the 1950s and 1960s in order to invert and redirect the notion that queer representation came later—and that trans representation comes way later, with both appearing only long after programming is established as resolutely heterotransphobic. Queer gender production is as constant as the over-the-top obsession with binary male-female segregation in sitcoms. No matter how insulting, jokes at the expense of gender nonconformity and gender nonconforming characters are a part of trans history. Furthermore, being relegated to the butt of the joke is far from the whole story.

I focus on the 1950s and 1960s and on the commercial art form of the sitcom in order, additionally, to depart from the notion of subversive TV content covertly "worked into" programs transmitted across "thin" air. This "thin air" rhetoric erroneously suggests that minority representations are encoded while dominant representations just are.⁷ The mindset that this metaphor represents, and the metaphor of queer makers and readers smuggling LGBTQ+ content into, or alternatively poaching LGBTQ+ content from, a mainstream, implies that the wavelengths across which television feeds traveled were suffocating. These ways of thinking legitimize the epistemology of the closet, and the presumption of straight identity and cis gendering in cultural meaning as well as in people. The general idea about this period is that at the time you would have had to work hard to sneak minority and especially queer content "into" broadcasts. This idea, however, is simply naturalized heterosexuality, a taken-for-granted confidence that new media technology starts out straight, and in this case persists as straight for at least the first two decades of commercial TV, in spite of abundant evidence to the contrary. As this book will demonstrate, the thing that is believed to be missing is already there, in the form of queer gender—a form of camp that, as Jack Halberstam argues, "profoundly disturb[s] the order of relations between the authentic and the inauthentic, the original and the mimic, the real and the constructed."[8] By virtue of television, in particular, camp was a part of popular culture in advance of the late-1960s, before the time that scholars have, so far, expected it.[9] Camp was ubiquitous in the 1950s during the solidification of a volatile system of Hollywood studio production both synonymous and in tension with white middle-class family privilege, a production culture and infrastructure linked to what was initially a primarily East Coast phenomenon grown locally in and gradually rerouted to LA. Camp was the status quo in the industry and social context of Hollywood TV, which developed over the course of the 1950s and 1960s. Counter to commonsense assumptions about queer representation as among the first material to be censored, spikes in sitcom camp during the period correspond with the imposition of stricter limits on explicit representation.[10] The possibility of pseudonymous script submission and the practice of dispersed series conception, writing, and revision in the sitcom business makes TV in the period of particular interest for trans scholars of popular culture, whose subjects of interest (whether trans or not) may change names, use pennames, adopt nongiven names for their poetic/commercial resonance, and have given names that evoke self-invention in how they look and sound. *Camp TV* theorizes and historicizes forms of expression such as naming as *trans gender queer*, and as a resource for people in the present invested in mobility among multiple genderqueer positions. This term *trans gender queer* is a placeholder for the genderqueer within pop culture products assumed to be exclusively cis.[11]

The concept "trans gender queer" refers to the possibility of reading gender cues that are more specific than male and female, masculine and feminine. This is a possibility that existed (even though the term genderqueer did not) in the 1950s and 1960s, for example, people classified as "women" who at that time produced, through performance and embodiment, effeminacy, the principal queer gender this book relates, understood as a stylized nonhegemonic antimasculinism, or, in other words, feminine and masculine "of center" at once.[12] *Trans gender queer*, which positions *gender* as a multiplicitous switch point between *trans* and *queer*, accounts for prototrans subject positions and for nonbinary orientation missed and misidentified because of the conventions surrounding categories such as "women." The phrase signals affinities among the contemporary terms transgender, genderqueer, and queer, and among those three labels and lethal vestigial categories such as "spinster." These overlaps signify "homoerratically," in an eccentric space, in other words beyond straight-gay, female-male, and trans-cis binaries.[13] In the ephemeral TV broadcasts of the 1950s and 1960s, producers signaled some of the ways in which *male* and *female* were insufficient for conveying the depth and surface details of personality, self-conception, and attraction. Situation comedy made in the 1950s and 1960s, and the materials that remain documenting its making in the context of reshuffling identity norms, show that, in the early years of incorporating radio, film, literature, comics, game shows, and vaudeville and stand-up comedy for commercial TV formats, much of the medium's cultural power came from trans gender queer camp, in situational humor about social norms and taste distinctions and in seemingly throwaway punch lines and bit performances.

According to Judith Butler, gender in the context of cis-heterosexism *is* situation comedy, a kind of real-life system of typecasting. Butler's *Gender Trouble* notes that subcultural identification of dominant white gender norms as absurd generates knowledge-power as the foundation of minority perception: "Heterosexuality offers normative sexual positions that are intrinsically impossible to embody, and the persistent failure to identify fully and without incoherence with these positions reveals heterosexuality itself not only as a compulsory law, but as an inevitable comedy. Indeed, I would offer this insight into heterosexuality as both a compulsory system and an intrinsic comedy, a constant parody of itself, as an alternative gay/lesbian perspective."[14] This also describes the daily practice at the site of production of what Chris Straayer calls "a queer viewpoint," a perspective that "raise[s] questions and propose[s] strategies that reveal subtexts and subversive readings in a more complex system than the patriarchal heterosexual system assumes."[15] Gender is, as Mark Booth also indicates, a site of camp production. Camp transforms perception: "In the extent of its commitment . . . parody informs the camp person's whole personality, throwing an ironical light not only on the abstract concept of the sexual stereotype, but also on the parodist."[16] Concurrent parody of gender norms and self-parody (genre parody) characterizes the ironically "more complex system" in sitcoms of the 1950s and 1960s. This programming displays a "guest-star system" that parodies the star system of classic Hollywood cinema, meaning that in terms of casting and characterization, queer representation, generally in the form of queer gender (intersecting with constructions of ethnicity, nationality, and language) was metamarginalized.[17] In the 1950s, many popular entertainment precedents contributed to TV's instantiation of hierarchies of respectability and value by advertising the "intrinsic impossibility" of white gender norms."[18] The guest-star system evident in sitcoms in this period provides evidence of the industry production of camp as part of that process rather than as purely a response to a preestablished normalcy.

The guest-star system that positions the incisive absurdity of sitcoms as evidence of queer knowledge is a system of signification that highlights character actors, people considered supporting players who are, within and against the grain of the system, a central attraction, performers such as Richard Deacon, Kaye Ballard, Charles Nelson Reilly. Actors of this stripe are marked as eccentric (a productive euphemism for queer spatial maneuvers vis-à-vis the centrifugal force of norms), through a structured matrix of hierarchies in role.[19] Directors often cast Deacon, for example, as characters "of some importance—a doctor, lawyer or state department official—who suffer foot-in-mouth disease."[20] I am concerned with issues encompassed within this system of typecasting character actors into idiosyncratic roles, that is, with actors who are from a camp point of view the stars of network television. According to TV scholar Jeremy Butler, "Most of the time, we do not concern ourselves with the work the actor used to create the performance. Indeed, the television program erases the marks of that work by emphasizing the character as a 'real' human being rather than a constructed collection of character and performance signs."[21] Butler refers to dominant modes of reading; the work of acting is historically the audience's starting point in the context of camp.[22] Character comedians draw attention to sitcom performance as work even as TV naturalizes these performers as their characters and the characters as real friends to viewers. Camp actors, especially character actors, are historically publicized for eccentricities in their own private lives. These eccentricities often relay an askew relation to marriage and involve a realm of associations that play with and against gender expectations. In one indicative case, a reporter remarks that Deacon lives alone on "a steep, slightly winding street in Beverly Hills... except for [a] pet schnauzer. (It's [identified reductively as] a female but Deacon calls her 'Fred.')"[23]

Ingrained publicity patterns, part of casting and performance tropes manifest onscreen and off, render the character actors of television comedy consistently and iconically eccentric. The example of Kaye Ballard, a talented camp performer as an unruly Italian, illustrates how a typecast actor's career may be marked by queer gender across many venues, in this case musical theater, cabaret, clubs, summer stock, burlesque, off-Broadway, vaudeville, and, in the broadest sense, street theater, or everyday behavior from red carpet shoots to Internet presence.[24] Ballard began working in television in the early 1950s and scored a series role in the 1960s opposite Eve Arden in the Desilu-produced *Mothers-in-Law*, one of many series set in Southern California, this one self-reflexively featuring a TV writer as one of a set of husbands.[25] *The Mothers-in-Law* is camp TV. Many deem it worthless, or if not worthless too painful to watch. Yet countless viewers have absorbed some subset of the repetitive queer gender in the around 1,232 minutes of the series, as it originally aired, during rebroadcasts, and beginning in 2010 on commercial DVD. Ballard also appeared in TV specials, anthology programs, comedy variety hours, as a guest on and guest-host of talk shows, and in single-episode sitcom roles.

In the *Patty Duke Show* episode "The Perfect Teenager" (March 4, 1964), for example, Ballard, as Selby of Selby's School for Models, makes a parade of strict white gender norms for an audience of young people. Ballard-as-Selby represents the modeling and advertising industries and, broadly, the social phenomenon of "schools... designed to instill self-confidence," or upward mobility by way of aestheticized and sculpted gender norms. Ballard's short haircut with stylized sideburns, and bolero jacket featuring suitifying contrast pockets are examples of the queer gender the guest-star system of sitcoms ingrains in TV, creating comedy through contradiction. The costuming and accessories showcase a typical sitcom irony, that gender nonconforming characters (such as Phil Leeds's Mr. Pell, "the famous commercial photographer" who twice visits Selby's classes in the episode) dictate *and* undermine "male" and "female" as natural conditions.[26] Ballard's accent as Selby morphs for comic effect, taking up normative, ostensibly impressive English to intone, "The world judges you in how you move, talk, and look."[27] In this case this expert in coaching the most prized forms of femininity unmistakably deviates from those characteristics, and is shown to be in control of the behavior, as if it is a choice to be different to be funny—within both

FIGURES INTRO.1–INTRO.2. Kaye Ballard in the *Patty Duke Show* episode "The Perfect Teenager," March 4, 1964.

the story world and in the context of its construction—as when Ballard's Selby abruptly trades effusive French for a skeptical Brooklyn accent. In general, Ballard was coded and self-coded as non-white-normative and transgressive, as an energetic, over-the-top white ethnic type within a harshly but incompletely segregated racial landscape.

These signifiers at play in Ballard's camp persona and in performances in programs from *Mel Tormé* (1951) to *Hollywood Squares* (1967–75) may seem to have nothing to do with trans representation as defined in terms of personal identity. However, as I will show, such character actors are powerful conduits of trans gender queer content, aesthetics, and affect. Not everyone's self-identified sexuality category stems from a strict quantification of gender of object choice, the conventional means of calculating social role. Queer gender for genderqueer trans people can entail nonbinary modes of attraction as well as self-conception. This is a link between queer and trans discourses more commonly manifest in trashy sitcoms and classic TV than in contemporary quality subscription programming. In a 2017 episode of the half-hour episodic series *Transparent* titled "They Is on the Way," the brilliantly blundering Sarah Pfefferman character (Amy Landecker) declares that someone (a sibling) isn't trans but rather is genderqueer, nonbinary, in dialogue painfully implying—without riposte—that nonbinary and genderqueer people are not trans.[28] I have written *Camp TV* to insist on the opposite: to argue, by way of ridiculed sitcom characters, for the continued value of recognizing nonbinary and genderqueer expression as trans. A cultural legacy excessive of the increasingly narrowing conceptions of trans representation in dominant discourse has a widespread history in television, long before digital programming such as *Transparent* and the spate of sexual minority characters in the 1990s conventionally understood to anticipate queer TV. Pre-1970s situation comedy is considered not to have lesbian or gay representation, but there is no dearth of lesbian/gay representation. There is an excess of queer trans signification, the queer gender of which signifies as all of the above at once. The camp and queer insight here aligns with but exceeds the knowledge of producers: sitcoms are constructed texts.

Sitcom Characterization as Camp Drag

The queer and trans history intertwined in sitcom history foregrounds white typologies of social difference, such as secretary-playboy dynamics at once emblematic of white patriarchal ideologies and indicative of camp. Industry processes rather than any one person or set of queer workers produced the queer trans camp within dominant discourse.[29] To explain this dynamic, I address the art within the typecasting of performers such as Rose Marie, Ann B. Davis, and Nancy Kulp. Kulp, Davis, and Rose Marie are TV icons, camp icons, and icons of camp performance in 1950s and 1960s sitcoms. Rose Marie is Sal, Sally Rogers, a comedy writer character in the acclaimed 1960s series *The Dick Van Dyke Show* who works on the staff of the TV-variety-show-within-the-sitcom *Alan Brady*, and by virtue of serving as the typist of the writing team is often recalled as a secretary.[30] The *Dick Van Dyke* episodes "The Pen Is Mightier Than the Mouth" (February 19, 1964) and "Dear Sally Rogers" (February 23, 1966), among others, showcase Sal's talent. In these two programs, Rogers, who is usually positioned behind the scenes, appears in the spotlight of the late night talk show *Stevie Parsons*. As is consistently the case, Rose Marie's performances as Sal showcase modes of embodiment such as finessed limp wrist action symbolic of the shared affects and affectations of gay/lesbian and queer/trans social formations.[31] Across many series, Rose Marie is an explicit signal of traditions of industry camp and queer gender production, as a character actor, and, more specifically, as a character actor conducive to ironic coupling scenarios due to typecasting as an industry insider. Rose Marie's Sal in *Dick Van Dyke* and Rose Marie's many appearances outside of *Dick Van Dyke* mediated the marginalization of previous comedy production modes, through characterizations speaking to the continuation of early sound film, vaudeville, and various stage tropes and traditions in the simultaneously consolidated and dispersed forms of situation comedy.

Ann B. Davis, best known as middle-square housekeeper Alice Nelson on *The Brady Bunch*,[32] and Nancy Kulp, who is typically memorialized as the self-satisfied and superior assistant Jane Hathaway on *The Beverly Hillbillies*,[33] appeared in structurally similar positions, as did many character actors. Together, these three performers alone spent a combined 140 years as actors transcending stereotype, in other words inventively escaping that pigeonhole of phobic projections that is the stock persona of the "man-hungry old maid," a stark lesbian type desexualized, vilified as sexually aggressive, and often portrayed as lacking self-awareness despite quick-witted intelligence. "Secretary" is a telling code, one enmeshed with common stock roles and conventionally defined, through cis sexualized insult, as secondary. These actors and others who played to the type appeared in pairs with gay playboy counterparts, where "gay" refers ambiguously to a light, humorous, camp sensibility and to gender and sexual nonconformity. Instances of Kulp, Davis,

FIGURES INTRO.3–INTRO.6. Rose Marie in the *Dick Van Dyke Show* episodes "The Pen Is Mightier Than the Mouth," February 19, 1964, and "Dear Sally Rogers," February 23, 1966.

Rose Marie, and other performers, such as Eve Arden, Imogene Coca, and Mary Grace Canfield, in versions of the recurring stock role, whether secretaries specifically or some other version of "career woman," and the rote but idiosyncratically passionate attraction they perform, constitute the core of the camp TV archive I assemble for this study.[34] As the compendium of typing involved in camp TV demonstrates through the workings of stigma converging in sitcoms, unmarried characters and other characters through which producers constructed queer meaning sustained "opposite-sex" interest (a misnomer in that there are no fixed binary opposites) as a signifier of nonstraightness with respect to white norms. This is a trans pattern.

The sitcom is a standardized format, a category of industrial production, designed to optimize advertising profits and investment returns through long- and short-term audience investment. Sitcom production involves freelance writers, writing teams, staff writers, consultants, rewriters, sponsor and ad agency representatives, network censors, story editors, executives, actors, talent agents, directors, and others. The material records of the process of producing sitcoms combined with the often instructive camp content of sitcom programming reveals in a formal way what Matthew Tinkcom calls "the specificity of how subjects come to have consciousness of the conditions of their labor" in specific historical moments.[35] The sitcom is, as Jane Feuer writes, "the most basic program format known to the medium" of TV and an integral component of what Raymond Williams described as TV "flow."[36] The role of sitcoms in the arrangement of TV content is indicative of what Mimi White calls television's "dispersed mechanisms of continuity," and emblematic of characterization and casting across TV genres.[37] Sitcoms foreground, as part of the pleasure, "clear narrative patterns" for continually inflecting, rather than developing, characters, through static and sometimes temporarily inverting characterization.[38] The guest-star system standardizes this contextually absurd formal element. As Gilbert Seldes writes, in an analysis of episodic scripting and casting practices, "Each new guest is supposed to be utterly ignorant of the qualities of the star-comedian, and by their astonishment, the familiar tricks are lifted to a level of freshness, the audience willingly sharing the delight of the guest."[39]

The many forms and ordinariness of drag in 1950s and 1960s sitcoms are tied to comedians' willingness to take on stigma within this structure. Character actors in particular attract perspectives that consider ridicule survivable. They inspire points of view that are queer in affirming the appeal of stigma. An episode of *The Bill Dana Show* preserved at the UCLA Film and Television Archive that originally aired December 6, 1964, includes the most conventional understanding of drag in narrative fiction: one-off guest characters scripted as men who change into clothing designated as women's and are then perceived as women by other characters. In this series Don Adams (*Get Smart*) is a hotel detective, and Bill Dana plays a character Dana would later decry as racist, bellhop José Jiménez.[40] This Theodore J. Flicker–directed episode, based on a script written by Dick Chevillat (*Green Acres*) and Ray Singer (*The Lucy Show*) titled "We'll Get You for This," features a plot about two older white criminals identified as men attempting a heist of the hotel in middle-class white women's clothing. The punch line is notable for its gender neutral address: "Not only are you mean, nasty robber persons, but I hate your dress." The phrase "robber persons" is a trans gender queer construction in that it makes space for recognition of nonbinary orientations to meaning. "Robber persons," here a witty, comedic phrase, is applicable regardless of gender identification and assignment. This is an example of writers inventing gender neutral terms for humorous effect, and not entirely at the expense of the gender nonconforming. With or without the drag costuming, this type of moment showcasing the performance of dialogue indicates camp strategies of wordplay.[41] Studio television productions display significant queer trans dimensions by virtue of such investment in creative language.

Other forms of drag range from impersonating someone of the same gender to taking a stage name. In show business in general, and especially in Hollywood studio sitcom production, names that may or may not be second (taken, as opposed to given) names are a denaturalizing default, especially in cases of second- and third-generation Hollywood workers. One touchstone in this respect is George Burns, who claimed to change names more than anyone in the business, beginning sometime after fourth grade, with one inspired by advertising on trucks on the streets of the Lower East Side of New York City.[42] I use the poetic and referential value of names to reproduce the queer character of the television texts I resurrect. I spotlight a range but only a sliver of performers with intriguing and compelling camp TV credits. I lay out this network in order to establish the continuity of queer television textuality and the texture of the broader social scene from which these sitcoms construct trans meaning. I track this constellation of type and typing to pursue trans representation in abundance.

In reconstituting this history as a history of queer production, I seek to rescript expectations about what television crews, casts, and writers were capable of producing in their own time period. Their presentation of nonconformity through a combination of dispersed authorship, dispersed continuity, the guest-star system, and the norm of episodic eccentricity brings queer and trans representation into being together in the same moment, over and over again in the "ethereal" past and present, in print culture and the remains of aired and unaired material.[43] Sitcoms adapted drag performance as banal, everyday sitcom content, in the tropes of crossed wires and missed connections that Lynne Joyrich and Ron Becker spotlight in work on the simultaneously regulatory and queer work at play in sitcom form. Sitcom camp was amalgamated from vaudeville, film, theater, and radio conventions during the transition in broadcasting from radio to TV comedy.[44] In accordance with advertising, sponsorship, and branding demands, the sitcom production context established formulaic deviance in character actors' personas over time as well as in corresponding conventions of casting, acting, costuming, framing, direction, set decoration, sound editing, and other aesthetic concerns especially prominent in studio production. In *Writing for Television*, Seldes describes television comedy as "a highly formalized, almost mechanized product."[45]

Camp as a mode of production constituted these formulas. In the corpus of TV comedy, camp draws attention to the context of Hollywood racism. Sitcoms are camp because they emphasize the industry conventions that establish who is marginal rather than central, in terms of hierarchies articulated both through the language of programming genres and in the narration of the history of the medium of television as a history of television programming. Comedy about commercial pressure to sanitize, standardize, and profit from social variance illuminates, along with the reliable appearance of queer gender in supporting, extra, and star characters, sitcom production as a Hollywood specialty of standardizing whiteness as the dominant norm.[46] This process of race-class-gender construction circulated as part of the discourse of programming from the time of television's initial mass marketing well into the liberation and civil rights era, during which time television broadcasts became somewhat accessible across the United States and its borders, in some places ubiquitous. The relevant literature, as Guillermo Avila-Saavedra states, suggests that in venues other than television such as vaudeville, stand-up, and comedy variety performance, comedians are free from "the rigidity of a sitcom character."[47] However, the supposed constraints of stasis create ironic possibilities for variety within the repetitious predictability of sitcoms, in specialized recursive forms. Sitcoms of the 1950s and 1960s are saturated with sexual representation and yet perceived as prudish. This is the artistry: that's "the camp," a critically queer payoff of exploitation, available to viewers (and self-defined nonviewers) in the historical period.

Hollywood TV at midcentury was a next phase in the simulation of heterosexuality. This corpus is replete with queer codes, or connotative signs of gender and sexual minority status. Straight gender relations consistent with white norms became an increasing priority for the television networks as the 1950s progressed. Relatedly, the importance of prepackaged advertising grew in its significance for global markets. As a result, the orientation toward white femininity and white masculinity further intensified. The initial period, featuring product endorsements performed live, was mixed and mostly unrecorded. With homogenization came wacky white-centric diversification, but much of what aired has been lost and forgotten. Despite scarcity, archives preserve evidence of queer coding and with it inventive ways of rejecting racist norms of perception, identity, and attraction enacted through binary gender.

The specific historical detail of midcentury US sitcoms is especially useful for understanding the workings of queer gender. Sitcoms are not usually recognized as camp productions, but they are important to look at in terms of camp, because they demonstrate how and why nonbinary and genderqueer constructions not only are trans but also are crucial to understanding the significance of trans oppression within systems of structuring inequality. Sitcoms are camp even before they age, due to their studio-produced efficiency aesthetics, their hyperreal content, and the calculated, self-evident white-centrism of the TV schedules. *Camp TV* shows that television's camp value is as immediate and powerful as its racism and gender policing, precisely because camp is so intertwined with both the perpetual whitening of TV comedy in the 1950s and 1960s and also simultaneously the multiply minoritized energies that constitute queer representation. I argue that there is queer representation in the sitcoms of the period. Further, in this queer representation, there is also transgender representation.

The operations of whiteness evident at the site of queer gender are instructive. Looking at sitcom texts and their production contexts while examining the simultaneity and correspondence of trans and queer representation demonstrates how camp became ingrained in media production through the popularization of television. Camp is smack dab in the ambiguous overlap of trans (genderfluid, transsexual, genderqueer) and gay (asexual, aromantic, lesbian, bi, pan, poly) identity—in other words, in the crossover space of the highly heterogeneous categories used to conceive of gender and sexual minority status. Camp is the experience of being both, of embodying supposed contradictions. I use my analysis of the material history of situation comedy in archives to shift camp's detection more equitably, away from the notion of white cis homos behind the scenes as the epitome of queer production. My account of the racializing binaries that proliferate this dominant image of queer Hollywood producers as white and not trans retools a set of prominent limiting presumptions: (1) that camp found its way to television only recently; (2) that camp consists of drag, defined as cross-dressing, understood as swapping hair and makeup; (3) that camp is sexist, homophobic, and transphobic; and (4) that queer representation is primarily about sexuality, whereas trans representation is primarily about gender.[48] In redacting these clichés, I show how the camp of 1950s and 1960s sitcoms is queer and trans as opposed to queer because it is trans. I question why censorship is presumed to eradicate this representation, and I hope to convince you of how abundant queer gender is in US sitcoms and popular culture. I show how queer gender complicates the idea that transgender history is a minority history not included in general television archives.

My focus on the production process sidesteps the general preoccupation with gender stereotypes as conservative and constraining. Genderqueer sexual expression, camp, and queer gender are examples of *trans gender queer* representation because they reference multiple queer gender representations in ways that move, or create imaginative space through language for the possibility of movement, across queer gender positions and expressions. This formulation *trans gender queer* guards against the kind of simplistic thinking that might, for example, in appraising some queer textual feature, consider naming elements of signification lesbian or gay but not both; transgender or genderqueer but not both; queer or trans but not both. In a time before the popularization of the term transgender and before the emergence of the word genderqueer, there was trans gender queer representation. Queer gender in sitcom production of the past is genderqueer camp and queer trans representation, in advance of its historical solidification in dominant discourse. Now, the term genderqueer and the notion of what it can entail is increasingly rendered distinct from the category of trans and what that concept is perceived to encompass. I articulate genderqueer culture as trans by analyzing queer gender in US sitcom history. Analyzing queer gender in the context of television history is a project of queer temporality encouraging TV texts to speak across time toward future transformation.

Television Archives, Unbinarized

The stakes involved in perceiving camp TV are high, in that perceiving this sitcom camp can mean reconceiving of gender. In the United States, television emerged as a linchpin of social cohesion during the decades following World War II, when it began to color daily life and recalibrate the experience of color. Television programming was the new media of the 1950s and 1960s and a major force in social relations and the reconfiguration of the techniques and terms of white cis privilege. Power relations shifted with the introduction of TV sets to the consumer market and the attendant proliferation of broadcast stations across the 1950s, which all transpired as the medicalization of categories for gender and sexual nonconformity continued, principally through scientific racism and class hierarchizing. While further instituting hetero norms, the shifts in TV created more space for queer signification within the representational system of the dominant culture, space for the representation of what Judith Butler describes as "desiring subjects who either fall outside the heterosexual norm, or operate within it... in 'perverse' or illegitimate ways."[49] Butler writes of subjects, but objects, including the intangible objects of television studies, also operate within and outside of norms, with productively perverse and "illegitimate" discourses such as slang as standby genre elements.

To document and analyze queer gender, I avoid classifying media makers, especially character actors, as female or male, rejecting the binary formulated categories of actors and actresses, queer men and queer women, and comedians and comediennes, male and female comedians. An approach that segregates by gender (or, worse, a naturalized "sex" status) is inadequate for understanding how producers animate live-action eccentrics through writing, casting, performance, and collaborative character typing. The beginning of regional television infrastructure coincides with the experimental stardom of Gorgeous George, a wrestler in a tutu whom historians recognize as achieving an indisputably queer fame by performing camp in the context of matches, through self-conscious parody of widely recognized stereotypes. So who comes between Gorgeous George and Charles Nelson Reilly? Who else is there besides Milton Berle and Liberace? Who else in addition to Eve Arden, Mary Wickes, Sheila Kuehl, and Kathleen Freeman? Beyond Judy Garland, and Agnes Moorehead's Endora? On top of Raymond Burr and Tab Hunter? More "manic" than Danny Kaye and Jerry Lewis?[50] In the construction of sitcom texts, scripts call for many actors and characters assigned to different gender categories to produce a lot of divergent, flamboyant, overlapping styles and eccentricities, which involve connotations of taste, race, ethnicity, appropriation, sexuality, class, and ability. The combination of these signifiers produces queer gender.

My analysis of this queer gender production process in *Camp TV* draws on additional names, centering the uncredited, to inaugurate a new reality, in which sitcoms revamp binary gender along queer lines, creating queer gender as part of the format. In this discursive space, there is no need to classify the people who made sitcoms as men or women. Any comedian may be untransitioned, in which case classifying them according to convention is wrong. Instead of appraising the historical record using an idea of the truth of "sex," which contradicts the self-assignment of trans people, I read sitcom production with genderqueer sensory perception keyed to both the material record and the ephemerality of performance in the production of prerecorded weekly US comedy series. Situation comedy of the 1950s and 1960s is not typically considered camp, yet these shows are camp and operate in the manner of camp in helping us "grasp a reality . . . totally separate from what is taught," thereby allowing us to "literally create a new reality."[51] Camp, as Michael Bronski writes in *Culture Clash*, is a way to "criticize social mores and structures while shielding [yourself] from retribution," which is what Michael Warner argues queer counterpublics do, and which was broadly necessary during the Cold War lavender scare.[52]

Bronski argues that you can create a new reality through camp, so why not do so with the history of sitcoms, the ultimate platform of complacency, the media technology definitive of the duped masses? According to Andrew Ross, camp is the "highly individualistic interpretation of role-playing within what is often a very restricted repertoire of stock characters. There is little room to maneuver, but the art lies in the virtuoso skill of maneuvering."[53] This applies to television in terms of consumers, producers, producer-consumers, and consumer-producers. As Julie D. O'Reilly, in *Bewitched Again*, explains, "As antithetical as it may sound to some, television makes me think, even television programming that is considered 'bad,' 'mindless,' or 'forgettable.' . . . Television programming makes me think long after I have turned off the set or closed the browser window. The thing television makes me think most about? How gender is depicted within its fictional realms."[54] Doty, whose writing advocates celebrating queer pleasure as a way of learning social justice, explains, "If television didn't exactly make me queer or a feminist, it provided an almost daily feeding and provoking of what became the queer and the feminist in me."[55]

The autobiographical writings of two well-known trans activists, Jamison Green and Leslie Feinberg, concur: fluff TV is fodder for critical self-production in terms of gender. In the 2004 book *Becoming a Visible Man*, Green describes NBC's 1955 broadcast of *Peter Pan*—starring Mary Martin as Pan—in Fred Coe's *Producers' Showcase* as "one of those lucid moments" that countered everything he was otherwise experiencing in being denied self-identification as a boy and continually discredited as a girl even though many other people also perceived him as he perceived himself, as a boy. "I clearly remember thinking," he says, "during Peter's first scene in the bedroom as he tries to retrieve his shadow, 'If she can be a boy, then so can I.'"[56] Seeing this show one time rendered maleness accessible to him on terms he considered his own, which was exactly what he needed to become the man he wanted to be and eventually become legible in general on cisgender terms. The world insisted he be a girl, but television supported his trans subjectivity, as well as a sense of parody as camp play evident in his desire to not just be a boy but to be a "much better boy" than Martin.[57] Trans experiences of programming are part of television history. This is less a fact to be proven with conventional historical evidence than an axiom along the lines of one of Eve Sedgwick's: "People are different from each other."[58]

On the flip side of Green's exhilarating self-recognition is the pain and punishment in forging queer gender that everyday life and TV viewing often involves, principally for some because of the use of studio or canned laughter (edited laugh tracks) constructing a butt of the joke and positioning gender-variant characters as subhuman outliers. By many accounts, the ridicule of queer gender resonates traumatically, as a stinging betrayal. In a 1996 manifesto of note titled *Transgender Warriors*, Feinberg recalls the impact of hir parents' periodic enjoyment of the drag routines Milton Berle performed throughout the 1950s. Feinberg writes, "[I] cringed as my folks guffawed when 'Uncle Miltie' . . . donned a dress," because "it hit too close to home. I longed to wear the boys' clothing I saw in the Sears catalog," but "boys were expected to wear 'men's' clothes, and girls were not."[59] For Feinberg, as for Green, time in front of the set is prominent within a lifelong process of opposing gender oppression. The pain is part of it, but it can't be the whole focus, especially if you take the actual lived existence of trans people (such as myself as a researcher formed by these texts in my own childhood) into account. Anecdotal evidence confirms that the medium was doing more than inflicting harm in circulating compensatory escapist entertainment in the 1950s and 1960s. The same critical consciousness that Green achieved through light TV fare came to Mary Ellen Cohane, a feminine cis folklorist, through the same broadcasts that stung Feinberg, inflaming self-conception. As a kid, Berle's performances informed Cohane's choice to butch up appearances to gain access to a neighborhood scene dominated by boys.[60] The *Texaco Star Theater* or *Buick-Berle Show* performances that stung Feinberg actually alleviated, in Cohane, a kind of gender dysphoria. For Cohane, Berle's facility with makeup and manners marked as feminine rejected the misogyny of the playground culture that curtailed Cohane's participation based on expressed femininity. Cohane wanted to wear dresses like Berle did, but also wanted equal access to a sexist social sphere, and Cohane saw Berle as a sign of future gender freedom and fortified femininity. Fans applauded Berle for the markers of femininity—dark lipstick, lush shimmery fabrics—to which Cohane was drawn.

In the context of the cissexist violence of the time (and of today), camp TV is an ironic resource. Many people commonly perceive the very appearance of queer gender in pop culture as a weapon that harms and polices. The context of the appearance of queer gender is conditioned by sexism, homophobia, and transphobia, and by intersecting ableism, racism, and classism. Moments of televisual rejection can be distinctly raw because the medium purports to be universal while obviously excluding. However, even in the context of this—yes, ultimately unfunny—cis-hetero "comic" othering, television is about a unique cultivation, for corporate profit, of intimacy, immediacy, and routine. Sitcoms in particular are familiar. Their racism, sexism, homophobia, and transphobia are predictable. The brutal rejection is a tradeoff: easy to ignore if you are attracted to gender and sexual deviance; possible to diminish through attention to the detail of the simultaneous queer trans camp comedy. The "invert" stigma that the dominant medico-juridical discourse assigns to "ugly" "females" and "emasculated" "men" has appeared inventively, deployed ironically, in devalued popular genres.[61] Alongside pulp novels, physique culture, Hollywood film, and pornography, fuzzy TV broadcasts transmitted the "stimulating aether of the unnamed," within what Sedgwick describes as the "stigma-impregnated space of refused recognition."[62]

My aim with the project is to express the possibility of attraction to queer gender (in terms of erotics and embodiment), using archives to open up contemporary discourse beyond antitrans logics of perception and sexual assignment. The classification of characters and performers as female or male is compulsory within academic discourse and popular mores at present. However, this practice actually prevents recognition of queer gender, and it is not a necessary part of cultural history or textual analysis. The parody of camp produces queer gender, queer gender I attempt to maintain by minimizing the commonly gendered pronouns "he"/"him"/"his" and "she"/"her"/"hers." I avoid these in my study even though conventions instituting their ubiquity and, in particular, normative patterns of relying on these words in close analysis and academic argumentation, by alternating between subjects' names and these pronouns, may make my diction seem off to some readers. Pronouns are a site at which the discourse of binary gender excludes. The rhetoric of only two possible categories for performers (male and female, comedienne and comedian) does a constant disservice to nonbinary-identified people. This discourse enacts violence material and symbolic—even when it is facilitating the legibility of lesbian, gay, and bi identities. Camp offers a better system of gendering for a better feminism.

Overview of the Book

In the chapters that follow, I reconceive of sitcom history on the basis of the imaginative evidence that sitcoms and sitcom records provide of queer gender. *Camp TV* presents sitcom art spurred on by reorganization after *Red Channels: The Report of Communist Influence in Radio and Television* (1950), a publication listing the Hollywood Writers Mobilization as subversive and the Hollywood Anti-Nazi League as defunct.[63] The rhetorical force of *Red Channels* had residual effects through the 1960s and its slant continues to contribute to a Cold War climate of xenophobic fear. In this context, camp TV is inventive and interrogated the workings of cis privilege in its own period. Yes, the emphasis in the industry on socially sanctioned heterosexual gender roles reinforced the idea of stable gender assignment, through a notion of sex perceptible on the body. At the same time, looks, size, movement, and differences of appearance, behavior, and taste became the substance of situation comedy. Increasingly, especially across the 1960s, sitcoms addressed discrimination in an oblique manner, through surreal civil rights analogies that articulated witches as women as queers as monsters as people of color.

During the 1950s and 1960s, the period of the emergence of commercial television, networks and agencies perfected tactics for profit. The system commodified broadcast and leisure time, providing free programming to viewers by selling them, as audiences in the abstract, to advertisers. Making television schedules and TV programming involved multiple traditions of showbiz insight into popular entertainment but also the type of demographics research that constructs mass markets. Situation comedy programming is emblematic of this commercialized sphere.

Sitcoms present "charged" humor, a transmedia phenomenon linking stand-up performance to social justice,[64] as familiar, in the context of ad-driven programming flow. In TV, prerecorded advertisements and sponsor messages organize sitcoms and, overall, the medium's self-reflexive address. Broadcast episodes are built around product placements, while patterned juxtapositions and sensory repetition feed the habituated rhythms of everyday life. Anna McCarthy highlights programs (such as sitcoms) as "supplemental necessities in the TV production sector."[65] McCarthy explains that, "in purely revenue-based terms," the "business purpose" of shows is "to secure an audience for the advertisements that appear within and between them." The charged content of sitcoms is notable in light of the ways in which "overinvolvement and excess are often defined as the normative goals of commercials [and] advertising researchers' perceptions of [advertising's] effects are ... based in a notion of mimicry."[66]

Sitcom writing and repurposing is crucial to the success of this system. Sitcom writing is an exclusive craft, and yet the rules of the art have been evident on the surface, in the repetition of sets, character typing, and situations of a broadly interchangeable sort, providing plot structure for joke after joke and performance play.[67] As Feuer states, "The situation has always been a simple and repeatable frame on which to hang all manner of gags, one-liners, warm moments, physical comedy and ideological conflicts. In fact, one could say that it has been the *ideological flexibility* of the sitcom that has accounted for its longevity."[68] In addition to characters and settings that continue from week to week, episodes of 1950s and 1960s sitcoms featured, as indicative of their conventions, witty wordplay performed by mugging actors, presented in medium- and long-shot combinations, with a laugh track mixed from recordings of coached in-studio audiences. Writers and actors were instrumental but disposable in legitimizing standardized ad breaks, audio-visual branding, and promotional rhetoric depicting television viewing as a way of life. *Camp TV* is a rendering of queer critical insight and antitransphobic camp from this disparaged body of work,[69] largely the result of the playful expertise through which freelance and contract laborers deliver camp as if it were normal, in incredibly crafted hypersurreal situation comedy.

The industrial apparatus of sitcom production and television textuality is still largely in place from the 1950s and 1960s. Studio-oriented sitcom production procedures continue to generate queer gender like clockwork in episodic comedy fare, through the norms of casting, scripting, shooting, editing, and scheduling half-hour comedies, and these elements continue to characterize web series and the comedy content circulating across digital distribution platforms. The networks claimed to censor sexual perversion, homosexuality, and deviance from all formats in the 1950s and 1960s. Sitcoms especially were expected to affirm wholesome values. Yet sitcoms were camp upon release; they are not only camp in retrospect, when an additional datedness sets their repetitive patterns in relief. Sitcoms debut as camp, and then much of that camp passes by most audiences, today and likely into the future. Some sitcom camp admittedly registers consciously with only a rare subset of viewers, those who can identify Elinor Donahue in an episode of *The Golden Girls* as Betty from *Father Knows Best*, for example. Dialogue, performance, costuming, and casting call up other roles, past and contemporaneous, as "Easter eggs," or hidden caches of instructive camp sensibility, whether these associations are deliberate, overdetermined, or specialty-fan based. Synthesizing the historical details of these referential connections as intertextual buoys for trans gender queer meaning making changes conceptions of US programming made in the 1950s and 1960s.

The first chapter explains how sitcoms—a category of standardized filmed studio productions formatted for commercial advertising segments—emerged in the aftermath of *Red Channels*, as the power of the TV networks (NBC, CBS, ABC, and for a time DuMont) increased relative to the influence of sponsors in the industry. Initially, during the era of live TV broadcasts, sponsors would finance shows and use them to promote products. Later, when the use of telefilm became more common, the networks sold short advertising segments to multiple advertisers, moving toward standardized commercial breaks. Changes in funding and formats, namely the delineation of situation comedy from comedy variety, dispersed authorship in sitcoms. The use of pilots, initial test episodes, and a weekly in-season production schedule meant that new episodes in each season could be written, rehearsed, staged, filmed, and edited in four or five days, at the same time as recently finished episodes were airing. This system solidified first after the crackdown on and reform of scandalous Jewish and other complexly appropriative ethnic comedy in the early 1950s. It then intensified following the quiz show scandals of 1958, which prompted the industry to promise the public more respectable, family-friendly TV fare. As the industry and many workers migrated west to Hollywood, and live broadcast productions were replaced by filmed and taped telecasts, schedulers sanitized programming of sexual, gender, and racial diversity while relying on a nonethnic-ethnic model of success in mostly segregated sitcoms. A screwy star system of character actors in guest appearances played off of conventional celebrity, facilitating the perpetuation of planned obsolescence and social inequality while occasioning queer gender and camp, all as a result of different industry entities vying for control over content and for influence with program producers, like Hollywood studios.

Chapter 2 narrates sitcom history within a trans gender queer frame, using archival research to explain the dispersed system of authorship, personnel relations, market research, talent management, and publicity strategy that Hollywood sitcoms involve. Across the 1950s, prime time comedy programs, initially broadcast live and associated for the most part with New York City, were increasingly made by studios in Hollywood, a home of industrialized film and media operations that has, as has New York, historically cultivated queer culture and collaboration as it constitutes and exports vicious hierarchy. Middle-class norms defined as white increasingly steered TV programming through the image of the audience. Early stars of the small screen that were at odds with ideals of pure whiteness faced program cancellation as audiences grew, and as the networks reshuffled shows in terms of day and time placement to optimize advertising profits and brand identity. With the move to the West Coast, television studio production processes meshed with a local system of racist stardom with global reach, in the form of radio, film, and music industry infrastructure. To draw out the dimensions of this, I focus on Bob Cummings, an icon of white-defined desire and identification.

Chapter 3 explains how Hollywood studio production proliferated queer gender through the mundane everyday process of creating comic distinctions set against social norms. Queer gender is expressed in moments and objects such as a look or a lilt, a scarf or a sweater. Queer gender corresponds to a discursive system inventively unhinged from ideas about "born" sex, binarized sex organs, sex practices, and secondary sex characteristics, "biological" gender, and other rhetorical instruments of racism, cissexism, ableism, eugenics, and genocide. The multiple meanings produced with and through queer gender signifiers in movement, costuming, and my principal concern here, dialogue, link up with a dominant system of signification in which the vast majority of people somehow consume, without recognizing, the queerness of gender. Using material records from archives, I question the rote presumptions about queer invisibility in network TV before the 1970s.

My argument about invisibility and the possibilities of supposed invisibility—possibilities I evoke through the stylistic use of pronouns and names in genderqueer combination—sets up an analysis in chapter 4 of a 1968 series I call *Girl*, which I discuss as if the property were still in process. The starting point for queer trans fan labor with *Girl* is that the series is not well known and is generally derided when it is discussed. The project is to trans feminize the text in concert with queer labor onscreen and off, while counteracting the medium's white-centrism, formulaic ethnic-nonethnic orientalism, and colorblind casting, a system of casting actors and writing characters within a white/other framework deflecting attention to ethnic specificity.[70] My research into *Girl* and the connection between a queer subset of transgender practice today and the comedy production of the TV industry in the 1950s and 1960s articulates the problems of recounting the history of sitcoms as if this history were straight (not queer). I use the convergence of sitcom wit and queer trans critique to counter the intertwined limited tendency to assume that television history is all cis. By contrast, the queer discourse of network TV very apparently, on the surface, participates in the production of trans culture, through comedy about attraction, dating, devotion, sex, and marriage; standard sitcom narrative formulas of character doubling, mistaken identity, makeovers, and miscommunication; and considerations of power relations and subject-object positions in commercial art production.

The concept "trans gender queer" refers to the possibility of reading gender cues that are more specific than male and female, masculine and feminine. This is a possibility that not only existed in the 1950s and 1960s but became rudimentary in the appreciation of TV comedy. Television is, as many scholars have long argued, about intimacy and immediacy, affect and affiliation, as something the medium uniquely cultivates, through routinized viewing. The camp TV archive of queer gender records nuance in a system retrospectively perceived as absolute in its relation to, in terms of its representativity of, heterosexism. Today, this archive enables a vision, or retranscription, of pop culture far beyond the scope of what television is supposed to entail. It demands a sense of history as more variegated than commonly understood in the present. The material and methods transmit the potential to attune to the heterogeneity of nonconformity. To model this research mode, *Camp TV* explores the process of recognizing within archives gender dynamics more complex than expected. The book advocates for interpretation of queer gender as a way to register its historically specific appeal in violently dehumanizing hostile contexts.

Camp TV and Queer Gender
SITCOM HISTORY

Camp, a critically queer mode of production attuned—even in highly appropriative commercialized mass culture contexts—to everyday theatricality, gains incredible momentum from casting, especially those cases when multiple camp actors perform together. In an exemplary instance, Martha Raye, Paul Lynde, Wally Cox, and Charlotte Rae, all luminaries of queer gender, brought their craft to the September 28, 1954, episode of *The Martha Raye Show*.[1] The combination of these actors in any situation comedy setting in any series would produce queer gender, from the recombination of their respective idiosyncratically characterized personas. However, this episode is extra special to note for its camp self-satire and coupling of Raye and Cox. Lynde portrays a television personality named Royal Gunderson, a newscaster who also hosts a talk show, *Gadding with Gunderson*, and is hysterically in love with the station's lipstick sponsor (the actual sponsor of Raye's program, the Hazel Bishop company). Cox's character is defined as a "Martha-murderer," a timid person on an absurd killing spree whom Raye, in explanation of Cox's comically-presented fixation on offing one Martha after another, diagnoses as likely "a hypersensitive chap who was raised by a miserable aunt named Martha." This premise, ironically resonant with homophobic and transphobic rhetoric while airing queer gender, prompts an abstract chase-dance routine featuring Cox reading Raye's diary and wielding an affected weapon, a left-pocketed scarf. Cox's characterization as an ambiguous threat devoid of muscles prompts Raye to go by the name of Irving, which Cox seamlessly uses to address Raye in an iconic deadpan manner. Following elaborate cross-cut choreography, Lynde's Gunderson character stages a reenactment of the unfolding news story of the "Martha murders," showcasing Raye and Cox, the actual participants. Orchestrating their encounter as a live entertainment scoop that feeds into an advertising segment, Gunderson exclaims about the surreal macabre news, "You just put my show in the top ten! Commercial!"

This self-reflexive emphasis on ratings and ad breaks, part of the matrix of associations productive of queer gender, came at a moment when the broadcast form of commercialized airtime was beginning to change in accordance with shifts in the overall balance of power in the industry.[2] Lynde's Gunderson character speaks of trading in twelve different sponsors for one, which, in the hyperbolic and inverting manner of camp, points to a real relatively recent increase at the time in the "magazine" strategy of juxtaposing consecutive short commercials between story segments instead of having hosts and announcers plug brands and products by directly addressing their audience. The comedy, that is, indirectly invokes the ascendance of the sitcom, a half-hour format that helped institute the magazine style of advertising in tandem with more covert product placement in place of explicit sponsor plugs. In the context of this uneven transition, queer gender resulted from casting. The combination and loose partnering of people with different vivid, idiosyncratic gender expressions in the comedy-variety-influenced form of the sitcom inspired the scripting and staging of ironic coupling. Writers, performers, and crew created queer gender by developing tropes of ambiguously believable romantic interest and sexual devotion. These easily repeatable character and narrative formulas were keyed to the changing rhythms of product shilling and industry-investor brand building.

This chapter explains queer gender as camp productive of a straightforward irony in characters and coupling that generates a discourse of trans representation. I analyze circuits of assimilation in the development of the television sitcom, choosing examples that are multiply iconic in terms of the performers, offstage producers, and intertextual references they involve. In other words, I intersect the robust resumes of exemplary producers of camp TV in order to argue for the significance in the present moment of the trans gender queer representation common in 1950s programming. Across changes in production and commercial context during the period, dispersed group efforts into situation comedy—including in comedy variety programming such as *The Raye Show*—consistently resulted in queer gender. I connect the trans gender queer camp in sitcoms to situation comedy in comedy variety in order to reconnect sitcoms to their influences from black minstrelsy and blackface vaudeville performance, which came to television by way of radio, film, and other entertainment traditions.[3] I use this multiply sourced queer gender in the context of my concept of camp TV as a retrospective antidote to the representational violence of the early commercial television era. The inequities of that period are still manifest today, in the persistence of broadcast airtime, including as a model for new media-commodified advertising, and in the differential value conventionally attributed to various TV-related objects, archives, and embodied practices of everyday life.

A Variegated Field of Trans Gender Queer Representation

The broad history of media industry appropriation of marginalized culture for the construction of whiteness appears within the history of sitcoms and their middle-class assimilationist norms as a kind of drag and as an infrastructure for unconventional forms of drag. Emerging formulas for network success, for example, briefly brought Gertrude Berg back to series TV in 1961. An intimate Jewish icon from *The Goldbergs* (1949–56, CBS, NBC, DuMont), a program generally considered with respect to the blacklist backlash and as the first sitcom on TV, Berg returned as Sarah Green in *Mrs. G Goes to College* (*The Gertrude Berg Show*, CBS), a less explicitly Jewish version of Berg's character Molly Goldberg in *The Goldbergs* who faced stiff competition from Screen Gems series about culture mixing like *O.K. Crackerby*, a sitcom about a New Englander tutor for the grandkids of a tycoon from Texas.[4] In this context, a queer Jewish context, understandings of drag tethered to conceptions of biological sex obscure the variety in trans gender queer representation interwoven with ridicule. The way that conviction in some noncultural meaning or information in "sex" can interfere with the process of appraising TV history is evident increasingly across the 1960s but also in the case of the most famous drag artist of US television in the 1950s, the Jewish comedian Milton Berle, a counterpart in the comedy variety format to Berg's success with situation comedy. Known by gender binarized appellations making "television" Berle's last name following a gendered honorific and construing Berle as an assigned-male member of the family (as "Mr. Television" and "Uncle Miltie"), Berle set a standard for facility with gowns, wigs, and makeup and is thus sometimes mistaken as the only one who participated in TV drag, which is far from the case no matter how narrowly drag is conceived. The post-*Goldbergs* cleanse of Jewish variety from the network schedules channeled the trans gender queer energy indicated by Berle's inspired version of standard drag into sitcoms.[5] Unlike Berle's notable guest star role in the 1959 episode of *The Lucy-Desi Comedy Hour*, "Milton Berle Hides Out at the Ricardos," camp forms of sitcom drag—and much of the camp of variety shows—did not strictly follow the binary gender rubric relied on in most scholarly analysis, including in feminist and queer media studies.

Trans gender queer representation excessive of "conventional" drag is evident in some striking camp characters in Berle's *Buick-Berle Show / Texaco Star Theater* ensembles. Ruth Gilbert's Max and Arnold Stang's Francis are two recurring gendernonconforming characters that center marginalization and indicate how the creative energies of the makers of television comedy crystalized in camp producers' characters onscreen, as a kind of drag.[6] Berle's situation-based sketches were self-reflexive, depicting the making of the show itself. Max is a "script girl," sexist/camp industry code for a continuity expert, a gendered labor position. Producers presented Max as indispensable to the production and as emblematic of the backstage setting from which television programs emerged. This character refuses to be overlooked or ignored, hovering, getting in people's faces, withstanding insult, and emphatically pursuing Berle and other celebrities sexually. This Max character controls the whole scene as an odd underling. With extreme deadpan, Gilbert decimates norms. You really can't miss the parody of gender conventions, even if you don't appreciate the eccentric details, because the actor delivers the dialogue idiosyncratically, punctuating trans gender queer lines with iconic nonnormative bodily and facial accent. In the basic comic scenario and characterization, Max is relentlessly, ridiculously devoted to Berle. The producers present this basic conception of Max's pursuit of boss Berle as itself comic, as an absurd takeoff on conventional hetero norms.

This parody, fundamental to TV in comedy genres and beyond, produces queer gender. The September 21, 1954, *Buick-Berle Show* episode, for example, illustrates how gender signifies independent of assigned and popularly perceived sex. In this episode, host Milton Berle looks about comically while farcically fretting over a short, suave Marlon Brando clone introduced as the president of the Milton Berle fan club and the club's one member. As Berle performs characteristic nervousness, conveying classically effeminate, queer Jewish TV poses encapsulated in the affected wringing of hands, the Brando tribute, performed by Nancy Walker—the future Ida Morgenstern, one of the Rhoda character's parents in *The Mary Tyler Moore Show*—is built from sullen bravado, ironic recklessness, utter disdain, and superiority in rejection of social convention, in counterpoint to Berle's attempts to manage cast and crew. Walker does Brando's signature brooding with a white, working-class rebel image especially evident through the chest and torso and in the hair and cap. While Berle refers to this person, "Marlane Brando," as "young lady," the fictionalized production culture that the situation comedy of this comedy variety program represents entails queer gender, even if it is popularly perceived according to a limited binary gender-crossing model of camp. As Berle self-deprecatingly remarks about the *Buick-Berle Show*, in confronting Walker's Brando and identifying with them and the other trans gender queer staples of the program, "I got a Max, and I got a Francis, and now I got one that looks like both of them put together. We should all be put away together." The details and finesse of stylized gender presentation supersedes performers' legal and social "sex" status in a space of trans gender queer camp.

The production of queer gender within the frame of nonbinary drag that carries over to sitcoms from comedy variety is clear in a sketchlike set piece from an episode of *My Friend Irma* (CBS, 1952–54), a series set in New York City, made in LA, and part of a franchise built around Marie Wilson. While cisnormative, heteronormative, and sexist in terms of the conventional "working woman" frame, this text is also trans gender queer camp productive of queer gender. Dialogue and performance question the logic of gender assignment. When, in the course of relating love trouble, Irma excludes Kropotkin, saying, "Only a woman would understand. . . . You're not a woman." Kropotkin's first retort is, "Only if you want to be technical."[7] The second is, "I can't help it—I got off to a bad start." In the world created by this exchange, gender expression does not require or benefit from a particular physical or biological makeup (even if that is what many viewers think that the laugh track implies). Narrative devices that start out gender essentialist veer. Kropotkin says, "I have qualifications: I cook, I mend, I sew. Why only last month I took first prize at the church bazaar with my afghan." As

FIGURES 1.1–1.4. Milton Berle and Nancy Walker in the *Buick-Berle Show* episode "7th Season First Show," September 21, 1954, invoking Marlon Brando.

Irma and Kropotkin practice twirling their cigarettes, femininity becomes a behavior cultivated through style and experimentation, with an unsettled relationship to bodies and looks prefiguring the publicized insights of trans people and the work of gender studies scholars. Femininity, though devalued, is fun and explicitly not a natural possession of white women, in the context of this TV comedy. In this indicative "sketch" element in one of the few preserved episodes of this program, producers represent an entirely different world than what is remembered or expected of the 1950s or would have generally been thought possible at the time. In this camp space, the legitimacy of gender presentation does not hinge on or necessarily even benefit from alignment with sex in medical, legal, or popular definition. This 1952 episode features Sig Arno, a German Jewish immigrant actor, as Professor Kropotkin, an artistic intellectual associated ambiguously with Europe. Arno is a trans gender queer performer in a trans gender queer role, with both the character actor and this particular part exoticized through formulas for building situation comedy from contextualized eccentricity.

The significance of this bit in which Kropotkin teaches Irma how to impress an affluent date is not in being any kind of "first."[8] It's not that this never happened before or did not happen elsewhere. My point is the opposite: there is so much queer gender in ephemeral embedded routines such as this that the history of queer gender resists conventional narration through tropes like "firsts." In camp TV the confluence of diegetic performances (scenes in which characters perform for one another) and dialogue that denaturalizes sex assignment produced a queer trans form of camp readily apparent in prevalent queer gender. In the case of this Marie Wilson–Sig Arno pairing, *Irma*'s producers treat "female" as a category that people who are not designated female or perceived as female can self-apply—or at least attempt (as part of a contest in which everyone fails). Twirling a cigarette, Kropotkin explains and embodies Hollywood femininity, while Irma, the ostensible ideal, looks on. Collective authorship is crucial to this representation. The producers use the Kropotkin character's queer relationship to gender as the focus of comic exposition. This strategy creates multiple forms of queer gender, as well as movement across these configurations. This is trans gender queer textuality, ethereal in its sources yet material in its effects, producing queer gender without attributing potentially incriminating culpability to any individual maker. Crucially, the name "Kropotkin" situates queer gender as ethnic-nonethnic; it potentially signifies as Russian, as possibly

Jewish, and carries an anarchist ring in the context of the widely translated Peter Kropotkin, while also resonating as simply quirky.

This surface-level character-actor-based characterization represents how queer gender persists through the 1950s and into the 1960s in the nonethnic-ethnic typing of sitcoms more strictly calibrated to white middle-class norms of decorum and consumerism seemingly antithetical to trans gender queer representation.[9] As white-centric norms gained further prominence in TV formats, and production processes established idealized boundaries of appropriate behavior, sitcoms swiftly deconstructed social codes in fleeting moments of wordplay and performance. The 1950s clampdowns on camp whitened the schedules, and the whitening of the schedules was an attempt to send camp packing. But it simply percolated more campily, with excessive semi-detectable flair. When the networks tried to disinvest in comedian-driven comedy programming in the late 1950s, producers responded sarcastically with more: more versions and variations of camp; more subtle rebuttals; more unexpected viewpoints, expressed through references, specifically the performance of scripted reference. Comedians continued to work with gender in all kinds of sacrilegious and intertextually charged ways, combining the unruly antics of screwball film comedy with traditions of stage and radio performance transferred to TV.[10]

Sponsors targeted vibrant, versatile Jewish shows for cancellation or reform, while people of color had a chance at mostly token roles. The queerer material was more often canceled. Sanitizing TV content—ridding it of anything unsavory or unpalatable, including evidence of queer existence and expression—was the overall business strategy. According to Susan Murray, practitioners understood the variety format "as a modern extension of turn-of-the-century vaudeville, an industry populated largely by working-class performers of particular ethnic backgrounds, the most predominant being Irish and Jewish."[11] Initially the networks promoted the stars of their comedy variety hours by playing up ethnicity. Situation comedies starring comedians with Jewish queer gender such as Phil Silvers appealed more than "traditional Anglo-Saxon heroes in the form of cowboys, drifters, or tough guys," but in the late 1950s westerns took over and sitcoms went more domestic.[12] Trans gender queer camp persisted in television comedy from the 1950s into the 1960s despite the fact that, after anchoring schedules with "vaudeo" (vaudeville on video, i.e., vaudeville by way of television broadcast), the networks pulled the plug. A "retreat from Jewish TV images" escalates in the late 1950s and into the 1960s despite "declining anti-Semitism" in US culture overall.[13] Vaudeo appeared "unsavory... particularly [in] its explicitly ethnic Yiddish humor and overly suggestive 'adult' content."[14] Comedy variety and other forms of talk television continued, taking on a bigger role in corporate synergy, such as through multimedia promotions, while sitcoms supported magazine-style advertising segmentation as well as sponsors. Scheduling and syndication strategies for profiting from the industry's fluctuating oligopoly solidified.

The expansion and consolidation of the industry included a streamlining of the practice of profiting from nonethnic-ethnic signification in the context of a racist, segregationist, white supremacist culture. The Chitlin' Circuit, the black network of vaudeville theater halls, hardly transferred to the new medium, with artists seeing more open avenues in music than in small-screen acting derived from stand-up comedy success. Comedians of the Borscht Belt, a circuit of East Coast Jewish summer camps in the Catskill Mountains, migrated unevenly but more successfully to TV, although in the views of many they did so at the expense of Jewish specificity. Their legacy became central to the sitcom, as did influences from newspaper comics to screwball films. The white normativity that emerged through the sculpting of the prime time schedules over the course of the 1950s and 1960s relied on Jewish entertainment traditions, including the disavowed legacy of racist blackface performance, which carried an appropriative trans gender queer charge through to the sitcom. This transmedia continuity of an industrializable comic repertoire sits at the nexus of settler camp orientalism and single/dating/marriage comedy, such as with Guy Marks's "timid" "cowardly Indian" scout character Pink Cloud in *Rango* (an adaptation of a comic book's collision of native and queer stereotypes), who is indicative of the nonethnic-ethnic absorption of queer and trans of color reference and other minority representation in the mass camp of camp TV.[15]

Racism, Economics, and Censorship

Given this connection, understanding how sitcom camp fared requires a closer look at how television markets expanded amid segregation and explicit racism. Producers worked the ideologies of white-centrism and white supremacy. In contrast to what many assume, television did not start out at its most conservative, no matter whether you mark the beginning of programming with the rollout of military signals and city broadcasts or with the imagining of a national audience as stations moved out from metropolises and in from the coasts. Accounts of the industry and its programming generally construe changes in programming across the 1950s and 1960s and then beyond as unidirectional, toward increased diversity in depicting more varied living arrangements and more people of color. In these accounts, the conventional white middle-class family unit is stable at first and becomes increasingly disrupted by outside forces as time goes on. In fact, families took over more in the 1960s, even as camp comedy with unmarried characters continued to expand. The work of television production in the 1950s and 1960s actually involved an interconnected, idealized, but ultimately impossible straightening out, whitening, and upper-middle-class-ification. This whitening is well documented, and it continues—actually worsens—after the 1950s and 1960s, in a period associated with better representation. According to Patricia Mellencamp, "From 1970 to 1980, . . . whites enhanced their overall domination, . . . blacks had a representation of only 6 to 8 per cent, and . . . other minorities were virtually excluded from portrayal."[16] The producers of situation comedy channeled sensibilities variously coded as urban or rural, private, public, and domestic within contested contexts of signification and taste stratification that produced these signifiers as especially raced in the context of the seeming all-whiteness and ostensible and readily deconstructable homogeneity.

The television sitcom of the 1950s was a new product, in part something never previously encountered, "television's own form of comedy."[17] The form uses over-the-top acting in stories ranging from the mundane to the absurd and supernatural. Programs aired weekly or in syndication for afterschool and daytime consumption in the home, for those who could afford not only somewhere to live but also a set. As the United States reabsorbed the cultural mixing of the World War II years,[18] the House Un-American Activities Committee and senator Joseph McCarthy led to the *Red Channels* blacklist and to other "do not hire" lists, and to family-focused programming trends, first in the early to mid-1950s and then again in the very late 1950s, around the time of the cancellation of *The Bob Cummings Show* and *The Phil Silvers Show*, both semi-salacious, perennial Emmy contending sitcoms, in 1959. The power dynamics of the mid-1950s that led to a dip in camp TV in the very late 1950s and early 1960s stemmed from advertising and regulation practices, as did a previous dip initially, during the early adopter period. The industry solidified its formats and honed its image to bounce back from the quiz show scandals, which brought pressure from sponsors, the FCC, journalists, lobbyists, set manufacturers, and other investors in the network system to purify the airwaves of potentially offensive content. White bias and the blacklist defined this period of the TV sitcom. With three networks devoting prime time schedules to fictional programs recorded in advance, the sitcom was "shaped and reshaped," as Lynn Spigel states, "over the course of the early fifties until finally it emerged as one of the networks' staple program types."[19] By the end of the decade the thoroughly corrupt, thoroughly white-dominated US media system enshrined television as its foundation, with the sitcom as a cornerstone. Over this period, culturally specific performance traditions mixed further, recombined, and reemerged, behind the scenes and onscreen.

The National Association of Broadcasters, a major arm of the media-industrial-complex, faced congressional inquiry as full television schedules (with daytime and nighttime programming, if not yet continuous twenty-four hour feeds) came together in the late 1940s. Press coverage of the networks' process of adopting a Code of Practices for Television Broadcasters, a system of self-censorship modeled on the Hayes Code for Motion Pictures but with less centralized oversight exterior to the networks, peaked in 1951 and continued sporadically, with regular references in newspaper coverage to program practices and program standards departments and representatives as well as to sponsors playing similar roles out of house. This "code of ethics" insulated programmers from routine government interference from the FCC, the Federal Communications Commission, on the basis that television was "one of America's most important media of free expression" and should not be subject to state prescreening of programming.[20] The code required networks and stations to limit commercials and refuse ads for certain products, such as liquor and guns, but notably not cigarettes, the copious ads that, Marsha Cassidy shows, attempted to performatively instantiate, through vivid, sensuous, easily camp-able overkill, heterosexual gender as a gateway drug to capitalism.[21] This code also banned profanity, smut, and vulgarity, categories of representation central to the historical conditioning of heterosexism. It emphasized "wholesome entertainment" and notions of social responsibility. A *New York Times* report in the fall of 1951 described a code "designed to eliminate obscenity, preoccupation with sex... and other abuses."[22] The role of this code in various crackdowns and cleanups across the 1950s and into the 1960s is unclear. An elaborate system of cultural codes, with the classic Hollywood film coding of queer characters among them, interfaced with "the code," the official policies of regulation implemented or overlooked. Like the overall industry and its rhetoric, the code naturalized idealized white settler colonial American nationalism, promoting family units with disposable income, credit, and gender conforming togetherness.[23]

The emergence of queer gender in camp TV illuminates white normative operations in terms of heterosexism. Generalized ethnicity, or "nonethnic-ethnic" representation, in which Italian and Jewish and Irish cultural markers signified interchangeably in an off white way, was in league with the white-dominated "cultural forum" model of commercial television, in which sitcoms fit awkwardly but assuredly.[24] As part of the process of establishing the role of sitcoms within the television schedules, and whitening them for broader distribution, writers cast ethnicity askew, into the realm of trans gender queer representation. This sitcom infrastructure in place by the 1960s makes use of a guest-star system of casting, specially honed in TV (amid sexual harassment/assault and cissexist discrimination), in which people of color are marginalized, often as extra or one-off characters if they appear at all, except in the context of black cast sitcoms. These characters are often portrayed by lighter-skinned actors, actors often of a different ethnicity, namely by white actors. Producers tailored sitcoms to shifting censorship processes within white supremacy.[25]

Censorship is not the issue here. Queer culture took many forms, some that censorship and general social expectations of propriety could not eliminate. Queer content, content indicating that another way of life besides conventional heterosexuality was possible, could not be banned from television by declaring references to homosexuality obscene. Queer expression can travel through language that seems neutral. Stipulations in TV regulating astrology were as relevant, if not more relevant, to the camp mode of situation comedy than sexual perversity clauses and proscriptions against illegal behavior and incendiary beliefs. Nevertheless, it is important to note the context in which the broadcasting association moved to "clean house," scrub up for show, on its own — without aid, or intrusion, from the kind of national advisory board recommended by the FCC and on the floor of Congress in 1951. In rescripting the relations among networks, stations, and sponsors, advertising agencies lost some of the leverage they'd had to oversee and censor programming, much of which they — rather than the networks, including the soon-defunct DuMont network — had, up to that point, developed and produced. Competitive alliance among these parties and manufacturers contributed to a strong stance forbidding "sexual perversion," according to a *New York Times* report.[26] "Sex crimes and abnormalities" were supposed to be, but were not entirely, "unacceptable material for programs."[27] Consolidated network control with respect to stations worked to the detriment of straight-laced hypocrisy in sponsor input. As US TV further commercialized throughout the 1950s and 1960s, gender norms were reported to be under threat. Television was a scapegoat of this upheaval—a feminized object purported to corrupt.[28] Sitcoms rehearsed the confusion of social change through camp. Camp, if not directly appropriated from, can be traced to close connections with, queer and trans of color culture. Assimilation set the stage for trans gender queer representation and camp TV, in a context of celebrity starkly gendered and raced as it relates to sitcoms. Sitcom camp is instructive in this context because it registers whiteness as race when considered through feminist terms that supersede binary gender.

Rose Marie Does Liberace, and Queer Gender All Over the Dial

As the industry grew, it reinforced existing systems of US white privilege through some of the social norms surrounding the new medium of television, but in terms of programming, trans gender queer camp proliferated. At the time, FOX, cable, HBO, and digital distribution were decades away. The DuMont network folded in 1956; NBC, CBS, and ABC solidified their position in telecommunications. Nick Browne explains in "The Political Economy of the Television (Super) Text" that the survival of the network system has depended on its ability to accommodate the "set of manufactured objects that can efficiently be advertised . . . products intimately linked to the ongoing biological and social maintenance of the . . . family unit."[29] This entailed moving away from live-broadcast comedy series, namely variety shows, which were often sponsored by a single company, and toward comedy series (with less showy product plugs) prerecorded on film, standardized in segments for the smooth insertion of multiple prerecorded commercials. The importance of ratings only increased across this shift. Ratings calculations measuring audiences through commodified viewer data facilitates profit, setting airtime costs to companies for strategically placed commercials. The system developed involves series vying, throughout a seasonal calendar, to fill (and maintain or improve their standing in) predetermined half-hour blocks of carefully, ideologically crafted prime time programming schedules. Historically, it is those proposed properties most conducive to embedded sponsor messages, tie-in merchandise, and long-term and potential spinoff profits that have been rewarded. Queer gender is a liability within this product-oriented system but also, ironically, a result of its routines.

Although many people were involved in trans gender queer camp, queer gender was routine in network TV simply by virtue of the consistent appearance of Rose Marie, "an appealing hunk of femininity" and a nightclub singer since the age of three, described as sassy and known for a husky, lusty voice.[30] Rose Marie's association with unmarried characters in sitcoms is legendary. Up until and including a top billing in the 1972 mini series *Honeymoon Suite*, an anthology program, Rose Marie specialized in roles that exemplify the connection of "single-ness" and the guest-star system, and, in this respect, the propensity for situation comedy to produce queer gender amid segregation and assimilation. The traditions of trans gender queer production Rose Marie encapsulates are especially prominent in the context of popular entertainment commenting on its influences. A 1959 vaudeville-themed nostalgia episode of Dinah Shore's *Chevy Show* (NBC, 1956–63), for example, indicates both Rose Marie's stature and the broader repertoire of camp conducive to television comedy.

In this program, host Shore introduces Rose Marie as a favorite of "anyone who's ever hummed the tune 'There's No Business Like Show Business,'" at which point Rose Marie performed the Irving Berlin song, which celebrates the queerness of the entertainment industry with lines like "There's no people like show people. They smile when they're low."[31] Beginning there, Rose Marie performed a medley including dancing, juggling, and singing that as a whole recounted in hyperbolic terms a true-to-life melodramatic showbiz upbringing. In reciting established song lyrics, Rose Marie self-identifies as "a bum" destined for a life in entertainment. The performance recounts fabulous tales in a career as an underage traveling musician, which includes circus appearances as a lion tamer and a bearded lady, finale acts that involve swinging from chandeliers and modeling for magicians in nightclubs, and a stint pitching for the Chicago Cubs. Rose Marie's continuing character, defined by repetitive reference to this work history and to remaining unmarried, linked up with queer showbiz migration tropes that *The Shore Show* presents as broadly appealing.

This confluence of fandom and participation in the industry is evident in a 1953 episode of *The Jimmy Durante Show*, which indicates how at this time, mobile ethnic signifiers figured prominently in situation comedy-based skits. Rose Marie ambiguously adopted and often impersonated the unique singing style of Jimmy Durante, the host of the show, a mentor of Rose Marie's, doing so throughout the 1950s and after, including on *The Dick Van Dyke Show*, a renowned sitcom about TV comedy writers. Durante mentored Rose Marie, whose Polish ethnicity was eclipsed in programming and publicity by codes of Italianness, due in part to this link to Durante as well as to mob affinities dating back to her child star days and nightclub tours.[32] For this *Durante Show* sketch, Durante and Rose Marie enacted a typical Hollywood romance story, as versions of themselves, for laughs, with most of the routine consisting of their breakup, instigated by Rose Marie.[33] They end their relationship, absurdly, in a pool hall located under a bowling alley. The dialogue plays off of the setting; they filter romantic movie trademarks through the vernacular of pool sharks.

In this skit, Rose Marie's character dumps Durante's amid loud noises and falling debris, continuing to shoot pool while saying goodbye, telegraphing the queer gender parody through camp tones of voice, acting absorbed in their feelings for each other despite the destruction surrounding them. Rose Marie calls for a round of beer to commemorate the relationship and refers to an invitation for a final game of snooker as a "sentimental" gesture. While climbing on the table to attempt a difficult combination shot, Durante remarks, "I want to remember you that way. Always." In other words, as the typical rhythms and clichés of a Hollywood love story proceed, the performance diverges from popular expectations of what romance entails. By the time the script calls for them to stage-kiss goodbye, they have showcased their inability to keep a straight face while playing lovers, breaking the "fourth wall" with uncontrollable laughter multiple times, as if the idea of them together is utterly ridiculous.

Standard paradigms for representing relationships construe men and women as complementary opposites, an approach that reinforces traditional understandings of masculinity and femininity. In the *Durante Show* skit, in contrast, both performers, coconstituting their masculine qualities, wax poetic in feminized roles and pile on sexual innuendo. While the producers depict Durante as attracted to pool prowess, Rose Marie's character leaves specifically to move to Southern California in order to become a star in Hollywood, a popular trope communicating camp. As Rose Marie says again, as Sal in the 1965 *Dick Van Dyke Show* episode "Fifty-Two, Forty-Five, or Work," "Hollywood, here I come." A line reminiscent of Sal's wisecracking, given in direct address, re-marks Rose Marie's type: Rose Marie "would make a wonderful [parent], if I could only get her out of the pool room." The comic situation of a form of love based on shared passion for billiards creates queer gender through mutually parodic ethnic-nonethnic performance, meaning in this case that the sense of Italian and Polish and Jewish and Irish American culture as a touchstone for erotics of sameness is articulated through New York City, New Jersey, Chicago, and other mafia and street culture landmark voices and accents.

Another example of comedy variety program situation comedy as trans gender queer camp from this time, an episode of the 1954 season of *The George Jessel Show*, demonstrates how queer gender can be a product of ethnic-nonethnic parody even when—or especially when—the parodied person remains anonymous. In this guest appearance, Rose Marie offered a parody of the entertainer Liberace, a pianist popularly remembered both as one of the most closeted and as one of the most obviously gender transgressive and queer television personalities of the 1950s and 1960s.[34] Rose Marie did the impersonation without a costume. This is significant in that it is indicative of the assimilation of vaudeo drag into more subtle forms of trans gender queer sitcom camp. Instead of dressing like Liberace, Rose Marie crafted the impression around Liberace's facial movements, voice, and physical demeanor, invoking the musician's queer image and camp edge through a slight arch of the eyebrows and a soft singing style. Slipping into character at the outset of the segment, Rose Marie uses Liberace-style run-on superlatives to describe the pianist about to appear as my "very wonderful favorite . . . television performer." Liberace played a lot and exaggerated a lot, and so Rose Marie's monologue introduces a medley of "six or seven thousand songs." The camp exaggeration is classic comedy by way of incongruity, in that recognizing Liberace as the object of Rose Marie's impersonation requires noting minute details of the gender presentations of both the impersonator, who is present, and the impersonated, whose image and demeanor must be recalled from memory.

Such details include the precise flair of fingers at the keyboard, unsettlingly soothing vocal inflections, and a televisual composure in posture and facial expression, all of which Rose Marie performs with intricate fidelity. Less delicately, Rose Marie punctuated this musical performance, an amalgam of parodies sung in duet with Lenny Kent, by handling a candelabra made from a soft material that flopped over instead of standing up straight, in reference to Liberace's trademark prop, a décor item holding multiple candles.[35] This routine is training in tertiary "sex characteristics," through trans gendered signifiers capable of replacing primary and secondary traits in the cis sexist paradigm of perceiving gender truth in anatomical sex. Rose Marie and Kent repeatedly laughed out loud as they handled the prop, which doubled as a rack of appendages, or an excess of phallic symbols. Modifying the trademark object of Liberace's stage persona, these droopy candles made Liberace's candelabra seem scandalously erect, exploring the gendered and sexual implications of bodies through props in a camp manner, flaunting the open circumvention of ineffective censorship in an example of trans gender queer representation.

Through props and performance, the *Jessel Show* sketch mediates queer gender with televisual discourse instead of reductive sexual identity categories. Combining the gender signifiers associated with two different celebrities compounds the otherwise independent cultural charge around deviance that the TV industry cultivated on the model of eccentricity. Over the course of the sketch, the candelabra comes to represent not a dominant notion of impotence or emasculation but rather, in the words of Alexander Doty, "desperate attempts to deny the queerness that is so clearly a part of mass culture."[36] The bent candles of this situation sketch comedy construct Rose Marie's single persona as part of this queer context at the same time as they represent Liberace as a comic muse spectacularizing its denial. Adding an additional layer of irony and stressing the intertextual reference, host George Jessel, throughout the routine, feigned ignorance of the artist in question, which is funny because Liberace was so popular and such a flashpoint in gendered taste wars. Rose Marie responded to Jessel's obvious put-on with an incredulous gasp, saying, "You don't know?"

This gesture, one toward opacity as opposed to an endorsement of "the closet,"[37] adds an additional thread of trans gender queer connection to the joke, and indicates the genre elements of comedy variety that were shaping the narrative structure and flow of sitcom episodes solidifying at the time. Continuing to play coy, Jessel pointed to the prop candelabra and asked Rose Marie if they meant Mister Peepers, Wally Cox's character in *Mister Peepers*, a camp TV program starring a trans gender queer icon that had recently won a Peabody Award. The segue of the Liberace impression into a Wally Cox joke is the kind of broad, self-reflexive "situation" comedy appearing in variety formats. This construction, or situation, offscreen, of the "situation" of the industry as situation comedy overlaps with and influences sitcoms. Sitcom writers developed scenarios that rescripted the punch lines of vaudeo monologues as exchanges between fictional characters. They adapted stand-up strategies and standard comedy material just as sitcom producers continue to do as they pitch concepts and develop series.[38]

As this look at trans gender queer industry camp through just a few of Rose Marie's many variety show appearances indicates, the work of producing television comedy in this period consolidated queer codes from multiple media formats. Sitcoms, in particular, mixed performance traditions through invigorated camp practices. In modifying variety conventions and a variety of conventions, including tropes sourced from radio and classic Hollywood film coding, sitcom writers and actors purveyed codes of eccentricity—and eccentricities exacerbating eccentricities—capaciously and at an amplified pace. The work of TV comedy producers ingrained camp into the patented procedures for scripting and performing in sitcoms, which were becoming a prime example of how, as Browne attests, "television's serial forms serve to continue the subject along the itinerary of habituated consumption."[39]

Ed Wynn, Edwina, and the Fluttering of Hands

The TV industry's assimilation of ethnic specificity into a more homogenized whiteness,[40] a major dynamic at play in this Shore–Durante–Rose Marie–Jessel–Liberace strata of celebrity, is a trajectory evident throughout the work of Ed Wynn, a Jewish performer with a signature kooky look and sound signaled by name, voice, and image. Wynn had been big in radio, and is particularly interesting in representing camp as it emerged in the transition from videoed vaudeville–type programming to distinct forms of comedy variety and situation comedy. Ed Wynn worked a perfect fool persona, somewhat like Mary Grace Canfield and Imogene Coca. Wynn's brand, which consisted of fluttering hands and general scatteredness, modulating giggle fits and a lilting delivery of lines, offered a distinct combination of queer gender adaptable to different formats across the 1950s and in league with the many prominent illogical types of the day, who were feminized and definitive of the sitcom form of cross-category "dumb blonde" typing.

There are two main *Ed Wynn* TV shows. The first *Ed Wynn Show* is a Wynn-hosted CBS half-hour vaudeo series (a relevant distinction from the conventionally hour-long later comedy variety) broadcast opposite the DuMont network's *Morey Amsterdam Show* at 9 PM on Thursdays during the 1949–50 season.[41] Not much of this series has been preserved. However, the Seaman Jacobs Papers at Syracuse University includes a subtly risqué and temporally astute bit from the first series that is textbook camp in its unobtrusive reference to the "intercourse" implied but never depicted in classic Hollywood cinema. Wynn describes a play being put on in Brooklyn and delivers, by way of a grammatical pun, a punch line that can be taken as sexually suggestive but, characteristically, need not be. "[One character] says, 'I don't want to be a Hollywood movie actor. One day you're kissing Lana Turner, the next day you're kissing Loretta Young, the next day you're kissing Joan Crawford, and the next day you're a has been.' The other says, 'Yes, but look where you has been!'"[42] This is camp TV because in many ways, including some wholesome ones, it resonates as queer in terms of gender. The joke is a way of poking fun at the movies, where many and women especially are "washed up" early due to ageist norms. The joker (likely Wynn or the unnamed scene partner, if Wynn was in it and it was in the final broadcast) complains about kissing women, when, within the dominant discourse, this is the "heterosexual" desire universalized at the time as a condition of white masculine privilege.

Despite this discourse, queer gender was especially valuable as sitcom currency. Characterization through queer gender facilitated ongoing episodic narrative and provided a rich context for camp and the cyclical reproduction of queer gender. As Chris Becker and Mary Desjardins detail, TV programming presented performers with opportunities to speak back to the machinery of the motion picture industry through productions for the small screen.[43] The trans gender queer traits and physical habits that made Wynn and many other radio and vaudeo performers stars presented queer gender as part of a broader "speaking back" connected to a more dispersed form of camp authorship. Wynn animatedly flicked fingers from hinged wrists. These mannerisms coordinated with Wynn's fluttery vocal delivery, which Susan Douglas describes as a voice that "shot up octaves as [Wynn] whinnied and giggled" in a kind of "vocal cross-dressing."[44] Wynn is iconic in voice and gesture in terms of inspiring parody, prompting other performers to speak in the modulated dippy voice, place their hands in and out of their pockets repeatedly, and to flutter their hands around with Wynn's characteristic ethereal affective gestures. Such "gestures" and sonic stylings give texture to specific roles as eccentric, as evident in a comparison of variety and sitcom performance that follows.

The original *Wynn* TV series was a variety format, a self-reflexive forum in which the producers questioned whether Wynn's persona as a Jewish gendernonconforming person would appeal to viewers. Would a corresponding image be too much for potentially hostile consumers? For the variety show, Wynn drew on fifty-five years of experience in show business but discarded the fire captain character famous from radio. Wynn performed as Ed Wynn, television host shilling for sponsors while captive to network interests. The program was notably smutty, urban, and ethnic, with Wynn performing frantic, fey, and mischievously scatterbrained, training for voicing the unruly Mad Hatter in Walt Disney's animated *Alice in Wonderland* (1951). Wynn still engenders a host of imitators and iconic appropriations, some in tribute and some explicitly phobic. The variety show contained a significant amount of camp and genderqueer comedy. In this respect, it is indicative of the many live comedy variety shows that helped generate situation comedy and the sitcom form in the 1950s. This *Wynn Show*, and programs like *The Ken Murray Show*, and *The Wynn Show*'s direct competition, *The Morey Amsterdam Show*, showcase the collision of industrial self-reflexivity and queer gender in early variety programs. In the variety hour, Wynn presented meandering stories framed as pitches to studio executives, voicing media producer perspectives on everything from melodramatic conventions in radio, film, and theater to television's trashy reputation and its wrestling matches.[45]

The name Ed Wynn itself is interesting (as many of the names of camp TV producers are). It is phonically and rhythmically queer in that it sounds like Edwin, the full name Ed might be short for. It is seemingly sonically unmarketable, which becomes its marketability. Wynn is also a homonym for "win," with the intrinsic comedy of repetition in the suggestion of Edwin Wynn as Ed Win Win. This is one of countless cases of a stage name that transcodes Jewish assimilation through camp orientalism, or the construction of appeal in foreign and unusual or "exotic" looks vis-à-vis the straight cis white norm.[46] This one, easily misheard, references the deconstruction of language so common to sitcoms and, within them, so conducive to trans gender queer representation. According to the somewhat depoliticized version of Wynn's biography, Wynn split a middle name given at birth in order to spare family embarrassment about having a relative in entertainment.

Like the rest of the trans gender queer television icons that I reconstruct from the consumer culture that generated them, Wynn's persona as well as the programing crafted around it are collectively authored by writers, agents, designers, and other collaborators, including critics and fans. Wynn performed on a genderqueer register, observing with shock, for example, "I lisp!" This is a variety show, not fiction, but its scripting participates in the emergent formation of punch lines through visual verbal delivery of eccentricity. Situation comedy is a recursive system of high-concept one-liners. In this mode, Wynn lanced the looks discrimination and gender policing encroaching on TV comedians as the market grew. Faux horrified in anticipation of being thrown off the air, Wynn's attitude was sincere and frivolous simultaneously, a hallmark of camp indicatively genderqueer and conveyed through eccentricity and capacity for parody. The commentary was on assimilation, as in a revealing sketch on the first *Ed Wynn Show* with Garry Moore and another guest star.[47] Both, dressed in Wynn drag on stage with Wynn, created comedy from their own obvious likeness and lack of likeness to Wynn in terms of ethnic and body typing. All three are dressed identically, including the one identified as Edwina,[48] who is in a long-skirt version of the pants the other two wear. Through costuming, blocking, scoring, lighting, and cinematography, the producers put forth as comedy the fact of differential male privilege—including for people who appear to have been (and might or might not be mistakenly) assigned female. Edwina's Wynn confirms Ed Wynn's opinion that Moore's Wynn—an appropriately fluttery imitation from someone with an inappropriately normative white look—is too odd for TV. The recurring command "You can't lisp in television," is rendered triply ironic by Wynn's lisping replicas. The ethnic-nonethnic difference is pronounced through contrast between Moore's Wynn and Wynn and Edwina's Wynns. Together, all three break the so-called rule several times, in a sketch that, all told, involves the labor of hundreds of people lampooning television's heterosexist gender norms through successive sanctioned lisps.

A similar drag formula runs across the variety show *Wynn Show* episodes, in the form of a repeated gag that, staged at the liminal moment of an introduction, hinges on swapping names, identities, and appearances.[49] In one version of this trans gender queer routine, Wynn introduced the Three Stooges as a group of CBS executives—among them William Paley, the chief executive who, as heir of an expanding cigar company, developed CBS as a radio network out of Philadelphia. In another, Wynn introduced models in swimsuits as important executives. In another, the Three Stooges appear when Wynn calls out the models. This draglike situation-based humor lays bare privilege, hinging on contrasts in gender, class, and comportment. The actual executives would not be so unruly, nor would they be likely to wear swimsuits, whether those modeled on stage or any others. Routines like this highlight the visual component of television in comparison with radio. They turn on the rituals of variety shows, their curtains, announcers, and applause signaling a studio audience under direction from offscreen crew.

Sitcoms consolidated this material as narrative formula. The *Wynn Show* joke itself actually has an antecedent in a Three Stooges movie, *Movie Maniacs*, a short from 1936 indicative of their working-class personas.[50] Camp was useful, because camp transmediates. TV producers in the 1950s and continually throughout the 1960s adapted material from other textual systems and performance traditions, appropriating and incorporating across media through the mode of camp production. They made drag "televisual," including by rendering it at a simultaneously less visual and hypervisible register, by infusing drag elements into comic situations, exploiting without necessarily relying on wardrobe, looks, props, décor, styling, and other elements of cinematography, as was the challenge in radio comedy.[51] During the addition of a visual dimension to broadcasting, as prerecorded Hollywood production took over network programming, much camp involved sound. As Robert Shandley writes, "The presumed harmlessness of sitcom banter allows a level of commentary that had proven difficult in any other arena of primetime television."[52] Television technology allowed consumers to differentially privilege sound and image (such as while vacuuming, doing laundry, entertaining, or napping). Producers tailored image, dialogue, and scores for a commercial market in which television-recording devices were unavailable and camp could potentially circulate out of range of censors, in spite of script approvals, rehearsals, and surveillance.

Before the second *Ed Wynn Show* but after the first, Wynn guest hosted and acted as a rotating host along with Jimmy Durante, Jack Carson, and Danny Thomas on *Four Star Revue*. This *Ed Wynn Show* came after Wynn won acclaim with a straight dramatic part in the Rod Serling teleplay "Requiem for a Heavyweight" aired by *Playhouse 90* in 1956. In the second *Ed Wynn Show*, Wynn appeared as John Beemer, a dreamer and an endearingly rascally grandparent raising kids. This second *Wynn* series indicates the intensified assimilation process television comedy underwent in the late 1950s as compared with the late 1940s and early 1950s. This *Ed Wynn* show, which debuted and ended in 1958, was a domestic comedy that NBC scheduled as a lead-in to *Twenty-One* the autumn the quiz show scandals broke. Wynn's John Beamer character partly repeated but also significantly departed from the version of Ed Wynn that fans knew from vaudeville, radio, and comedy variety TV. The characterization is notable in making Wynn seem less Jewish, less frantic, less fey, less feminine, less effeminate, less idiosyncratic, less queer, more gender conforming, and more conventional in terms of sexual energy. The divergent family premise of the second *Wynn Show* situates

Wynn's Beamer character as a widow and the sole caretaker of three grandchildren. This *Ed Wynn Show* represents overarching industry trends at the time it aired. Without a backstage setup, the late 1950s program liquidated the queer and Jewish cultural markers that had suffused Wynn's earlier work. At the same time, in the aired pilot program available as a part of a *Lost and Rare Film and TV Treasures* DVD from Festival Films, trans gender queer camp is again central.

Queer gender is also central in an episode script featuring a one-off character named Lydia. This script, and the repurposing of the concept by the same writer, Seaman Jacobs, for an episode of *The Real McCoys* (ABC, 1957–63), "Aunt Win Arrives" (guest starring Joan Blondell, aired February 17, 1963), suggests that the camp interwoven in comedy variety hours continually reappeared in sitcoms. The script for "Aunt Lydia Comes to Town" uses a stock plot that many family series incorporate for one-off inflections of their usual story worlds. Aunt Lydia visits Uncle Beamer and Beamer's grandchildren in their hometown after having lived the past fifteen years in Paris. The situation is that, previously, Lydia was shy and studious. Now Lydia is cheeky and cosmopolitan. Explicitly modeling the character on Tallulah Bankhead, this *Ed Wynn Show* script gives Aunt Lydia a snobby poodle named Napoleon, a penchant for the words "darling" and "divine," and an array of sexual witticisms beyond the perceived bounds of the family hour. Danny Thomas had cleaned up earlier. Wynn did with this and Disney's *The Gnome Mobile* ahead (in which the prolific Richard Deacon also appeared). In the script for "Aunt Lydia Comes to Town," one among a season's worth of episodes, the Lydia character solicits from Wynn's banter of the kind rife in the variety program but left untapped within the sitcom's domestic setting. As a temporary addition to the cast, the Lydia character motivated new locations (a roadhouse bar) and scandalous themes (cross-generational romance in which, atypically, Lydia is the older partner) conducive to double entendre and queer identification. Arriving at the airport, Lydia notes, "I simply adore pilots. I wouldn't think of flying without one."[53] Comments like this may seem inconsequential, but this is camp TV: quips from shamelessly unconventional characters that open onto a performance mode traceable back through vaudeo to traditions of popular entertainment that were more racially integrated or even non-white-centric.

The guest-star system guarantees queer gender in situations such as those conceived for the episode with Lydia. Lydia's Tallulah Bankhead drag is an opportunity for Wynn to channel a comedic persona shelved for the sitcom, a revival of the shtick about Hollywood has-beens scripted for the variety program. Lydia represents an earlier historical moment, the one in which producers reestablished Wynn's trans gender queer persona from radio. Lydia also represents the persistence of producers repurposing Hollywood glamor in the sitcom production context. The questions of fame the script taps, which metaresonate with contextual questions about the cast, are questions that preoccupy queer artists and audiences. The writers map codes of foreignness onto the Lydia character, and this character occupies the eccentric role Wynn used to take up from the position of host (and would return to in a different context with *Mary Poppins*). The script offered Wynn the opportunity to play against the cultural connotations of the Lydia character's cosmopolitan image in a self-aware manner associated with a former role from a program in a different vein.

The basic plot of the episode carries an implicit call for Wynn to match Lydia's innuendo. Wynn effectively has a free pass to one-up Lydia, according to comic formula. "Aunt Lydia Comes to Town" recirculates a camp history of TV comedy even as it takes a straighter and more de-Semitized form than Wynn's earlier work. Standardized television conventions that followed from the sitcom's guest-star system kept camp alive after the more raucous incarnation of first wave TV comedy had been informally banned. Various performers—from the famous to the unknown and unidentified—have appeared in Wynn drag in comedy variety skits; performers continue to lift, or pay tribute to, Wynn's vocal delivery, in audio drag; sitcom characterization in standalone episodes tailors drag performance to a specific person or combination of personas, as in the meshing of variety-style-Wynn antics with the class, gender, and camp sensibility markers of Tallulah Bankhead in "Aunt Lydia Comes to Town." Ironic commentary scripted for sitcom characters turns on heightened gender markers, binary and not. An actor impersonating another actor while in character is camp. While asserting trans gender queer agency through the dialogue of sitcom episodes isn't the same as having Garry Moore and another comedian ricocheting physically in queer gender parody of Wynn on stage in front of a live audience, as in the episode of the earlier variety program, the trans gender queer residue in Wynn's capacious persona reanimates a constellation of queer gender production to which the industry on the whole was at the level of law and policy explicitly opposed.

Couple Camp and Close Encounters with Queer Gender

Camp also flourished in the context of couples, fictional, actual, and, in the case of Ida Lupino's show *Mr. Adams and Eve*, both real and performed. Lupino's *Adams and Eve* is an example of a CBS series full of industry wit. Running originally from 1957 to 1958, the program features in Lupino one of many major players to move from film to television in the 1950s, and to work onscreen and behind the scenes.[54] The lead characters of this series, glamorous but down-to-earth film stars Eve Drake (Lupino) and Howard Adams (Howard Duff) advertised pricey products and services like traveler's checks. Camp permeates the episodes "Dear Variety," "Typical," "Bachelor," and "Come on to Mars' House," the few episodes available at UCLA. "Dear Variety" caricatures movie studio economics as an interpersonal rollercoaster contingent upon long-distance communication between East Coast bigwigs and West Coast crews and management, quite the opposite of the situation on set. This series investigates marriage norms and the relationship between film stardom and the television medium. "Bachelor" looks at the interplay of onscreen and offscreen romance among industry professionals, also the subject of the series pilot, and "Come on to Mars' House" lampoons Hollywood types for their adherence to astrology. Starting from a point of seeing something like astrology, like showbiz history, as a potentially queer vocabulary, the situational superstition suddenly acquired by the character played by Howard Duff, listed as subversive in *Red Channels*, takes on the form of a feminized interest conscripted for queer code, a cultural difference prototypical of the ethnicization of gender and sexual and racial minority difference and the discriminatory appropriation patterns of the network system.

"Code" is a misnomer, though, because in exposing the fictiveness of the dream factory's products, camp incorporates explicit references to sexuality and frank discussions of queer culture. For example, in one episode, Howard, just after returning home from a "boys' night" out on the town, speaks of the drawbacks and benefits of single life, waxing poetic about datable recent transplants to Hollywood, listing Seattle, Omaha, Dixie, Cucamonga, and Kansas City Mo among them. These monikers are like good drag names. They work as standalone jokes. Just imagine the characters! This is trans gender queer representation. All are more gender-neutral than the average name your parents might impose upon you. They reflect a Hollywood stage name-change history and sensibility coincident with queer and trans cultures. Cucamonga, short for Rancho Cucamonga, a suburb about an hour's drive, these days, from Hollywood or downtown Los Angeles, is a long-standing metareference associated with Jack Benny and Mel Blanc. In the camp mode, this suggests, among other things, that Cucamonga is, for some people, conceptually speaking, as far away from LA as Omaha despite the proximity.

Like perennial references to Pocatello, Idaho, referencing the vivid vaudeville history now absent from that city's landscape, Cucamonga is construed as at once foreign (and decidedly outside the bounds of the jet set life of Los Angeles–area celebrities), familiar (and thus name-dropped by SoCal residents), and vivid within the imagination of the media industries (as part of a legacy of creatively supplementing reality through representation). The litany of locations taps into a metronormative migration narrative that posits even relatively large cities such as Seattle and Kansas City as narrow-minded places to escape. The tone and cadence of the names signals indigenous and displaced populations and histories that exceed mainstream narratives of national identity in step with the ongoing history of colonization in and around LA.

Camp inflections in the acting of the scene suggest scandalous valences without specifying any particular transgression. Lupino and Duff deliver their dialogue such that the laundry list of aspiring Hollywood workers seems timeless and familiar, as in references to "Zsa Zsa" Gabor in an episode online currently, in which the dialogue implies the global star is a dear friend or family, and may be. This is the instigation of queer gender in sitcomic imagination. Using language perceived—from a dominant white point of view—as unusual, and speaking at a highly abstract level of meaning, Eve and Howard suggest, to one another, that they have been everywhere, they have seen everything, and they see aspiring industry workers come and go, over and over again, from their vantage point of consistent Hollywood employment. The ones lost are trans gender queer. Eve recognizes Kansas City Mo, a name that puns on the state abbreviation "Kansas City, MO," saying, "Oh, Kansas City Mo is a fella. I knew him well." Without taking note of the fact, much less denying, that Howard has grouped someone Eve perceives as "a fella" among the people Howard might be sleeping with, Howard checks to make sure they are referring to the same "Mo," a term (adapted from the second syllable in "homosexual") that was, at the time, at least in some circles, slang for "queer people," and especially "trans gender queer people," although history books often categorize the culture as white male.

The label "fella," especially in this context of camp delivery, is loaded in that it can be a synonym for boyfriend as well as friend. It can mean both and be used ambiguously (as in *Dick Van Dyke* humor around Rose Marie's Sally Rogers character throughout the 1960s). The witty wordplay around this Mo character creates space for representation distinct from dominant norms. To confirm the mutual acquaintance, the writers highlight the components "one" and "a million" in the phrase "one in a million," in common logic synched up with the focus on Mo. Howard asks, "A million laughs?" and Eve replies, "That's the one!" This and the other few episodes of *Adams and Eve* preserved all correlate a trans gender queer set of producers, including actors who deliver no dialogue, to Hollywood's core.[55] This show and camp TV generally renders more tangibly textual a set of unspecified workers behind the scenes of media production. The sequence is fleeting, but the perspective may stick, even after the line and image long fade from memory. In this period, situation comedies came to make regular trade of the camp mode of self-characterization as drag.

While the industry whitened its programming, the camp context of a broader sphere of cultural production that did not (want to or was not allowed to) make it to TV exploded. Gestures, costuming, vocal inflection, and appearance all contributed to trans gender queer expression in the context of iconic character acting and guest-star system circuitry in sitcom formulas. This prime time programming and rerun fodder was queer culture, and it featured trans representation.

2

Queer Gender and *Bob Cummings*
HOLLYWOOD CAMP TV

This chapter establishes connections between feminism and the need to read across gender in a "trans" way even when talking about seemingly cis straight people. It analyzes moving image and performing arts archives, backstage communication records, print media, and digital culture in ways that are feminist and trans gender queer. I focus on *The Bob Cummings Show* and Mary Elliot Cummings, whom I call MEC and refer to as Cummings. Camp producers populate the fictionalized Southern California and actual SoCal spaces that this series and others depict. I position MEC's spouse-creation Bob Cummings as indicative of the gay playboy character type, a camp characterization that feminizes, effeminizes, and queers the emblematically hetero role of the misogynous "womanizer." Cummings, the less privileged of the pair, was Bob's business manager and spouse from 1945 until their divorce, which, when finalized in 1970, earned a massive headline in the local paper. "MEC" marks the records of Laurel Productions and the Ten-Sixty

Corporation, two of the companies that MEC and Bob established.¹ Although I was researching with a feminist mission from the start, it still took me years to wade through sexism, internalized and contextual, in order to apprehend Mary Cummings's (MEC's) important role in Bob's now-neglected success and in the orchestration of "Bob" as a hybrid fictional and star persona. The methods of historical analysis I present emphasize the work MEC did as an independent television executive, running, day-to-day, these and other international business ventures. There is more sexism than presumed and more women working in such roles than generally suggested.

Bob Cummings, the TV series with which MEC and Bob Cummings were most directly and for the longest time involved, indicates overall the complicated trajectory of camp in sitcoms. The program spotlights Hollywood producers' unique social mores and sexual practices. It chronicles the life of commercial photographer Bob Collins, a local celebrity and an avid dater with a studio on Sunset Boulevard and a bit of an entourage. My analysis disperses credit for this popular queer icon of the 1950s and 1960s into the recesses of ephemeral character comedy. In terms of camp, it is a dream cast. Rosemary DeCamp—whose very name, based on the "hidden" camp in it, surfaces as a punch line in the watershed gay play and feature film *The Boys in the Band* (1970)—starred as Margaret MacDonald, Bob's wise and competitive sibling. Dwayne Hickman appeared in the role of Chuck, crafty, cohabiting teenager. King Donovan's Harvey Helm, Paul Fonda's Lyle Talbot, Dick Wesson's Frank, Lola Albright's Kay, and sundry other producers-within-the-text, including Nancy Kulp's Pamela Livingston/e, Rose Marie's Martha Randolph, and Joi Lansing's Shirley Swanson, along with the behind-the-scenes producers (including crew) who created Bob's gay playboy photographer type in *The Bob Cummings Show*, created trans gender queer representation that conventional analysis blithely tramples, in displays of cis and straight privilege. Repetitive camp casting fueled camp acting and episodic situations. When Kulp kisses Bob, it is hyperpassionate—as John Cleese and Megan Mullally (as Lyle Finster and Karen Walker) kiss in *Will & Grace* so many years later—in parody of over-the-top hetero display in the everyday as exemplified by dramatic Hollywood film conventions.

The most that is typically mentioned about the characters in which I am most interested is that they were unattractive, and that is an assessment I reject.² First, I look at Bob's relationship to different personnel, in the context of MEC's role in production. Then I discuss publicity of Bob as a gay playboy and work in other media contributing to this characterization. Next, I analyze TV programming specifically, within that broader constellation of contextualized signifiers of queer gender.

Eccentric Star Study

Mary Elliot Cummings was a working producer in the television industry in the 1950s and 1960s, innovating in what later came to be known as narrowcasting techniques, mediating information from talent agencies, networks, production companies, and trade papers. Cummings worked behind the scenes as a major player on four TV programs starring Bob: the Emmy-winning and mostly disavowed show *My Hero* (1952–53);[3] two *Bob Cummings Show*s (the first, 1955–59, [aka *Love That Bob*, which netted eleven Emmy nominations, including in writing and editing, and two wins for Ann B. Davis], and the second, 1961–62 [aka *The New Bob Cummings Show*]); and *My Living Doll* (1964–65). All four were California sitcoms. *My Hero* took place in and around Los Angeles, where the Thackery Realty Company, the main setting for the series, did business. In that program, Bob played Robert Beanblossom, a naive, hyperactive loafer whose image producers animated with special effects in postproduction, a sore spot for the actor despite an Emmy nomination. The next series, the first *Bob Cummings Show*, featured Bob as a commercial artist who stationed the Bob Collins Photography Studio on the Sunset Strip. The second *Cummings Show* moved Bob a ways up the coast to a San Francisco Bay Area airfield. In that program, Bob was Bob Conway, a suave private detective using a fleet of planes in personal rescue missions. *My Living Doll* brought Bob back closer to Hollywood, to work as a psychiatrist at a scientific research center working up prototypes for the US Air Force. In *My Living Doll*, Bob, Dr. Bob McDonald, is responsible for Rhoda Miller (Julie Newmar), a robot just barely passing as human. While MEC's role in these series varied, the behind-the-scenes influence was consistent.

By the time of Bob's last series, *My Living Doll*, some peers saw Bob as passé, but Bob was a "boyish" brand. Known as the "perennial youth of television," and as "vital" and "versatile," the name Bob signaled a second life (in TV following film stardom for Robert Cummings). Bob reportedly chirped.[4] New episodes of the second *Bob Cummings Show* debuted at a time when *My Hero* and the first eponymous show—recirculated as *Love That Bob*—were airing every weekday in daytime syndication. Bob was suited for television, which for economic reasons sought "personalities," accessible celebrities with flexibility, stamina, and charm, as the medium's corollary to

Hollywood's feature film stars. Bob actively chose to work in TV, reporters noted, following publicity strategies incubated by MEC through the selecting of projects,[5] roles, and promotion tactics.[6] Reporting, in the early 1960s, that Bob was about to begin yet another network series, newspaper columnist Eve Starr celebrated this news as a symptom of Bob's freakishness. Starr described Bob's announcement of a third TV series as "a statement no other top-ranking star can make—or would probably even want to make." Cheeky journalists commonly coded Bob as queer by stressing the "college boy" act and suggesting that Bob self-publicized by engaging, excitedly, in behavior that other celebrities actively avoided or rejected, often at the behest of their agents and employers.[7] Speaking of astrology, for example, Bob told a reporter, "People make fun of almost anything you delve into. They make fun of anything they don't understand. Now I make a hobby of trying things that people make fun of."[8] When critics dismissed Bob, which they did routinely, they painted the star as a faddist, a dilettante, a fruit, and, above all, as an eccentric.

As David Marc details, the sitcom was a platform "in the service of personal expression" at that time.[9] It was also, however, a mouthpiece of opportunistic industrialists, and the ideology of consumer capitalism came out in kooky ways in those twenty-two-minute melodramas of escape and stasis designed to peddle merchandise. Marc shows that Paul Henning's artistic vision and authorial signature are evident in *The Beverly Hillbillies*, *Petticoat Junction*, and *Green Acres*, as well as in *The Bob Cummings Show*, for which Henning is credited as having penned over one hundred episodes in a row, that served as a custom crossroads of the film, fashion, and military industries. At the same time, the notion of sitcom auteurs is absurd.[10] Indeed, Marc argues that Henning, who was some combination of creator, producer, and writer on those and other programs, including *Fibber McGee and Molly*, *Burns and Allen*, and *Where's Raymond?*, equally represents, in articulating some personal vision through sitcoms (beginning in radio), "the complex machinery of the production and distribution system."[11] So does MEC.

The Intertextual Landscape of Camp TV

In the 1950s and 1960s, camp TV synthesized sponsorship models and other modes of monetizing airtime: it assisted programmers in juxtaposing segments of broadcast content for a pleasant consumer experience. Sitcoms tailored TV affects and televisuality through constructed flow. The prime time TV schedules were organized around programming fragments integrated into commercial slots to flow with advertising, matched to times of day, week, and season, and tailored to emerging markets and the built environment of mobile privatization.¹² In the 1950s and 1960s, TV and industry (advertising, quality control, ideological state apparatus proliferation) interlaced. Marketing and demographics research exploded, in step with legal, medical, and psychosexual identity models reiterating, ad nauseam, straight white American norms, immediately fomenting countercurrents, backlashes, and culture wars. Censorship was rampant. Yet queer gender remained prevalent, in comedy products and their promotion.

This prevalence of queer gender prompts reassessment of many presumptions in media history. One prominent existing narrative implies that, historically, television kills cinema, in dealing a sizable blow to an honorable industry, "film," as if entirely distinct. In the binarized teleology, Hollywood as film industry ingeniously recovers over time, justifying its existence and discriminatory status quo—"regain[ing] an audience which in its demoralization had been captured by pathetic television fare consisting of pratfalls and the banalities of Milton Berle."¹³ One snapshot presenting 1958 as the final round is a special feature in *US News and World Report* from that year, titled "What TV Is Doing to the Movie Industry." This group-authored, unattributed piece delivers "gloomy findings," supported by statistics supplied by the US Commerce Department and the MPAA (the Motion Picture Association of America) from a report "prepared for the industry."¹⁴ The dire projection: "Television appears to be strangling the movie business."¹⁵

Yet, as a "top consultant" cited in the unattributed article points out, white flight, DIY culture, social fragmentation, and "difficulty in parking near downtown theaters" (read: car culture, suburbanization, and white fragility), "among other things," were interacting with television, or were "to blame," as the authors put it, projecting insecurities about social change. The supposed shift was simply more white supremacy, given that the number of drive-in theaters opening (and "holding their own [but] not making their owners very rich") matched the number of city theaters closing.¹⁶ A sidebar to the article, "Slump in Movies Hits Britain, too," reports on three hundred movie theaters closing in a period of about a year and a half. Mobile privatization at that time meant "millions of people . . . stay at home and watch old films on TV rather than pay to see a new movie at their local theater."¹⁷ By early 1958, approximately 175 features were playing on New York City TV every week, of the kind that prompted Frank O'Hara and friends—in "communal viewing" sessions in which the "television was almost as instructive as the chatter"—to imagine that, in between the time of the making of the movie *Secrets of a Secretary* in 1931 and the time of its broadcast in 1960, the actor Betty Lawford, according to a quip from the group's host, painter John Button, "became Peter Lawford."[18] Camp TV and its trans textuality operate within this field of medium interactivity.

These practices were part of a dynamic intertextual landscape full of references to movies, music, and more, which camp TV producers helped create.[19] Hollywood fandom and trans cultural touchstones—such as Ed Wood's feature *Glen or Glenda*, which came out in 1953—were part of an expanding communication system, alongside physique magazines and pulp novels.[20] Print publicity and reports of television programing offered commentary about writing, casting, acting, and sometimes directing, costuming, set decorating, editing, and sound production. Critics addressed individual episodes and made comparisons across seasons and series, often with respect to specific choices producers made. Alongside coverage of trans people, writers considered issues of censorship and assimilation, relaying conflicting perspectives on network trends, gimmicks, spin-offs, hybrids, and branding initiatives. Anonymous producers wove trans gender queer camp into the fabric of this media array.

As my use of this archive of queer gender so far suggests, camp considers everyday life and mass media as "an aesthetic phenomenon . . . not in terms of beauty but in terms of the degree of artifice, of stylization."[21] Susan Sontag's "Notes on Camp" presents camp as an "answer to the problem: how to be a dandy in the age of mass culture."[22] Camp circulates through self-presentation. It is a mode of production and consumption both within the story worlds of 1950s and 1960s texts and within their industrial contexts. In this realm, prejudice fuels camp's queer representation as much as it quashes it. Noël Coward, for example, a literary icon from London, worked and appeared in US TV.[23] According to Coward, in various professions, as on the street, "a polo jumper or unfortunate tie" could "expose one to danger."[24] Coward once warned a friend that recognizably queer dress could "close . . . doors" in Hollywood and is known now for presenting an "out" flamboyance in terms of queer and trans gender presentation at the time.

In the 1950s and 1960s, camp ways of relating to and within the industry created increasingly subtle and displaced forms of everyday "queer semiotics."[25] According to Shaun Cole, "the styles of clothing and grooming, mannerisms, and conventions of speech" fashionable in the gay world were not "intelligible to straights."[26] However, a range of industry participants, from the queer-savvy to the homophobic, interacted with systems of queer meaning, making camp use of clothes, taste, sound, gesture, and comportment. Screenwriter Leonard Spigelgass described camp as Chauncey and disciples do, as a closely guarded form of subcultural knowledge exclusive to (white) gay men: "Those who were strictly straight in Hollywood were kept out of it—to their ostensible envy, because they were thus barred from the cultured world of Cole Porter, Larry Hart, George Cukor, Somerset Maugham, and Noël Coward. On the one hand, if you said, 'They're homosexual,' 'Oh my, isn't that terrible' was the reaction. On the other hand, if you said, 'My God, the other night I was at dinner with Cole Porter,' the immediate reaction was, 'What did he have on? What did he say? Were you at the party? Were you at one of those Sunday Brunches?'"[27] This line of questioning, with its emphasis on embodiment through speech and wardrobe, attests to what José Esteban Muñoz calls camp's "artificial respiration," and to its workings beyond white-centric culture from within.[28] Select coteries self-policed by surreptitious individuals no longer need be considered the definitive source of camp, given that, as my analysis suggests, popular entertainment circulated camp beyond the bounds of such cliques, and, as Ernesto Javier Martínez states, camp has "a rarely documented feminist and critical race tradition."[29]

Like Martínez, Muñoz argues for an identity-based understanding of camp as "strategic response," in which camp counters "the breakdown of representation that occurs when a queer, ethnically marked, or other subject encounters [their] inability to fit within the majoritarian representational regime."[30] However, in the case of trans gender queer camp TV, the camp "response"—strategic in terms of profit within a corrupt system—extends beyond classifications of subject formation and deliberate acts of individual minority agency, in part because of the industrial context of ambiguity around ethnicity, such as in the Bob persona of Scottish and US Southern or Midwestern (Ozark, Missourian; MEC grew up in South Carolina) representation cleaned up for a world of white-oriented consumption. Camp TV proliferates what Matthew Tinkcom calls "productive valences" around the question of "whether a queer *person* had some hand in the making of camp texts," while also stoking that ambiguity in terms of race and ethnicity, in light of cycles of cultural appropriation.[31] Operating through this speculative discourse, camp in the context of situation comedy represents the self-archiving insight of those who "live within their labor through camp," in a context where, as Annalee Newitz puts it, "making a living often feels like dying."[32]

Camp traveled through a broad contingent of industry producers who were more fluent in queer vernaculars than official experts on homosexuality. In 1960, for example, Donn Caldwell, a writer who was "quite familiar with the homosexual subculture," taught UCLA psychologist and gay advocate Evelyn Hooker about queer gender cues.[33] Although Hooker's research focus was on gay men and involved extensive interviews, Hooker was not yet in the habit of reading self-presentation from an insider stance. Based on Caldwell's and Hooker's different professions and the distinct Southern California social circles in which they traveled, Hooker was oblivious when it came to camp, while Caldwell, Hooker's partner, was fluent. According to Hooker's biographer, after Hooker invited Sam Fromm, a former student, to dinner one night, Caldwell remarked, "Well, you told me everything else about him, why didn't you tell me he was queer?" Hooker knew Fromm was gay because Fromm had told Hooker directly. What Caldwell showed was that someone else might know without being told.

From the point of view that the goal of antihomophobia is to avoid making presumptions, the idea that one may identify someone as queer without that person's own explicit self-identification may seem homophobic—it might imply that the knower is merely marshaling cis-normative gender stereotypes. In some contexts, however, not needing to be told represents a disruption of normative presumption, indicating the recognition of queer gender. In one instance of such perceptive practice, actor Mamie Van Doren realized Rock Hudson was gay on seeing Hudson at their studio cafeteria, following a first date that included sex on the kitchen floor; notably, the evidence was in the daytime setting and social scene, not in the sex.[34] At the time, gender and sexual minorities employed in the media industries faced a combination of acceptance, ignorance, renown, and alienation. In response to continually changing codes of conservative norms and cutting-edge fashions, sitcoms cultivated characters whose queer-coded traits were based on their camp sensibilities and lines of work as opposed to some simple sexual equation or sense of gender pathology.

Antisexist Archive Study Surfaces Powerhouse MEC

Assessing queer gender in the context of the white privilege and conservative California politics that conditioned Bob's success offers a better picture of misogyny in the period and a stronger grasp of transmisogyny. It also emphasizes the speculation about producers on which camp thrives.[35] The television programs MEC made channel the queer force of that which is feminized and devalued, and so does much of what remains of their promotion and criticism, which, like camp discourse within sitcoms, is unpredictably resonant with trans meaning. Bob's image put subcultural vocabularies at the disposal of TV artists and advertisers. Writers, including Bob as an actor-director, leveraged details about military service, health food, flight, clothing, technology, and other personal passions into charged erotic banter, sly innuendo, and relatively wholesome displays of queer gender.

In a column for the *Los Angeles Examiner* on July 11, 1960, for example, Louella Parsons, a journalist who had been skewering fashion cycles in Southern California since the mid-1920s, described Bob, who—"believe it or not"—wore a "bright green" blazer to a Hollywood party, as "perhaps... three or four leaps ahead in style."[36] The column reinscribed the idiosyncratic reputation that Bob, an actor and TV personality who had been in the entertainment business nearly as long as Parsons had, occupied within Hollywood's star and celebrity systems. Bob joked that the dinner jacket was made "from an old Billiard table." The column ran next to an image of Bob and MEC with two other partygoers and a caption that, while using conventional pronouns and the gendered term "wife," emphasized the flouting of gender conventions: "Bob Cummings used a hand to straighten his hair. His wife (right) went ahead with her conversation." The photograph frames Bob in an affected pose as Bob draws attention to the haircut, midpat, while gazing across the room, away from the group pictured as well as away from the *Examiner* photographer. Bob seems oblivious to the surrounding conversation and quite conscious of the camera, as if taking time out from rubbing elbows to flirt, and posing for the camera by posing for an implied observer across the room. MEC meanwhile gestures in a rational manner to the group about what would seem to be a serious matter, signifying executive status. Bob is coquettish eye candy. Queer gender, in midtwentieth-century TV and its extratexts, was "a mode of erotic difference or ... a means to express or enact ways of being and connecting that have not yet arrived or never will."[37] The color green was a marker of sexual pursuit and self-identification from the time of early sexologist Havelock Ellis through Oscar Wilde's Piccadilly entourage and, into the 1950s, one of many "tactics that allowed [people] to move about freely [and] construct gay space in the midst of, yet invisible to, the dominant culture."[38] Bob's look with the green jacket, like Henry Aldrich's privileged shrieking about a "green Tyrolean" hat in *The Aldrich Family*, communicates what Christopher Nealon calls foundling discourse.[39] Simultaneously "leaps ahead" and stuck in the past (wearing "an old Billiard table"), Bob's style conjures via camp contradictory "marginalized time schemes."[40] Including details of color, texture, and temporality, Parsons, and the editors or staffers who conceived of the coverage, bank on MEC's purported reaction to the garment: "Isn't it something.... But I like it?" MEC's appearance amplifies camp even as it may seem to signal heterosexuality.

This was often the case. An article with an MEC-centered title and subtitle, "Don't Envy the Wife of a TV 'Glamour Boy': Bob Cummings' Harried Spouse Drove Herself to the Hospital to Keep a Date with Mr. Stork," devotes far more copy than usual to MEC's work but nevertheless perpetuates the hetero-possessive trope. This piece by John Maynard, which appeared in the summer of 1955 in *The Milwaukee Sentinel* and *Pictorial TView Sunday*, a section of the *New York Journal-American*, identifies MEC as a business supervisor, script reader, professional adviser, and majordomo who "plunged into . . . business law, business administration, tax problems . . . [and] plumbing" after stepping out of the silver-screen spotlight. It includes pictures of Bob handing an Emmy statue to MEC; Bob holding baby Laurel while MEC looks on; and Bob sidled up for a selfie behind Jan Darlyn, "one of the attractive starlets who are seen on the show."[41] "Perish the thought that wives of actors are ever jealous, but Bob does work with some gorgeous gals . . ." The captioning, like the titling, is melodramatic; the bulk of this piece presents MEC as incredibly enviable, as someone "in a field alone," and that it is actually Bob who is the harried one, "leaping up," letting out a "strangled cry," and "running in several directions at once." Mary Elliot Cummings, in contrast, is decisive, speaking with "crisp efficiency," and calling back home to do more work before birthing the baby after checking in at the hospital. Author John Maynard presents MEC's "many-faceted life" and "certain multiple relationship" to Bob, as well as this birth story, as a comic "situation" wholly originating with Bob, even though, again, MEC sculpted the Bob persona, selected projects, and placed publicity. Perhaps MEC merely went back to work shortly after having their latest kid, but, as Maynard puts it, "Bob is not the fellow to let narrative bog down just in the interest of unadorned facts."[42]

Maynard's approach is, tellingly, situation-comedy based, along the lines of a single panel comic. This graphic camp comedy was common, and in fact Maynard's article isn't the only place to find a photo of MEC holding an Emmy awarded to Bob. Here, Bob hands the statue to MEC, as if presenting it to the rightful owner, and in a photo published with the headline "A Family to Cherish," a profile by Bud Goode in a *Radio-TV Mirror* from the same year, Mary holds "Emmy" (a kid-ified incarnation of the coveted award from the Television Academy).[43] Bob holds Pat on one side, mugging a put-out look at the camera as MEC holds out the Emmy in a gesture toward its status as a child, as something Bob and MEC produced together. The arrangement of the figures aligned on a couch, seated increasingly at the edge and photographed at an angle, correlates with a wry caption. This brief text introduces everyone else prior to mentioning Bob—implying an order of importance that puts Bob at the bottom—and identifies everyone but Bob as occupying the picture's foreground, asserting that, in the practice of TV production, star Bob, who is barely leaning behind that visual plane, is conceptually in the background. This behavior is part of a regular routine of queer gender production evident in this situation-print-comedy and other ephemeral materials in the BYU collection and elsewhere. These materials show how the guest-star system of sitcoms formulaicly generated trans gender queer camp.

Queer Gender Production, Unbinarized

The Bob Cummings Show is full of trans gender queer comedy. The series, which aired new episodes from 1955 to 1959 and was rerun as *Love That Bob* throughout the 1960s,[44] was produced on a soundstage at General Service Studios with a two-camera recording set up.[45] Whether characters were working a beauty contest in Hollywood or hosting visitors from Missouri in Beverly Hills—all part of day-to-day life at the Bob Collins Photography Studio—*The Cummings Show* gave prominence to cultural practices exceeding what Michael Warner has dubbed the "impoverished vocabulary of straight culture."[46] The extent of its trans gender queer representation stresses how misleading reconstructions of sitcom history are when programming is presumed straight and construed as cis, something further emphasized by Kulp's, Davis's, Rose Marie's, Bob Cummings's, and other participants' roles beyond *The Bob Cummings Show*. Kulp, for example, guest stars as Helga Peterson in "Passenger Incognito," a makeover-and-missing-jewel episode of *Oh! Susanna* (*The Gale Storm Show*), a late-1950s series set on a steamship line featuring an actively dating social director, that was popular at the same time as *The Bob Cummings Show*.[47]

Cultural appropriation was part of the TV sitcom trade, as in the days of MEC's and Bob's first series, *My Hero*. *My Hero*, made with Don Sharpe and

FIGURES 2.1–2.6. Nancy Kulp of *The Bob Cummings Show* (Pamela Livingstone), with Gale Storm and ZaSu Pitts, and guest stars Maurice Marsac and Paul Bryar, in the *Gale Storm Show* episode "Passenger Incognito," October 13, 1956.

FIGURES 2.1–2.6. (*continued*)

sponsored by Dunhill cigarettes, like *The Gale Storm Show* and occasional *Cummings* parodies, showcases the consistent whitening of mixed comedy traditions that established the industry's casting and coding practices of non-ethnic-ethnicizing, including in episodes titled "Africa Calling," "Arabian Night," and "Very South Pacific." Promotional materials including a publicity photo suggest its debut included a typically camp orientalizing, racist parody dream sequence, with the notable John Litel double cast, appearing as both Thackery, the regular boss character, and as an indistinct fantasy native, a "cannibal cook" in a grass skirt boiling the scrumptious Beanblossom in oil.[48] Queer gender, exoticized according to formula, was broadcast despite censorship and the high stakes of nonconformity in everyday life during the 1950s. The earlier series, *My Hero*, and proxy prototype episodes of *The Bob Cummings Show* embedded within *My Hero* testify to and complicate the industry history of white normalization. *The Bob Cummings Show* ended 1955 with "The Sheik," an episode Hal Landers, writing for *The Hollywood Reporter*, called a "hilarious satire on silent films."[49] By 1958 it was sending up westerns, the small-screen fad besting comedy genres at that time.[50] The character Schultzy appeared in appropriated Native costuming, which allowed Schultzy's portrayer, Ann B. Davis, and others to create trans gender queer camp erotics through dehumanizing stereotypes.

The column by Landers provides an example of what it is that print material contributes to the camp TV archive. The article is an example of the collaboration among dispersed producers of sitcom camp. Landers calls "The Sheik" "a wacky gem" in a review listing many producers by name.[51] Landers raves about the episode's actors, including Joi Lansing, Sylvia Lewis, Carol Conn, and Margie Tenny; its associate and assistant producers, Al Simon and Eddie Rubin; and director Rod Amateau, who "rates kudos"; and especially about the episode's "pencilers," William Cowley, Shirl Gordon, and Paul Henning (also producer).[52] Bob was "a heavy lidded Valentino-type in a harem with . . . Ann B. Davis as the siren." Schultzy also plays "a bearded Sheik(!)," in this episode in which Kulp is madeover, as in *The Gale Storm Show*, according to a more recent reviewer, Hal Horn, who calls the episode "one for the non-models."[53] As part of the overall comic frame of the program, writers and performers mimic social taboos through excessive fidelity to gender convention. In the case of this episode, Rosemary DeCamp and Dwayne Hickman, "usually Bob's sister and nephew, enact [the] wife and son, shocked by the 'orgy.'"[54] Camp is not anathema to the pop culture of this period. It is not purely a product of present interpretation. Camp reactions are in these texts, in scripting, performance, and more.

The camp sensibility of this series, its backstage setting, and the work of the writers, actors, and other crew members dissected dichotomous divisions, playing with language and oppositions of private and public, female and male, and what Robert F. Reid-Pharr calls "the (white) Man/(black) animal binary."[55] Upon its debut on NBC, a *TV Guide* reporter urged *Cummings*'s writers to script episodes with more substance, charging them to "fix" the show "by indulging in some soul-searching on the subject: how much farce is too much?"[56] Later the show moved to CBS for two seasons and then back to NBC, where new episodes ran through 1959, when, despite renewing Ann B. Davis's contract for another two seasons, it folded.[57] The cancellation was a long time coming, according to writer-producer Paul Henning, because MEC held out on signing Bob's contract with Winston Cigarettes, the sponsoring brand with the jingle "Winston tastes good like a cigarette should," which *The Bob Cummings Show* had from its debut inventively showcased in witty, gimmicky tag scenes.[58]

Queer gender, which has generally been written out of TV history, took center stage. As Chris Becker states, while hedging a bit or perhaps marveling at the feat, in *It's the Pictures That Got Small: Hollywood Film Stars on 1950s Television*, Cummings brought the Collins character to life "with a certain affected, even effeminate style."[59] Davis, DeCamp, Hickman, Kulp, and the rest of the regulars, guest stars, and extras were charmingly precise with their mannerisms, pacing, vocal inflection, and wardrobe, as well. Collectively, the cast represents a white Hollywood urbanity that is, as Becker indicates, inseparable from effeminacy. But *The Cummings Show* also links this queer gender and the sophistication of camp intellectuals in Hollywood TV to rural and southern spaces. Places purportedly unlike Los Angeles, in that they are not media capitals, contributed. Settings generally perceived to be judged as backward by insiders and queers were sources of camp.[60]

The series was panned from the outset and appreciated by many critics. In the estimation of *New York World-Telegram* TV critic Harriet Van Horne, Cummings "has a very funny show."[61] Van Horne alerted readers to the new series starring "just about the most gifted comedian we have today" and airing "at 10:30 Sunday night, if you're still up." That review began, "Watching the new Robert Cummings Show . . . one is frequently provoked to utter some stern words. Such as, 'Well, this is the most ridiculous piece of trash I ever——.'"[62] Van Horne's punch line: "Rarely is the sentence completed.

The words trail off in a burst of laughter or they explode in a loud snicker." By the time the show had been cancelled, after five seasons in au courant time slots, comedian Jack Paar was calling it the "dirtiest half hour ever." They played racy material as if squeaky clean.[63]

The basic *Bob Cummings Show* situation compelled producers to cultivate an ironic relationship to gender and sexual norms. Bob and Margaret are two single people, siblings, who expect each other, and whom others expect, to be marriage minded, but who never shack up with anyone else or seriously pursue settling down. This dynamic could be characterized as a heterosexual front, a function of the closet. However, producers' comic exposition of this sibling dynamic involves camp meditations on aging, desire, respectability, and appearance, which create trans gender queer representation through their negotiations of gender and sexual norms. According to the template of their character typing, Margaret mocks Bob's serial dating, while Bob teases Margaret for going out infrequently. Margaret performs knowing eye rolls in response to Bob's patented moves, and Bob attempts to convert Margaret to a decadent way of life, rehearsing sexist double standards presented as trite and absurd, with Bob as the butt of the joke by way of the inconsistency of social sanction and expectation across gender categories.

Cummings approximates the conventional setup of domestic family comedy series, in featuring two cohabiting adults and a child, but at the same time offers a cast of divas. DeCamp's Margaret, usually at least one step ahead, is a case in point, and Hickman, as in the later series *The Many Loves of Dobie Gillis* (CBS, 1959–63), delivers lines with over-the-top naiveté, and camp knowingness shining through. Ann B. Davis, who simultaneously appeared as Ammonia Dumont, a name that resonates in terms of network TV commercial drag, at an LA club, embodied in the character Schultzy more subtle doublings and finesse, while Nancy Kulp, on the air in dandy garb as Pamela (who the photographs in the BYU archives memorialize in queer gender costuming), acted to extremes.[64] The roommate arrangement between the characters Margaret, Bob, and Chuck can be seen as a smoke screen or an alibi, but more accurately in practice it provides scaffolding for trans gender queer signification throughout the series text. In a prime example of *The Cummings Show*'s parodic situational structure, Bob Cummings, who plays Bob Collins, the unfatherly figure, also plays Collins's spry, eighty-year-old grandparent, Josh Collins, a photographer in Joplin, Missouri, Bob's (Collins's and Cummings's) hometown. Hickman's Chuck character is another Bob double, another diva. Twenty-five-year-old Hickman plays a teenage version of Bob brought up between Beverly Hills and Hollywood rather than in the Ozarks. Some characters do fit the "average neighbor" type, but most characters work in the world of media production, and even everyperson characters such as Ruth and Harvey Helm and Grandpa Collins and Chuck are securely lodged at the periphery of showbiz and at times epitomize its unique mores. In the context of the fiction, they hang out at the Bob Collins Photography Studio. In a backstage sense, where much of the theatricality in showbiz is offstage, a genealogy of the actors, the question of which calls up a whole host of workers, contributes to trans gender queer connotations of the characters.

In a particularly interesting pattern, trans gender queer representation is strikingly evident in the cursory treatment of *The Bob Cummings Show* in TV studies. Of Kulp's Pamela Livingstone character, Marc writes, "Bob, Chuck, and all the male characters wince at the very sight of [Pamela] and are not bashful about making cruel comments concerning [Livingstone's] appearance. . . . Pamela is offered no reward at all for [their] virtues."[65] Attallah, in this same vein, describes Kulp's Jane Hathaway as a character "with all the traits of masculinity, right down to . . . manner of dress and comportment" who is "for all intents and purposes . . . a man," predictably conferring and denying the character potential entry to status as a man based on perceived assignment and, principally, physical form. Attallah reads sitcoms as perhaps most people do, without any idea that gender crossing of the kind common in camp is possible, pleasurable, and productive—without any idea that people can be queer, can be trans, and, even in combination, can be quite different from others in their same intersectional identity categories, and, additionally, contradictory in self-identification and behavior.[66] From Attallah's perspective, the comedy comes from the juxtaposition of Hathaway's gender presentation with "a pronounced feminine desire," a phrase that reflects the pernicious assumption that any sexual interest in or erotic pursuit of someone assigned male is fundamentally feminine, no matter how complex is the gender presentation of the object of desire, and even if the desiring subject is male-identified and masculine-presenting, and, perhaps especially, if they are, like Pamela, queerly effeminate.

Binary gender may appear pervasive, in the dialogue and in general, but comedy goes further, by signifying within constraints. Such is the case when Kulp's Pamela, on a date with Bob at Joe's, a raw food restaurant, appears as a camp double for Bob, surrounded by "mounds of carrots, celery, beets, oranges, spinach, parsley, etc." heaped on the back of the bar and "bowls of dried apricots and prunes and glasses of raw carrot sticks" on the counter. Dialogue calls for Bob to compliment Pamela's "dainty fingers . . . like five slender little carrots," "lovely arm like a golden ear of corn," "delicate lettuce leaf ear," "graceful neck . . . like a banana squash," "cute little radish nose," "and that tempting mouth—like a gashed beet."[67] In this scene, the script instructs Kulp to speak of the desire to spend "a glorious vegetarian week together" with Bob. As Bob lays on the ironic charm, Kulp's character interrupts abruptly in an ambiguously authored, ambiguously voiced vegetarian reverie, celebrating a stated aim to "convert thousands" to their shared way of life.

The possibilities of gender identity and presentation are crucial to understanding desire in this case. While presumed insulting, the comedy actually prizes queer gender. Kulp's performance, in a parodic mode, takes Bob's seducer persona to a further extreme. Attallah deems Pamela's sexual behavior a manifestation of "pronounced feminine desire" based on the hetero feminization of attraction to men and masculinity, which constructs liking men as a female trait. On the contrary, Kulp's character's aggressive pursuit of Bob takes the form of campily masculine, effeminate gender expression. The supposedly male or female nature of desire is rendered ambiguous, mobile, and unbalanced.

Labels such as "asexual" and "unattractive," closely linked in the existing literature and directed at characters like Pamela and Schultzy, indicate trans camp. Without an accounting of the camp dimensions of sitcom situations and the queer gender produced through their implementation, interpretations of TV programming and its significance with respect to power dynamics in the industry remain limited. The established *Cummings* crew appeared slightly revamped in 1959, with a five-year-old added to the cast in this fifth and final season. The program wrapped right after this assimilationist ploy, in time for two major players, Paul Henning and Dwayne Hickman, to launch, respectively, *The Beverly Hillbillies* and *The Many Loves of Dobie Gillis*, the properties that would come to overshadow their work on *Cummings*, and *Cummings*'s queer gender production, while continuing to generate trans gender queer camp through its formulas. Without an appreciation of how insidiously skewed to favor straight and cis "readings" most scholarly and popular methods of relaying TV programming are, media history misses much contradictory evidence.

Dispersed Authorship and Guest Stars in Camp Production

I have so far discussed the *backstage* element of camp TV in terms of backstage settings. However, examining trans gender queer camp appearing in backstage settings onscreen, as part of broadcast programs, is only one way of approaching camp TV. A preserved parody script, titled "'The Bob Cummings Show' (Emergency Script)," that unidentified writers composed just for kicks, rather than for broadcast, demonstrates how *Bob Cummings Show* producers so regularly collapsed the hetero signification systems of normative white typing into queer meaning.[68] In this case, the writers did so, indicatively, without disproportionately relying on the series' most recognizably trans gender queer camp characters. This five-page document, filed in a light Paul Henning folder in BYU's Robert Cummings Papers, includes roles for eight characters, five of whom typically appear as fictional characters in *The Bob Cummings Show*.

This fake, scandalous lampoon conforms to the conventions of TV scripts but incorporates these actors simultaneously as the characters they play and as themselves, two qualities signaling camp in print form. Bob calls Margaret "Sis," for example, instead of Rosemary DeCamp, while at the same time this Margaret and Bob embody the actors' political party affiliations and incorporate as Margaret's partner DeCamp's actual spouse (with the line "Judges don't make too much loot, you know").[69] Joi Lansing appears out of character, but only nominally, since Lansing's work as Shirley Swanson is more on the order of scene stealing, in anticipation of Jimmie Walker's J. J. Evans character in *Good Times* and Jaleel White's Steve Urkel in *Family Matters*. The setting is the McCadden Building at General Services Studio, and those that occupy offices there—Al Ellerman, George Burns, and Willie Burns, who was a writer for George Burns Productions—fill out the cast. The script namedrops still more executives: John Nicolaides, Al Simon, Maurice Morton, and the Nassers (James, George, and Ted). Jokes about the series losing money even though ratings were good and sponsors were thrilled lead into jabs at Ellerman, presumably a boss or bureaucrat. In this document created purely for amusement, lipstick and a coveted air conditioner are the crucial props.

Instead of buying an air conditioner for Al (because, in fast-paced relay team–style dialogue, "[Al] has to speak to John Nicolaides first . . . and John Nicolaides has to speak to Al Simon . . . and Al Simon has to speak to Maurice Morton . . . and Maurice Morton has to speak to Willie Burns"),

McCadden shuffles one unit around, from George's office to Al's, by way of Willie, who shows up with lipstick-smeared lips after Lansing takes one for the team, eagerly asking to speak with Willie, near where the buck stops, as the sure-shot in the group at persuading patriarchal overseers.[70] The main joke—Al's office is full of hot air (because Al is a liar by profession; because of how rapidly they churn out product so toxic it "wilts the flowers outside"?)—intertwines with questions of compensation and power structure, and is about sexual harassment.[71] Specifically, it nods to the way women can call the shots at a company without getting credit. Concurrent jokes take on the formal conventions of character entrances in sitcom scenes. Here, however, they are located within industry bureaucracy, in terms of a chain of command for requesting better conditions, and turn on knowledge of Davis's religious beliefs and practice of cursing.

This illicit play opens with Margaret, Bob, and Schultzy running into each other as they attempt to collect their paychecks. First Margaret and Bob negotiate the office as if there is a raging fire, "their flesh . . . seared by the unendurable heat."[72] Davis's first words are, in reference to the heat, "Jesus Christ!" As the writers put it, "What might become a nasty situation is averted as fun loving Schultzy enters." The exchange leading up to Schultzy's entrance plays on Democrat-Republican tensions and sets up a later joke about Bob's principal attractions. Bob is "venomous" in support of Dwight D. Eisenhower. Margaret is defiant, crying, "All the way with Adlai!" When Bob asks point-blank, "Do you like Ike?" Schultzy, the noncommittal outlier in the triad, brings it back to the paycheck question: "I like money." Cue Joi Lansing. "What might become a nasty situation is averted as Joi Lansing enters stripped to the waist."[73] Through Lansing, the writers bounce the ribbing back at Ellerman: "Don't tell me you idiots come in here with clothes on!" Camp performance appears in print in the form of dialogue, as it does in the program's actual scripts: Lansing, acting for Willie's benefit, has "heard" Willie is "a doll!" Giving away the air conditioner and taking charge of Joi's paychecks ensures George his own encounters with a topless Lansing. George gets the last laugh in the script, but not before the writers land one more quip about queer producers through Willie's dialogue, "Uh—George. I was just talking to—uh—Maurice Morton, and she thinks . . . I mean *he* thinks Al Ellerman should have an air conditioner": trans gender queer representation situated, multiply, at the site of sitcom production.[74]

The sexual exploitation in the parody script illuminates queer producers. Bob does not appear guilty. Bob may not be interested. Whether in tribute or as a swipe, the stage directions instruct Lansing to speak in a "sexy voice" while "sidling up to Bob in [a] most bewitching manner"—still half-naked. Bob, "looking [Lansing] over," responds with a campily modified Eisenhower campaign slogan that cannot but help read queer in context, "I still like Ike!" No doubt.[75] Queer implications are part of a shared comedic mindset attuned to power imbalances. Cue Dwayne Hickman's Chuck to comically avert "what might become a nasty situation." As is the case with a line about Ellerman's "heat prostration" (rather than heat exhaustion), which continues the literalized hot air metaphor that has Margaret hit the floor, "wriggle" into Al's office, and "dog paddle... to the desk" through "pools of perspiration ... streaming from him in rivulets," the repetition of this and other script cues for insider satire, pokes fun at the niceties of sitcoms, their casualties (such as the "pale gaunt shell of a man, hardly recognizable as the former Mr. Universe"), and their unsung heroes, the Joi Lansings who survive the misogyny of being passed from one boss to another while procuring perks for fellow cast members. The piece, while comic, references Lansing's acting expertise, kissing and being kissed—which is elsewhere simultaneously sexualized and disparaged. It presents this "bussing" as a legitimate skill as part of a discourse rejecting heterosexism.

This backstage camp is inspired, but it isn't so unusual. Just as this "Emergency Script" outlines networks within the industry, other documents open out onto a set of people interior to Hollywood studios generally presumed to have nothing to do with television, even in those cases where they and their work were on, or all over it. Lillie Messinger, who you could say created the classic Hollywood star system, was a fan. A letter to Bob from Messinger offers more evidence of backstage camp—beyond the very name Messinger, which, as you might surmise, is a witty "stage name" for a career behind the scenes and such talent at storytelling (to storytellers, for storytellers) that, as *The Judy Room* puts it, "Once Lillie got a hold of a story, no one was immune."[76] Messinger, a reader and editor at MGM who was integral in the making of films such as *Stage Door* (1937), *Meet Me in St. Louis* (1944), and *An American in Paris* (1951),[77] was on the invite list for a dinner party MEC and Bob threw in 1960 for David Levy and David Tebet around the time the four were trying to steal the post–*Cummings Show* spotlight back from *The Many Loves of Dobie Gillis* and competitors with a *New Bob Cummings Show* sponsored by Nutri-Bio, a health supplement pyramid scheme.[78] Messinger worked with people such as literary agent Audrey Wood, who represented Carson McCullers, shepherded three Tennessee Williams plays to the stage, and initially took on *Tea and Sympathy*, the Robert Anderson play—later a Vincente Minnelli movie—in which queer gender slips into sexual nonconformity and back again. Messinger had exclusive access to Louis B. Mayer, scouted material for Katherine Hepburn (after first directing Hepburn's screen test as a RKO talent agent), worked as a go-between for Arthur Freed,[79] and is counted among the many staff consultants who conveyed print properties by reading books, synopses, and treatments aloud to executives.

Within the sexist studio climate and now within persistently sexist industry lore, Messinger, when remembered, is lumped together with a batch of unnamed "Scheherazades" who in relaying stories in ways conducive to quick casting were instrumental in the making of studios as star mills and their subsequent celebrity deconstruction.[80] According to Richard Baer, a writer of camp TV who was a family friend and served as a "spotter" for relative David Sarnoff, feeding the General, the RCA executive behind RKO and NBC, the names of stars in social settings, Messinger "had a big job at MGM . . . and was palsy-walsy with every star on the lot."[81] Messinger is not only disproportionately unnamed. Messinger's names also consistently vary. Lillie is often Lily and Messinger Messenger. At present Messinger has two IMDb pages, each with one entry. Messinger lists the film *Panama Hattie* (1942) with Red Skelton (and Messinger as uncredited, in a role Hugh Fordin identifies as partial credit, along with four others, for the screenplay).[82] The entry for Messenger lists the 1962 TV movie *Arthur Freed's Hollywood Melody* (crediting Messinger as producer).

It was two years before *Hollywood Melody* aired that Messinger, who according to Fordin had left MGM for Universal sometime by the late 1940s, wrote Bob for a favor, soliciting a signed headshot "to put on the wall with a few of my most favorites" in a kind of metacomedy décor for the "nice new office" people at NBC were "fixing up" for Messinger in a Burbank building at 3000 West Alameda Avenue.[83] The Bob Collins Photography Studio, which producers placed just about where the Armani Exchange in West Hollywood was, had just a few, too, meaning a whole line of them displayed prominently by Schultzy's desk and along the walls of the office. Messinger's letter, signed "affectionately" and sent with "warm wishes" to Bob and MEC, ends with "fingers crossed this time again" for the second *Bob Cummings Show*.

This networking as interior design is a backstage corollary to the social mores on display in the series, which were also manifest in the practice of booking guest stars from the area. This practice contributed to trans gender queer camp. Five months before the first *Cummings Show* went off the air in 1959, Mamie Van Doren, an actor often compared to Jayne Mansfield, guest starred in "Bob Meets Mamie Van Doren" as Mamie Van Doren and Mamie-Van-Doren-in-drag.[84] Camouflaging a trademark busty-blonde look with the help of Schultzy and Martha, Mamie goes undercover in Bob's office as the nerdy Jewish Zelda Glutzmeyer, a guise these characters devise to help Mamie research an upcoming film role as a secretary without the distraction of Bob's inevitable sexual advances. As Mamie, and as Mamie-as-Zelda, Van Doren matched the *Cummings* cast's pace and sensibility in verbal sparring, in particular during sequences featuring Schultzy and Martha. These three have a lot of screen time together, in scenes that build to Bob's encounter with Mamie-as-secretary-in-training-Zelda. Mamie bests Bob, known for wordplay seduction, with a rival chain of slyly aggressive sexual innuendo. As things turn more broadly screwball, Mamie throws Martha's fur coat out the window. Bob, after failing to persuade Schultzy to retrieve it, teeters on the ledge, in an intense physical performance of fear, timidity, posture, and delicate wrist acting.

Van Doren in particular skewers binary thinking and overturns hierarchies of privilege while running circles around Bob. Mamie's appearance within the story world creates a camp context in which the production of queer gender occurs through the comparison of performance styles detached from established gender codes. This nonbinary gender crossing constitutes queer trans representation. Van Doren's performance remediates Cummings's characterization as an eloquent and skilled performer. Gendering typically implies characterization as masculine or feminine in relation to relatively stable masculine and feminine signifiers, but the performance dynamic here generates queer gender without gendering either character in the conventional sense. "Bob Meets the Mortons," featuring Larry Keating as accountant Harry Morton, a character from *The George Burns and Gracie Allen Show*, works differently but also produces queer gender. This episode merges the fictional worlds of *Bob Cummings* and *Burns and Allen* with the narrative ruse of Bob undergoing a tax audit.

Par for the course, Bob's behavior is policed, but in the manner of trans gender queer camp. The Harry character brings conventional mores to inflect the studio with well-established patterns of humor highlighting attitudes that do not hold water in the world of *The Bob Cummings Show*. As "Bob Meets the Mortons" repeatedly emphasizes, *The Bob Cummings Show* is an unconforming social space even compared to the wacky world of the *Burns and Allen* story world. During a scene in which the characters discuss the Bob Collins Studio's finances, March delivers comic lines describing Bob purchasing "feminine items of apparel . . . inadmissible . . . even for a married man," most notably a "shocking pink jeweled ladies' garter, with pom pom." Within the commercial art–centered story world, Bob works with women's wear without a second thought, shopping for women's undergarments as a routine part of the profession. Harry, an outsider to the scene, points out that, in other contexts, this action appears salacious. Structurally, the straight-laced Harry serves as a point of comparison for Bob's disregard for gender norms. The temporary addition of March inspires dialogue about Bob's unconventional habits. Harry questions Bob about receipts showing that Bob has purchased women's clothing and accessories, items that concern Harry, who states that these purchases will raise red flags for authorities. As the gatekeeper in charge of managing Bob's expense reports, Harry drily notes, "I'm apprehensive that the IRS may look with some skepticism upon a bachelor claiming as a legitimate deduction: One shocking pink jeweled ladies' garter, with pom pom."

"Shocking" carries a double meaning here, as it did in a 1958 Bob Hope joke on NBC.[85] The word references both the scandal of gender nonconformity and a particular color category, "shocking pink," a tone of pink commercialized in the 1930s. The "shocking pink jeweled ladies' garter, with pom pom" is an object of camp marked, though dialogue, by multiplicity and hyperbole—both in the exaggeration of a pink that "shocks" and the fact that the item has jewels and a pom pom in addition to being bright, pink, and a garter. This joke includes an implicit observation about a distinction between married and single men, one that resonates, in relation to the gendering of clothing and the implied textures and stimulating potential of visual cues, in complicated ways. This *Cummings Show* dialogue presents color classifications beyond the dominant dialect, incorporating, through intertextuality, the camp of commercial design systems, a domain of queer labor connected to gender transgression, self-determination, consumer culture, and sexual adventure.

The lines about the "shocking pink . . . pom pom" and "inadmissible purchases" are queerly critical in their sexual connotations. Implicit within the dialogue is an observation of a double standard—a reference to increased freedom in gender expression as a privilege accorded through marital status. The garter as gift implies a sexual relationship, potentially condoned in the context of marriage but likely to be viewed as an indication of sex outside of marriage. In a scenario in which married and unmarried "men" (a group invariably including some trans women) may actually be buying "women's" clothes to wear themselves, one has an alibi while the other appears indecent. The character of Harry suggests that such items are beyond taboo for people who are assigned male and remain unmarried, yet the writers trade in irony here. They are addressing the supposed taboo of a bachelor buying "women's" lingerie openly on TV, and they are presenting a situation in which such purchases would constitute work, if not unambiguous work or work universally considered legitimate, given its imbrication in Hollywood mores and modes of production. The comedy plays on the potential scandalousness of the garter, in terms of class markers and taste connotations. It also, simultaneously, plays on the ironic contradictions within hetero- and cis-normativity that make it acceptable for someone perceived as a man to purchase clothes understood to be for women only if that person has a wife. The category of person making these purchases encompasses trans women, even as they are undifferentiated from "men" in the primary social context for the comedy.

This conceptual use of color in the black-and-white telefilm also queerly interrogates the gendering of colors and clothing and, in a camp manner, represents Bob's behavior as both shocking and not. Later in the episode, when Bob dismisses Harry as "stuffy," the writers articulate Bob's conflict with the conventional mores of the accountant again in terms of color, as Bob refers to Harry as "the kind of square that thinks if you don't wear a dark blue suit you're automatically a playboy." Voicing a desire not to be stereotyped, no matter how accurate the stereotypical interpretation might be, this dialogue suggests that people who, in the manner of this character Harry, peg someone as a playboy based on their reputation or self-presentation in terms of style expose their own insufficient imagination, in terms of their reliance on a limited set of signifiers and denotative interpretation. With narrow understandings of cultural norms and of the ways in which it is possible *not* to conform, they are unable to comprehend nuance and variation in the self-representation of marginalized people who proudly depart from social conventions. In the context of the series, Bob's criticisms of Harry serve as a marker of *The Cummings Show*'s characters' camp approaches to social mores around clothes, sex, gender presentation, and artistic production. Bob's exchange with Harry indicates that Bob's facility with women's clothes could suggest queer, trans, or trans and queer identification, but the main point is that the classification of the item as appropriate only for women causes problems for Bob.

The characterization forming the basis of *The Cummings Show* situates Bob as genderqueer. Bob rarely disavowed interests construed as feminine according to social protocols for heteronormative behavior.[86] Instead, the character happily plays the role of matchmaker to friends and makeover artist to models. The comedy scripted for and performed in the program focuses on Bob's suave manner. This includes an ability to communicate across a range of purported gender, class, and language divides. It also includes expertise in charming people, particularly women and fashion models, but also sailors and city officials. *Cummings* represents Bob as "silver-tongued," that is, able to convince anyone of anything, and as like a woman in many ways, including this one, which values feminine behavior, especially the more flamboyant it is. Bob's manner, which undercuts the supposedly strict masculine norms of the day, was an obvious asset in the success of the program, treated with tongue in cheek in advertising the series, and an inspiration to television viewers, especially television viewers who were also television producers, like Jimmy Caesar as evident in Bob's appearance on *Burns and Allen*.[87]

Guest Stars Within

The guest-star system of sitcoms relies on performers who appear intermittently and often only once in a series. These same performers sometimes have regular series roles. Ann B. Davis is an example of one such character actor. Davis indicates not only how conducive overall sitcom formulas are to the articulation of the perspectives of supporting and minor characters within their story worlds but also how this system consistently produces trans gender queer representation. As Schultzy in *The Cummings Show*, Davis suffuses the camp-written "secret crushes" with camp performance, as prime evidence of collaborative self-typing. Schultzy is Bob's assistant: studio receptionist, stand-in model, printer, and production coordinator. Schultzy acts desperate for Bob privately, while the two function as pals day to day. (Kulp's Livingstone, in sharp contrast, attempts to seduce Bob with over-the-top seduction tactics, sexual aggression, and physical contact.) Codes for straight femininity and hegemonic masculinity resonate as femme and butch effeminacy, calling for nonce taxonomizing.[88] Queer gender occasions verbal repartee, flirtatious wit, and unconventional sex appeal. In a mundane and much-repeated trope, Patti (Eleanore Tanin), someone hanging around the front office as if they spend a lot of time there, teases Schultzy about Bob in a way that emphasizes their respective roles within the Hollywood production system.[89] After walking in on Schultzy kissing a framed photograph of Bob, Patti acts convinced that Schultzy and Bob are in a sexual relationship they hide for professional reasons. As part of the series' premise, Bob's success requires that people, especially models, assume Bob is available (an inversion of the conventional casting couch). Instead of speaking simply to communicate a clear message, these characters relish the form their conversation takes, as if the words are scripted for their delivery; they were. Davis, the performer, relishes this relishing. The scene might not pass the Bechdel test, a contemporary metric for gauging media sexism, but the conversation and the details of its execution are significant with respect to feminism. When Schultzy kids around with Patti, ad libbing a pretend secret as they amuse each other with camp banter, the script calls for Davis to "look around to make sure they're alone—then confidentially" deliver the lines. This look is not "to make sure they're alone" in the secured front office, but rather to amuse Patti (and with Patti, the audience). With each character as the other's knowing audience, the bit emphasizes the intimacy of the playful conversation, through physical proximity and easy demeanor with gender variance.

Another episode, titled "Bob Falls in Love," includes Davis's performance as Schultzy and as a Mr. Schultz version of the Schultzy character. This episode uses special effects, a dream sequence, and drag for a fantasy psychoanalytic satire featuring two versions of Bob. The writers develop a kind of anti-Bob with the urge to marry and a camp device in which this second, marriage-minded Bob levitates from Bob's body and interacts, as an ironic representation of the repressed unconscious of the unrepentant playboy Bob, whose commitment to bachelorhood is already ambivalent, consistently called into question as a deliberate and possibly highly embellished construction, a publicity strategy for the photography business, as sexual compensation, or both. After reestablishing Bob's trademark aversion to marriage and then calling this defining characteristic into question, the episode depicts Bob having a nightmare. This dream sequence, framed within the mind of the fantasy double, further compares Bob's staunch bachelor persona to a conjured married and monogamous version of the character. This segment draws out the subconscious as a trans gender queer space, highlighting Schultzy's role in Bob's bachelor equilibrium in a manner that ironically explains the usual departures from heteronormativity that define the series.

In Bob's marriage nightmare, daily life is a grind with wife Kay (Lola Albright) and three children, played by Bob and MEC's actual kids. Schultzy appears as Mr. Schultz, as Bob's boss rather than an assistant. Kay forbids Bob and Schultzy from working together out of jealousy. In other words, the plot villainizes heteronormativity, which the dream Kay character, the opposite of the regular, unconventional Kay, represents. In dialogue providing exposition for the nightmare trajectory, Schultzy's dream character Schultz commiserates with Bob about marital woes. Bob states, "You know how jealous Kay is. If [Kay] ever finds out you're a girl, we're both dead." In this vision of a nightmare marriage, Bob works in a less flashy field of photography and relinquishes designer purchases as well as time with Schultzy while Kay goes on shopping sprees. "A mink coat!" Bob cries out, "Kay, I haven't had any new clothes in five years!" The proximity of the dialogue articulating Bob's desire to shop and the line in the script concerning the mink coat create trans gender queer camp. While Noël Coward felt that those in the media industries had to walk a tightrope to dress how they wanted and not put themselves and their careers at risk on the basis of shirtsleeves that were "too tight," Bob was costumed in deep V-neck polos and patterned dress shirts often worn with the short sleeves further rolled, styling perceived in a range of ways as feminine, effeminate, and otherwise trans gender queer.[90]

As part of such innovatively formulaic plotting, *Cummings* conveyed basic backstage knowledge about the types of people at work within advertising-driven production cultures. Schultzy appears in *Cummings* publicity in this mode, for example in photographs from the filming of an episode in which Davis is incompletely ensconced in an ape suit, the most common nonhuman animal costume Schultzy dons, and in this case dons partially, wearing the body suit of the gorilla without the headpiece. *Cummings'* producers keyed Davis's performances of Schultzy's office tasks to systems of typecasting at work in the production of *Cummings* and the rest of camp TV. Schultzy, someone cast as a tiger and as a bull charging at the "Latin lover"–pegged Donna Martell, is also cast as an effeminate French artist chasing a femme model and as Señor Pancho Mendez in a takeoff of a *Real Confessions* tabloid story, "How I Fooled the Spanish Government Posing as a Girl by Señor Pancho Mendez." When Bob's friend visits the studio with a child and Bob asks them, in a pedagogically parental turn, to name the animal on set—a person fully camouflaged in a bull costume—the child responds by pointing at and correctly identifying, "Schultzy!"[91] When Bob explains the Pancho Mendez assignment with a compliment—presumably backhanded in context of dominant discourse—about Schultzy's "very versatile face," Schultzy jokes back, "I can be anything but a girl."⁹²

In an extensive early review, Van Horne paid tribute to Schultzy, analyzing Davis's initial stint in a gorilla costume, in a two-part episode, as high satire in the guise of a lowbrow costume gag. Addressing the concept of Schultzy as a primate at length, Van Horne argued that the merits of *The Bob Cummings Shows* were evident in its writers' and actors' ability to sustain the wardrobe without the conventional cinematic "motivation" for absurd set pieces provided by plot. Bob photographs "a beautiful blonde in the arms of a fierce gorilla" simply because Bob is Bob, a photographer in Hollywood, rather than because of some pointed backstory. Van Horne's review drew attention to *Cummings*'s producers' evident disregard for what would, in other production contexts, be considered required narrative justification. While developing photos and doing office tasks, Schultzy "potter[s] about the studio answering bells, taking prints out of the developer and obeying orders like any rational human being."

Van Horne's description of Schultzy's screen time in the gorilla suit emphasizes gender and class: a stuffy upper-class white character treats Schultzy, in the gorilla suit, as male or male-ish due to the way Bob compliments Schultzy's talents. Drawing attention to the art of scripted dialogue, Van Horne writes, "A middle-aged lady of unimpeachable refinement chose this particular time to call on Cummings. A conversation ensued in which Schultzy was praised to the skies for 'his' ability to type, receive callers, answer the telephone and so on. The caller, Mrs. Anderson, picked up her little dog and fled in terror." Van Horne's detailing of the situation also stresses the visual punch line of Anderson's retreat from the studio and shock at Bob's behavior. This sets up the flip side of Anderson's reaction in the second episode. Emphasizing the cumulative transformation in the initially square Mrs. Anderson's perception of Bob, Van Horne explains that, at the outset of the follow-up, "we had this elegant lady still under the impression that the handsome, eccentric photographer had a gorilla doing all [the] work. When Cummings asks if he can bring Schultzie to a party Mrs. Anderson is giving—('I want [Schultzy] to meet some nice people')—Anderson responds by getting a chimpanzee to be Schultzie's date." This is a camp take on the traditions of representation that produce "the default movie sex for costumed monkeys and apes [as] unspecified, genderless, in a literalization of the generic unsexed animal type."⁹³ Such dehumanizing anthropomorphism might seem insulting, but it builds on traditions full of trans gender queer representation.

These formulas are evident, for example in Ernie Kovacs's "Nairobi Trio" sketches. Performed across the 1950s and into the 1960s, these routines feature performers anonymized with ape masks moving mechanically as if figurines in a music box, appearing to play instruments and increasingly striking each other in syncopated unexplained violence instead.[94] Animalizing displacements of human interaction along these lines but through dialogue, like animal-themed double entendre, are common in *Cummings*. One example is Kulp's character's frequent birdcalls, motivated as much by basic patterns of eccentric typing and comically displaced dialogue as they are by the plotting of broadly metaphoric bird-watching situations.

Donna Martell's cameo, in a role notable for its racialized construction in the context of Martell's nonethnic-ethnic casting history, is in a second season episode, "The Silver-Tongued Orator," interwoven with the regular characters' scheme to convince another guest star, Mrs. Neemeyer (Marjorie Bennett), who represents the expanded space for eccentric *whiteness* in these sitcoms. With Martell offscreen, Bob refers to the actor character as "a lady bull with a Spanish accent" and Bob's friends register the effects of this character's "fiery... temperament" in the fact that Bob's butt hurts too much to sit down, emphasizing ethnicity, sexuality, tourism, and Hollywood as a cutthroat industry (as harsh as romance, and racist) and the place to be.[95] In the episode, Margaret and Harvey persistently circulate sexual references to Bob's sore ass, in commentary that Chuck does not understand. Although a teenager, Chuck is usually a full participant in the show's racy dialogue. In this episode, however, Chuck is portrayed as a perplexed bobbysoxer in relation to particularly "adult" material, which emphasizes a division based on people's ability to comprehend showbiz vernacular about sex. Bob joins the dinner table, intending to eat while standing. Chuck pleads for an explanation while Bob repeatedly snaps, "Stay out of it!" Margaret tells Chuck that Bob was "gored by a bull," and Bob interjects, "That's about as straight an answer as you're going to get." Camp production of queer gender led to queer sexual representation in the context of *Cummings*. In the face of Chuck's frustrations, Margaret continues the risqué play with words, suggesting that Bob learn from the fiasco that those "who live by the bull get caught in the end," referring to age, anal, and more.

Television historians and critics of *The Cummings Show* at the time the program aired have often—based on the perception of DeCamp as projecting a parental presence[96]—focused on Margaret's worry that Bob is a bad role model for Chuck, portraying this exclusively as conventional parental investment in propriety and wholesome normativity when it is also a camp device for more gay playboy and queer secretary dynamics. Previous treatments have missed the extent to which Margaret's ostensible concern with Bob's influence on Chuck is an opportunity for the writers, and, within the story world, the character, to rib Bob. They have ignored Margaret's own investments and active participation in the sexual culture of showbiz, at and outside the setting of the Beverly Hills abode. When Bob voices relief that the shoot for the travel ad is completed, Margaret again references Bob's affair with the Martell's model: "That's a good thing, otherwise you'd never be able to sit down." This dialogue highlights the expertise of *Cummings*'s producers. Positioning Chuck as a naive outsider on Bob, Margaret, Harvey, and Schultzy's conversation, the writers have Chuck repeat the BDSM/anal innuendo in ignorance, a strategy for scripting the conversation that compounds the camp slant. As Margaret and Harvey grow exasperated with Chuck's attempts to appreciate in full detail their commentary, the producers highlight taboos about keeping "adult" content from young people, which accentuates the salaciousness of the dialogue. In an ironic shout-out to teenage viewers, the writers include a comically displaced rejection of the interest they've scripted their characters stoking, with Margaret and Harvey yelling in unison with Bob, "Chuck, stay out of it!"

Engaging with queer signifying systems was a popular art in which this show specialized. Fans of the series recognized this. They lived it. Bob describes one fan letter as "wonderful . . . almost overwhelming . . . considerate . . . constructive and heartwarming." Written by Grizelda E. Grünwald and sent in the first months of 1964 from Fort Lauderdale, Florida, where *The Bob Cummings Show* was airing in reruns on CBS at 11:30 AM, the letter raves about *Love That Bob* (the program's title in syndication) and especially about Bob. Grünwald wrote the letter to Paul Henning, as a request that Henning work with Bob again. "There must be a laugh every 6 seconds, at least! It is exciting, has a good clean plot; yet if we must have SEX in TV, why not something that is fun and educational?" But Henning had moved on by the 1960s (perhaps dropping Bob as Bob had dropped Don Sharpe, the packager of *My Hero*).[97] Moving on included collecting residuals on *Love That Bob*, a name announced ostentatiously as a kitschy command. They went to coproducers George Burns and MEC as well as Henning. Reruns were in full swing as a second *Cummings Show* started to air, in anticipation of another upswing in camp during the ensuing era of further fractured, extended, fantastic, mixed, and amalgamated family comedies.

Moving on also meant repeating and elaborating on formulas from the first *Bob Cummings Show*, which was broadcast in a regular slot each weekday in many markets, along with *My Hero*, which by 1957 was already "being seen in some places in reruns for the 64th time." Henning was back on CBS again, with the "blockbuster" *Beverly Hillbillies*. Corn, a derisive name for camp TV's antiurbanism,[98] kept Kulp on the air as Jane Hathaway, and other character actors featured in *Cummings*, such as Rose Marie and Ann B. Davis, continued to work, without any credit going to MEC, who may very well have cast them in this marginally remembered but influential series.

3

Marriage Schmarriage

SEX AND THE SINGLE PERSON

This chapter and the next examine how the patterns of queer gender production common in the 1950s continued in the 1960s. Production cultures negotiated new media convergence for privilege within the "anti-indigenous self-determination" of structuring racism, which proliferated as a corollary of the social categorization sitcoms emblematize—simultaneously inventing and operationalizing difference—through their use of stereotype as a medium.[1] As high-concept premises moved from pitch to program, the production process curtailed many of their camp qualities. But sitcom formulas continually reinvigorated queer gender tendencies in a wide range of conceits. I highlight the continued white-centrism within the US network system of market- and ad-driven programming. Trans gender queer characters have remained regularized but appear more marginally, as seen in the 1970s, as sitcom producers began to solidify the gay-as-white-male type that has dominated sitcoms ever since. People perceive significant shifts over the decades, but what is the difference, considering the disparate identity discourses of the periods? The implications of my work are to redirect habits of assessing archives according to narratives of progress.

This chapter draws on archival print records to question rote presumptions about queer invisibility in network TV before the 1970s. Movement, costuming, and dialogue are queer gender signifiers circulating within a dominant system of signification. While the vast majority of people somehow consume, without recognizing, the queerness of gender, the multiple meanings constructed through these signifiers participate in queer culture and in this case particularly in queer critiques of marriage. The mundane everyday process of creating comic distinctions set against social norms, as part of Hollywood studio production, rendered queer gender so commonplace it was unremarkable. At the same time, the celebration of queer gender and trans gender queer camp in the industry was the subject of self-reflexive treatment. The resulting discursive system inventively unhinged from ideas about "born" sex; binarized sex organs, sex practices, and secondary sex characteristics; "biological" gender; and other rhetorical instruments of racism, cissexism, ableism, eugenics, and genocide. As a result, the institution of marriage, as a socioeconomic structure of reproducing white cis-heteropatriarchal privilege, became camp. Sex comedy and entire new transmedia genres, such as "apartment plots" in sitcoms, indulged sexist mores while presenting sexism and something else, something queerer and with trans textuality, queer gender representation.[2]

This chapter excavates the ephemeral yet indelible queer gender of 1960s sitcoms, documenting daily work on *Occasional Wife, Love on a Rooftop*, and *He & She*. I use the miraculous detritus preserved in the Harry Ackerman Papers and other collections to deliver a Rose Marie–centered reading of the canonized *Dick Van Dyke Show* (CBS, 1961–66), beginning with Nancy Kulp in a nonsitcom setting in order to emphasize the cross-format production of queer gender. *Occasional Wife* (NBC, 1966–67), in which Rose Marie guest starred as an orientalized astrologer, showcases an irreverent fake marriage between an aspiring fashion designer and an advertising agent. That program shared a wardrobe designer, Renee Firestone,[3] with *Love on a Rooftop* (ABC, 1966–67), a series that spotlights the money troubles of a newlywed former fashion designer associated with San Francisco style and an interning architect spouse, a wiz in the kitchen. *He & She* (CBS, 1967–68) features Paula Prentiss and artists involved in adapting a comic book into an animated children's show with a live-action hero, in New York. Looking at trans gender queer representation in these programs as synonymous with camp and comedy history further explains the TV production context of attention to queer gender and character actors aligned with Kulp and Rose Marie as one that constitutes trans discourse in the 1960s. The sitcom form is conducive to critique of sexism and sexual harassment and to a collaborative flirtation with queer culture presumed sequestered offscreen.

The *Password* Is Queer Gender

In the fall of 1966, just as the CBS network debuted the fifth season of *The Beverly Hillbillies*, a "blockbuster" Filmways series that amassed 274 episodes before going rerun-only in 1971, Nancy Kulp, who played the character Jane Hathaway, made a crossover appearance on *Password*, a celebrity game show, to publicize the 139th episode season opener written by Mark Tuttle and series creator Paul Henning. This fleeting moment, preserved for another fleeting moment on YouTube, records the trans gender queer camp circulating in comedy traditions in this period. Kulp is a character queerly comported in ways that eschew appraisals such as "plain" and "man-hungry" that are ubiquitous adjectives for Hathaway in histories of the *Hillbillies*. The vocal dexterity that codes Kulp's character as queer there also appears here. In conversation presented as impromptu banter, Kulp comments that *The Beverly Hillbillies* is about to air and does so "thanks to all of you," an officious gender neutral charm school mode of address invoking the audience in a manner reminiscent of Ernie Kovacs as Percy and Rose Marie as Liberace. The genderqueer character actor construction so central to sitcoms appears in this program, too, and is likewise not localized to one gender nonconforming individual. Kulp's character and persona may be generally perceived as the most visibly genderqueer, but the celebrity personalities of host Ludden and of Frank Sutton, who appears opposite Kulp as the other "all-star" guest on this episode, also contribute to the queer gender it represents. Sutton plays Vince Carter on *Gomer Pyle, U.S.M.C.*, and Ludden, likely working from a script, describes Sutton/Carter as the confidante of Gomer Pyle, the title character played by Jim Nabors—a principal performer (actor, recording artist) indicating how popular queer gender, a corollary of the epistemology of the closet, was in the period.[4]

The context of consumer capitalism provides the scaffolding for camp and the texture of queer gender, which combine to generate trans textuality. Postproduced (i.e., sound engineered) applause follows Kulp's gesture to an offscreen audience in this taped, cut-on-the-quick, serialized live studio talk format video, for consumption that holds up on YouTube today. Kulp claps for viewers, as studio audience members clap for Kulp, and host Allen Ludden,[5] a smooth egghead type with a self-reflexively canned-seeming voice, repeats the name of Kulp's program, adding, in an example of a throwaway plug flush with queer gender, "8:30 tonight." "Is Paul Henning going to let you get a man this year?" Ludden asks, emphasizing the continuation of Kulp's episodic storyline as a seasonal renewal of audience expectation. "Oh, don't be silly," Kulp replies instantly, and receives a great round of laughter. "You don't want a man?" *Password* host Alan Ludden asks. Nancy Kulp's answer: "This year, next year, never—No!" The excuse: "They just won't let me," ambiguously indicating executives, writers, and fans. The banter communicates shared pleasures in repetitive, formulaic queer coupling.

This pattern defines the sitcoms I examine here, produced in the 1960s by US studios for global markets. The lines "don't be silly" and "They . . . won't let me," which reference Kulp's understanding of the desires of the Hathaway character and Kulp's desires for and as Hathaway, involve queer gender in multiplicitous ways as an expression of this industrial mode of paratextual multiplicity. The producers edit rapidly to capture repartee, presenting a five-shot of the group, a two-shot of Kulp's team, and then a medium shot centering Kulp alone, as Kulp uses Hathaway's image as a sly, confident, adamant suitor, to self-characterize. When Kulp in another round of the game pairs with Hal Hines from Pasadena, California, and is told "for ten points, see if you can get Hal Hines to say that word," Kulp repurposes Ludden's instructions, quoting the host but dropping the last few words; "I'll see if I can get Hal Hines," Kulp says, first laughing at the line and then mugging after a few beats, amid delayed tittering, making an accidental, irrepressible faux pas in the manner of Jane Hathaway. More applause follows as Kulp explains, after Ludden jokingly reprimands, "That's not the game," "Oh, well, I'm so used to it"—so accustomed to repeatedly performing stylized stock expressions of sexual desire. "You don't need Paul Henning," Ludden observes, in response to which Kulp insists, "Oh, yes I do," a line that provocatively and poetically resonates as a possible answer to the earlier question about wanting a man. Kulp's "No!" seemed to translate to something casual, like "No thanks, I'm good." The "Yes" about Paul Henning slides into Kulp channeling Hathaway, in which case the line is an iconic ironic outburst also signifying "No, I do!"—don't ignore that desire (even if it is not mine) because of its (or my) unusual form.

Queer gender proliferates in the lopsided courtships, familiarly comic, of supposedly unattractive characters, like those Kulp played, or like those in which Nabors and Sutton and sitcom producers in general specialized. So many workers in the television industry and beyond collaborated to produce queer gender through such luminary figures without renown. Ludden, for example, who was married to Betty White, participates with a fast-paced cheekiness historically linked to queer gender, in interview portions before, after, and during the *Password* game playing. A dashing Kulp fiddles with a pair of debonair spectacles, repeatedly putting on and taking off the glasses. "They just keep you looking," Ludden states, to which Kulp responds, "I know." "It's funny to see you look," Ludden replies. Kulp answers, "It's fun to look," before a beat between warm-up wisecracks and more back-and-forth. The quick exchange is characteristic of the "mental ping-pong" for which the *Password* programs were known, a kind of situation comedy outside of the sitcom format.[6]

Kulp's fictional eccentrics in sitcoms were also all about verbal sparring. This *Password* episode transmits the imprecise but accurate sense that many producers in addition to Henning (including the workers on *Password*) flesh out Hathaway's and Kulp's already-known-in-advance queer fates, for which "recycled stars," as Mary Desjardins puts it, were perfect.[7] Sitcom stasis is the constant reiteration of queer pursuits, manifest in wardrobe, comportment, and sound minutia, established in the written formulations of the earliest part of the process of producing 1960s sitcoms, based on innovations of the 1950s and situation comedy and mixed performance traditions before. There was a climax in double-life sitcom concepts and a recycling of backstage conceits. The commercial artists in this chapter form a bridge between the fashion photographer who inflates his reputation as a wolf to chase women away that I discussed in the last chapter and those fashion photographers I discuss in chapter 4, built in as part of the premise around Peter Kastner's lead *Girl* character in the late 1960s.

Trans Proliferations in Unexpected Places

The famously self-reflexive *Dick Van Dyke Show*, cast by Ruth Burch,[8] demonstrates the connections among camp, queer gender, and trans gender queer representation and how these connections took shape and proliferated, particularly in marriage comedy in sitcoms in the late 1960s. These were programs with a significant science fiction/fantasy component, a sinisterness, and a camp attitude shining through in the writing that amounted to a dismissal of the institution of marriage along the lines of "marriage, shmarriage." This may seem an unlikely throughline to attribute to the wholesome and sweet *Dick Van Dyke Show*. However, this series involved trans gender queer scenarios, dialogue, and performance, a large part of which are positioned in opposition to marital norms. Richard Deacon, who played Mel Cooley and a hundred other queer nonethnic-ethnic Jewish parts (at least), is important to consider here, as one of a dynamic ensemble of character actors in *Dick Van Dyke* and as part of the matrix of characters at work across the industry.[9]

Deacon's stature, aura, and affectations as the married Mel indicate the everpresence of queer gender within sitcoms. Deacon had regular roles on *Leave It to Beaver* and *Date with the Angels* and twice turned down the chance to star in a series, explaining, "I don't want the responsibility."[10] After *Dick Van Dyke*, Deacon joined Phyllis Diller in *The Pruitts of Southampton* (revamped during the 1966–67 season as *The Phyllis Diller Show*).[11] In 1968, Deacon replaced Roger C. Carmel as Kaye Ballard's spouse on *The Mothers-in-Law*, in a swap as provocative if nowhere near as storied as Dick Sargent's substitution for Dick York as Samantha's partner Darrin in *Bewitched*.[12] Looking at Deacon's camp performances of comic whiteness as Roger Finley in *Date with the Angels*, a 1950s sitcom starring Betty White as Vicki Angel, and the resonance of this characterization throughout Deacon's work in the 1960s, illuminates the general eccentricity that sitcoms correlate to queer gender. Throughout this series and others, Deacon showcases a camp style of comic posturing and facial expression supported by costuming, props, décor, and dialogue. In "Shall We Dance?" (June 21, 1957), Deacon wears a white button-down untucked over black leggings to choreograph reluctant neighbors in a routine about the physics of atoms for a school fundraiser.[13] Minute gestures as well as comic contradictions of age and influence convey frustration and focus through straightforwardly fey behavior of the kind continually linked to the production of queer gender in the context of sitcom programming.

In "Francis Goes to School" (January 22, 1958), for example, Betty White's Vicki Angel character observes with alarm Deacon's Finley, who intensely yet obliviously ignores the phone while answering a call, after an all-nighter absorbed in psychological study of neighborhood pet Francis, the result of an academic interest portrayed as ironic, in light of the social friction Finley's behavior constantly causes in the context of hetero norms.

FIGURES 3.1–3.2. Richard Deacon and Burt Mustin, with Bill Williams, Maudie Prickett, and Richard Reeves in the *Date with the Angels* episode "Shall We Dance?" June 21, 1957.

FIGURES 3.3–3.4. Betty White and Richard Deacon in the *Date with the Angels* episode "Francis Goes to School," January 22, 1958.

Likewise, moments of queer gender in *Dick Van Dyke* include camp combinations of actors, characters, plot, framing, scripting, wardrobe, and stage setting. Margie Mullen merits mention regarding dialogue, in particular. Mullen is the always offscreen assistant to the *Alan Brady Show* writers. In frequently mentioning Mullen, *Dick Van Dyke Show* characters invoke Marjorie Mullen,[14] the backstage worker in charge of script continuity for *Dick Van Dyke* who directed four episodes of *Mary Tyler Moore* and worked on *Mary*, with Harold Sylvester as Harry Dresden, in 1986. Margie, by virtue of job description, recalls not only the Marjorie Mullen credited at the end of each *Dick Van Dyke Show* episode but also the unruly Max—the continuity expert within the fictional story world of Milton Berle episodes, whose camp crush on the host regularly compounded the queer gender evident throughout that backstage scene full of showbiz guest stars and local dancers.

Laura Petrie (Mary Tyler Moore), whose backstory as a dancer works in this fashion, is a similar trans gender queer hinge in the web of characterizations that structure and produce queer gender in this series. Moore's Petrie is a liminal figure poised between office and domestic spaces, the housewife laborer notoriously wearing capri pants. The Laura character is a fulcrum, as in a Jewish masculinity joke delivered by Lennie Weinrib as comedian Jackie Brewster: when Rob, ecstatic, says to Jackie, "I want to kiss you," Jackie replies, "If you really want to do something for me, let [Laura] kiss me." Conventional coupling and conventional gender roles combine in queer gender. In the case of this joke, which draws on Jewish comedy traditions, writers lampoon a mostly unspoken white fragility around the suggestion of men kissing. They position Rob as potentially gay, which is comic because of the perceived alternative masculinity (queer gender) commonly attributed to Jewish men, especially in showbiz.

"Anthony Stone," among other episodes, exemplifies Laura's role. In this telefilm, Sal (Rose Marie) receives "the third degree" about dating a character of implied ambiguous ethnicity (coded Italian and found in Jamaica), and Laura tells Rob to back off. Rob, unconventionally jealous, criticizes temporary boyfriend Tony's "attitude," "demeanor," and "slick veneer," and the fact that Tony dresses well. In a fan favorite tidbit, Rob is upset not primarily out of concern for Sal but rather because Tony is a better dresser than Rob; the Tony character is parodically vilified, actually glamorized, as an Italian American playboy dandy. Here, as elsewhere, camp treatment of queer codes scrambles the available sexual categories within dominant discourse, which produces queer gender. As Rob and Buddy guess at a secret they presume

Tony is concealing, they speculate about Tony as a floorwalker, a department store salesperson, which is one of no shortage of classic trans gender queer occupations in camp TV.[15] Moore's performance as Laura anticipates, in camp fashion ahead of its time, the flustered frustration of white fragility displayed in the face of genderqueer and other forms of transgender cultural difference today, but in the midst of the Cold War turn to neoliberalism.[16]

This advance critique in camp TV anticipates the "against equality" approach to social justice, which critiques the exclusive privileges sought in gendernormative and white-centric activism.[17] The critique, located within in the performances that constitute "Anthony Stone," relies on the writers' framing of the discussion. Leading into this scene, Rob calls Tony at work, learning on the sly, in a setup for jokes about "supersensitivity," Sal's new date is married. The humor extrapolated from Tony's marital status and job as an undertaker at a morgue creates discursive space for considering, unconventionally, two questions: Are either of these revelations a dealbreaker? Which is worse? (In the end, Tony's anger trumps everything.)

Rob and Laura's talk about Tony and Sal casts ironic light on their own relationship. The comedy culminates with Laura telling Rob about an affair she's not having. Laura, who does not yet know Tony is married, tells Rob that Sal "already knows" ... about the morgue. Confused because Laura does not seem upset by Tony being married, Rob presses Laura for a reaction. Surprised by Rob's concern, Laura channels Sal's subcultural vernacular, remarking, "You must be one of [Sal's] square friends." This comment appalls Rob. Van Dyke, in an extreme display of comic mugging in standard Stan Laurel tribute, mimes his character's shock at learning that Laura thinks open relationships, social arrangements in which committed partners consent to sexual (or romantic or otherwise intimate) involvements with others, are acceptable. In an elaborate moment of conceptual comedy instigated by brief verbal conjecture, the producers have Rob realize what it means to be in a nonmonogamous couple, all of the sudden. Van Dyke's mugging conveys a scandalous initiation into an implied divergent set of mores regarding relationships.

Rose Marie specializes in producing trans gender queer camp within this space. In collaboration with others who help perpetuate and embellish the conception of Sal, Rose Marie generated queer gender in excess of emerging gay type writing, typecasting, and character acting. *Dick Van Dyke* creator Carl Reiner (Alan Brady in the series) based this Sally Rogers character on Lucille Kallen and Selma Diamond, two former coworkers. Diamond wrote *Caesar's Hour* weekly with a staff that included Neil Simon, Mel Tolkin, and

Mel Brooks (who cocreated, with Buck Henry, the camp TV touchstone *Get Smart*).[18] In *Dick Van Dyke*, Rose Marie's Sal is a former writer for Milton Berle before joining the *Alan Brady* staff, true to the experience of Diamond. According to Deborah Schneider, Diamond embodied "the quintessential cynical, jaded character."[19] Diamond transformed the social pressure to marry into comedy. Sal and many other Rose Marie characters are in constant approximation, deflecting scrutiny of single status with distracting, defiant wisecracks. Diamond's and Sal's comic commentary on relationships draws attention to sexism, namely the presumption that women require or in any way benefit from having husbands. Schneider writes that Diamond was "again and again ... asked why [Diamond] never married," and developed, in response, comic tactics for "warding off nosy interviewers."

In spotlighting this set of skills, *Dick Van Dyke*'s producers generated trans gender queer representation connected to the lived history of the industry. Carl Reiner remembers Diamond as "the one who actually said one day in a writers' conference, 'Why don't we go out and find some girls and get laid?'"[20] In Reiner's version of this anecdote, Diamond's comment is about gender, not sexuality, even though it is spoken in terms of sexuality. Diamond was "not a lesbian," Reiner adds after relaying the line, as if picking up women was not the point, explaining Diamond "just said it because [Diamond] felt like one of the guys." It is unclear what combination of actual insight, contextual homophobia, and compulsory heterosexism Reiner's clarification represents, but, in any case, for Diamond, as for Sal in the fictionalized context, writers' room survival tactics create a force field of self-representation that displaces categorization as straight or gay, generating an open field for gender configuration. Representing marriage as a matter of (not much) convenience in a culture that articulates gender through marital dynamics deflates norms of femininity and masculinity, as does the queer gender common to Diamond's and Rose Marie's careers. Rose Marie married musician Bobby Guy, was proud Bobby was always "the man of the house," and nearly quit *Dick Van Dyke* after Bobby died, whereas according to Diamond, "The only reason for getting married ... is to have someone get up in the middle of the night to get you a drink of water."[21] At the same time, trans gender queer wordplay like that around "fellas" in Rose Marie's *Dick Van Dyke* role also resonates backstage, in the form of household knick-knacks and custom invitations referring to Rose Marie and Bobby Guy as "the Guys" as in, "The Guys live here."

Queer connections expand out from this camp foundation. The episode

"Br-oom, Br-oom," for example, is a sitcomified *Scorpio Rising* (Kenneth Anger, 1963), another queer classic.[22] Rob becomes Robby Baby, aiming for a macho persona but appearing to others as increasingly feminine, and attractive because of femme signifiers.[23] In the thirty-four-second vignette at the end of the episode, Laura and Rob wait in their garage (the garage being also the space of climax in *Scorpio Rising*) for Buddy. But the biker in black leather pants, bomber jacket, and helmet who drives in and revs the engine before lifting their mask ("I hope he does buy it"; "Here he comes") is Rose Marie, who doesn't miss a beat as the confused Petries pantomime shock. This butch queen coda to an episode showcasing Rob's femme appeal ends with a trans gender queer glamour shot of Sally. This fleeting ending image indicates how much sitcoms of the 1960s build on the sitcoms of the 1950s. Sally as Brando distills queer gender from *Cummings* comedy; Davis did Brando in prime time the decade prior, on a show in which Rose Marie regularly appeared.[24] Sal's bit is in the series more people have seen, but Roberta Shore had a bomber jacket and queer look constantly in the second *Bob Cummings Show*.

These connections point up the ways in which existing accounts of sitcom history skew characters and camp dynamics straight. Accounts that describe *Dick Van Dyke* as wholesome family comedy devoid of queer and trans representation represent the incomplete perspectives of their authors, not the full world of the program or the texture of life established within it (and within the experience of the audience). Yet a focus on black leather jackets and biker helmets risks distracting from the ubiquity of queer gender, as generated in response to norms, through sitcom formula. It is never just Sal alone navigating routine heterosexism but regularly so too do the characters of Buddy, Rob, Mel, Alan, Laura, and Richie; guest characters such as those portrayed by Wally Cox and Vic Damone; uncredited extras, as in the one-off biker roles in "Br-oom, Br-oom"; and intermittent supporting players and mostly off-screen characters such as Herman Glimscher and Herman Glimscher's parent. This trans gender queer camp is "meta" comedy in the nonethnic-ethnic ("in-between" [Ovalle], "passing") sitcom mode.

This broader view demonstrates Sal as key to traditions of sitcom effeminacy and as a part of a more complex view on characters that tend toward the 1970s solidification of a white, gay, supposedly non-trans queer character type. This type, considered merely stereotypical, develops in the 1970s by way of Billy Crystal, Tony Randall,[25] John Ritter (*Three's Company*), and Jim J. Bullock (*Too Close for Comfort*). Like Nancy Kulp (in my revised history) and Paul Lynde, or Edward Everett Horton, they are hallmarks of trans gender queer cultural production. Kulp, Rose Marie, and other sitcom specialists labeled "female" have not been considered within the set of performers conventionally imagined to perform effeminacy or to possibly play with codes of effeminacy in a camp manner. Reconceiving them within the lineage calls for reconceptualizing the stereotype itself.

The type is associated with sitcoms of the 1970s. However, the emergence of the white gay "male" characterization—later taken up for narrowcasting to yuppie viewers in the 1990s[26]—is already evident in the Broadway characters of *The Dick Van Dyke Show* in the 1960s. "Baby Fat" includes Buck Brown (Richard Erdman) and Harper Worthington Yates (Strother Martin), the type of characters who might displace performers such as Rose Marie in a genealogy of small-screen effeminacy.[27] The Brown and Yates characters are hallmarks of trans gender queer cultural production as well as of the white-centric ideology, diminishing nonconformity through conventional appeal, along a white gradient of attraction that comes to a head with the mainstream gay rights, marriage, and trans inclusion movements. In "Baby Fat," Alan asks Rob to doctor a script Yates is writing until the last minute. Performing on Broadway is a realization of a lifelong dream, Reiner's Alan repeats, cynical and sincere. Media producer vernacular and metaintertexual allusion (including to Alan's wig wearing) are in high gear. The producers build this serious-actor characterization upon personal backstory and routines of Reiner's with Imogene Coca and Sid Caesar.

Brown is a tailor appearing amid scenic dressings iconic of studio lots, and divulges much while interacting with the recurring characters of the series. Van Dyke, as Rob, is working undercover for Alan, fighting misapprehension as a rival clothing designer and actively closeted (at the level of plot, space, and absurd metaphor). Rob, trying to play the part and pass as a seasoned Broadway costumer, questions Buck's apricot bows. Brown, defensive, lists credentials, and after building to mild aggression, promptly apologizes for flaring.[28] Most viewers may have taken this "flaring," or unconventional self-reflexive in-text commentary on nonnormative emoting, as derisive stereotype reinforcing hetero gender norms. Nevertheless, Erdman's performance as Buck Brown, and the combined casting, directing, and choreographing of the character—like the very naming of "Buck Brown" (a playful anal animalism) and the scripting of the alliterative bows—present, for anyone at the time or after interested in an expanded view, a window into a world of queer gender more interesting than the conventional mindset allows.

Yates, another fleeting icon in the camp TV matrix that "Baby Fat" showcases, is dedicated to a big dog named Mister Ben whose partner has just died. The comic notion of a pet dog that's a widow provides Alan/Reiner with a prime laugh-track-less zinger based on a string of jokes stemming from this trans gender queer motif. The backstage off-Broadway situation of "Baby Fat" introduces incidental characters from the theater: someone in gold tights identified in a joke of delayed specification as a girl, and Sandy Kenyon[29] as Lionel Dann, the director of the play. Rob, intermittently hiding in the closet of Alan's dressing room, further elaborates a mistaken identity, taking on the role of Vito Schneider, in drag as Alan Brady's personal tailor. The name, a Jewish Italian mash-up, like many sitcoms, here signals commentary on ethnicity and assimilation, in a depiction of popular entertainment in some ways closely related to and in other senses distanced from the experiences in the industry of Rose Marie, Deacon, Amsterdam, Adamo, and other performers and producers on *Dick Van Dyke*. Life on *The Alan Brady Show* involves camp. This camp is shown to emerge in mediums with overlapping makers specializing in staging productions amid commercial constraints and self-censorship.

Links are continually prevalent between the story world established in *The Dick Van Dyke Show* and trans gender queer culture. Rob wears eyelash extensions in a flashback sequence in "Honeymoons Are for the Lucky," which offers an image of Rob presenting as Laura in the form of dialogue.[30] Rob is playing hooky from the army and leaves the barracks in a black chiffon dress. Pictured in the usual army fatigue uniform in a scene set in the visually comic lodge room the two rent for the night, Rob tells Kathleen Freeman, queerly coupled with Johnny Silver, that the eyelash extensions Laura is attempting to trim "kept me out of the air force," a reference to government practices regarding gender variance—and a common one, which Cliff Arquette[31] made later on *Hollywood Squares*[32] and was the premise of a movie, *The Gay Deceivers*, as well as the go-to formula for Jamie Farr's Klinger on *M*A*S*H* (and Farr shows up frequently as a delivery service runner in *Dick Van Dyke*). This moment in "Honeymoons Are for the Lucky" features a superstar of queer Hollywood cinema, Freeman, as the lodge keeper who mugs in reaction to the scene, in an example of heightened film-TV typing crossover and white privilege in casting and acting that camp TV programs such as *Dick Van Dyke* took up.

Sal's dating habits and ideas about relationships are a recurring source of camp in the series. Over the course of *Dick Van Dyke*'s 159 episodes, Sal went out with many people referred to as "fellas." Sal and friends constantly referred to a new fella, the latest few fellas, this or that fella from the past, and inevitable future fellas. Sal, Rob, and Buddy called each other "fellas," too. The term, which sometimes indicates masculinity, setting gender in repetitious relief, also sometimes signifies a lover. Or boyfriend. Or beard. Familiarly gendered male yet resonant with sameness and similarity, "fella" here connects to "fellow," a synonym that, in the context among such varied uses, plays up a gender spectrum. This work with words, like many running jokes, showcases Sal's witty self-presentation and the camp production of queer gender through the program. Sal's repetitious "fellas" gender neutralizes object choice, amplifying the sense of partner and peer while also proliferating incidental signifiers of gender, insights into heterocentric consumer culture femininity, and the dense and disparate discursive spaces of overlapping effeminacy, masculinity, signifiers of maleness, and more.

Spoken references to dates greatly outweigh any visual corollary, an economic innovation standard to sitcoms. "Fella" is a stand-in for "someone to date," as is "Diefenphaler," the rare Jewish ("fey," "fail") name Sal uses for dates prospective, past, and abstract: for "all my fellas." This is a camp gag, the kind that sitcom repetition enhances. Sal's oddball dates occasioned the casting of eccentrics, or second banana comedians: character actors. Sal dated showbiz hangers-on such as Doug Bedlork, a "new fella" who Sal can't stand (portrayed by Henry Gibson, who was later on *Laugh-In*) in "Talk to the Snail," a 1966 episode that also features Paul Winchell.[33] The exemplary "Sally and the Lab Technician" features Eddie Firestone in the role of another of Sal's one-time boyfriends.[34] Their femininity and Sal's public top behavior is one fruitful starting point for genderqueer comedy that consistently double-crosses cis expectations in the nonethnic-ethnic mode.

The trans gender queer camp of the formulas in these episodes is evident in synopses, details, names, and in episode titles. "The Sam Pomerantz Scandals" depicts the production of a variety show. The name Pomerantz is a tribute to the Jewish history of the form. In "I'm No Henry Walden," trans gender queer extras work in multiple camp modes.[35] "Jilting the Jilter" features Guy Marks as blank canvas of privilege Freddy White. "The Lady and the Tiger and the Lawyer," and "The Return of Edwin Carp," about radio talent being resuscitated through TV, are also of interest. "Dear Mrs. Petrie, Your Husband Is in Jail," "My Neighbor's Husband's Other Life," "My Two Showoffs and Me," "The Man from *Emperor*," "Like a Sister" (with heartthrob Vic Damone as a slightly transposed Rick Vallone), "The Secret Life of Buddy and Sally," "Romance, Roses and Rye Bread," "Three Letters from One Wife," "Bad Reception in Albany," and "Dear Sally Rogers" and "The Pen is Mightier Than the Mouth," with Sal on TV, repetitively develop trans gender queer camp through coupling.

Over time, many combinations of cast and crew explored queer gender through the Sal character. These same workers, among many others, made the range of important intertexts that constitute camp TV. These producers regularly used ostensibly straight coupling for queer representation. Many critics interpret Sal's vocal sexual subjectivity in witty dialogue as "spinster" desperation. Textual evidence, however, shows that the Sal character's fast-paced references to marriage usually constitute queer representation. In an exemplary bit of banter, Sal announces an intention to "pick up some shoes" over a lunch break. Buddy points out that Sal bought a pair of shoes yesterday. "So," Sal replies, "Today I'll pick up a salesman."[36] You see none of the feminist agency, however, if stuck within hetero attraction frameworks. Trans gender queer camp is a casualty of reading gender nonconforming characters such as Sal as traditionally invested in marriage when they are actually sarcastically critical of it.

For example, Marc pegs Sal as an archetypal "spinster" based on a highly partial sample of *Dick Van Dyke Show* episodes, as if several anomalously sincere treatments of Sal's single status discount the character's routine camp treatment of conventional coupling. Episodes characterizing Sal as pathetically lonely may dominate the mindsets of many, particularly those who cannot conceive of proudly gender nonconforming people who prefer single life. I am not arguing that there is a correct reading of the character that disregards the episodes with Sal's more self-pitying displays. I simply wish to point out that the disproportionate weighting of these out-of-character storylines within sitcom history and popular memory correlates with entrenched hetero bias. Recognizing Sal's resilience in response to judgment alongside the character's camp tactics for remaining independent challenges both characters within the *Dick Van Dyke Show* story world and critics who presume Sal is lonely and pathetic. Sal's fling with Rick, brief engagement to Freddy, double date to a Broadway show (*Love Is Love*) with Racy Tracy Rattigan (Richard Dawson),[37] fallback in Herman, date with Jack Carter's Neil Schenk (pronounced like "skank"), and *The Dick Van Dyke Show*'s plethora of "Diefenphaler" jokes are markers of the camp approach to marriage (and remaining unmarried) within supposedly wholesome family series.

Dick Van Dyke and other series brought to life the collective labor of collaborative comedy. They did so as camp began to fully arrive on the radar of general perception in the 1960s. Rose Marie, in a grand tradition, cleverly deflects scrutiny of the Sal character's single life by way of sexually explicit wit, as in the picking-up-a-salesperson line. In this manner, routine situation comedy suggests the possibility that these witty, envelope-pushing characters, and perhaps actual people assigned to the classification of female, such as Selma Diamond, are not presenting an unmediated otherness but, rather, are ironically producing a camp version of apparent but not actual sexual conformity. This cannot be relegated to retrospect.[38]

Trading in Queer Gender across the 1950s and 1960s

Much outstanding literature documents the nuances of pop culture and its intersections with hip, sexy feminism in the 1960s. Moya Luckett and Julie D'Acci have described the "swinging singles" of this era of prime time TV, showing, among other things, how the number of unmarried white characters in fictional television programming increased over the course of the 1960s.[39] As sitcoms remade marriage, they siphoned camp off from queer (uncoupling) couples, creating young newlyweds meeting the emerging minimum of sex appeal for celebrity in the TV medium. Queer gender was not quite as recognizable on the surface but still suffused sitcom story worlds. The self-presentation of characters such as Carolyn Jones's Morticia and John Astin's Gomez in *The Addams Family* represent one of many hybrid strategies producers used to continue to cash in on queer gender as camp comedy. Morticia and Gomez and many other camp TV couples represent a marital moment marking a spike in assimilation in TV of the 1960s and a corresponding high point in witty indirect commentary on assimilation. The intermeshing of a mainstream camp trend with the residual sway of vaudeo and other popular entertainment traditions proliferated trans gender queer camp as innocuous sitcom self-plagiarism.

As in the 1950s, censorship in the 1960s fueled trans gender queer representation. Screen Gems vice president Bill Dozier, who according to IMDb "made it to the top of the TV heap briefly in the mid-1960s," was the executive producer on *Batman* and an uncredited announcer providing the camp intro (not the first lisp in the medium on which lisping supposedly was not possible: "Get ready to cheer Batman and hisssssss his diabolical enemy"). This repetitive campy vocal delivery was more vividly punctuated and overall more emphatic than the Ernie Kovacs character Percy Dovetonsils, a trans gender queer camp TV poet who lisped like Ed Wynn, while also less drawn out and dwelt on. Dozier stiff-armed camp and its queer reputation (or tried, anyway, while hissssing in millions of homes). In pitch mode, at least (if not in implementation), Dozier construed *Batman*'s follow-up, the supposedly sincere *Green Hornet* starring Bruce Lee and Van Williams, as "not like 'Batman,' not campy." The executive told Judy Stone of the *New York Times*, "I hate the word 'Camp.' It sounds so faggy and funsies."[40] As the decade progressed, network representatives began publicly discussing their camp products and occasionally using the word "camp" in text, while continuing to keep most of the industry's camp production off screen, in hallways, on sets, in memos, and such. Meanwhile, reruns of 1950s sitcoms displayed the formulas the new and different programs continued to embellish.

Despite continued limitations on content (language, sex, intimacy, physical contact, "deviance"), network economics allowed—and actually encouraged—the subtly absurd story worlds of sitcoms to incubate trans gender queer representation. The written records of 1960s camp TV chart the continued fragmentation and interlacing of queer and straight representation. Queer gender sold, in that sitcoms were an indispensable part of television schedules, and queer gender was part of their formula. Series proposals, story ideas, scripts, revisions, memos, research notes, personal correspondence, and the records of merchandising and marketing campaigns offer insight into the ways in which trans gender queer representation inhered in sitcoms through standardized TV production processes, beyond the bounds of any particular programming cycle, subgenre, or set of authors.[41]

Yet many assumptions on the part of sitcom historians deploy what Judith Butler calls "restrictively normative conceptions of sexual and gendered life" contrary to sitcom logic.[42] Instead of reproducing cis norms, queer media studies needs an interpretive framework capable of recognizing that trans gender queer experience exists and is, persistently and tenaciously, a part of cultural history, pictured often, for example, in domestic family comedies of the 1950s. As Yvonne Craig puts it, in the introduction to Cary O'Dell's *June Cleaver Was a Feminist*, for the majority "it is simply easier to perpetuate an invalid conclusion or misperception than to re-examine it without bias."[43] Already in the 1950s, series presumed entirely normative, such as *Father Knows Best*, which began in 1954 and aired new episodes into 1960, contributed to the process of collapsing queer and straight representation through camp by circulating queer gender. This series, a radio adaptation indicative of the conservative turn in the scheduling, marketing, and studio production of television yet at the same time striking in its contributions to the camp TV archive, was a long-running hit for Screen Gems. Before continuing to investigate dynamics particular to 1960s sitcom production, I first take a closer look at David Marc's analysis of a *Father Knows Best* episode about queer gender, titled "Betty, the Track Star," in order to clarify how even feminist television historians rescript queer gender as ridicule in support of cissexism.[44]

"Betty, the Track Star" is from *Father Knows Best*'s 1956–57 season, the third of six. Written by Paul West and produced by Eugene B. Rodney and Screen Gems for CBS, it centers on a momentary change in Betty, one of the five-person Springfield family this Ed James series revolves around. Betty, played by Elinor Donahue, is the oldest child in the Anderson family, a teenager who is usually popular, fluent in social mores, and arguably charming to the point of annoyance. In this episode, however, Betty's confidence falters in the context of characters less beholden to gender norms. In the narrative climax, the track team and Betty unite to help win the track meet, and—after the track regulars help Betty change outfits in less than fifteen minutes—Betty also wins the local beauty pageant.

In an attempt to critique homophobia, Marc genders guest characters according to cis conventions, defending characters who are, in Marc's perception of the dominant meaning of the text, "pathetic," "overlooked," "unpopular," and "hapless." Marc's project is to critique the demonization of gender nonconformity in characters that are assigned to social categories such as female, women, and girls. Marc's analysis focuses, in other words, much as media studies does, on defending marginalized and underrepresented characters from ridicule attributed to the series' producers or to market-driven Hollywood logic. In this case, Marc uses terms such as "oddball girls" and "hardworking women athletes" to revalue them and teach readers to see them differently, in a more feminist frame. At the same time, however, Marc's critique takes the status of these characters as female for granted, and, indicatively, Marc's assumption that the text and production context condemn butch gender inflects the seemingly factual information he presents.

Marc's analysis of Elvia (Tamar Cooper), the guest character who takes center stage in the episode, indicates the pitfalls of close reading based on conventional gender assignment. The character's name, which is both rare and an "r" short of the more easily typecast "Elvira," indicates their unintelligibility within dominant discourse. To adequately address the trans gender queer history of camp TV, scholars must counter the presumption that characters like Elvia are simply unattractive or, in a word, ugly. I use "their" here, the possessive form of the nonbinary personal pronoun "they," to signal the trans gender queer resonance of the self-image that the Elvia character, through Cooper's portrayal, manifests. According to Marc, Elvia's main characteristics are "close-cropped hair, truck-driver grammar, and a vise-like handshake," but the text actually depicts Elvia as a leader, a persuasive speaker, and an ideal student. Likewise, the Elvia character's hair is actually on the longer side. It is styled to look undone in a fashion that the adjective "close-cropped" indicates but also overrides. Betty is, as I perceive this staged interaction, surprised not by Elvia's grip but rather by the equality and respect the handshake signifies. Elvia treats Betty like a person, not as a dumb prop, and Betty is unsure how to react. In the moment of the handshake, and several more times throughout the episode, gender is reformulated beyond the reach of the dominant discourse that demands a status quo of sex assignment and everyday sexism.

Marc, however, while seeming to protect, denounces Elvia and company as "grotesque period caricature."[45] Interpreting the episode's characterization as phobic coding of homosexuality, *Comic Visions* describes the track crew as ugly and offensive distortions of what "homosexual women" actually look and act like.[46] The comment that "Betty, the Track Star" "might as well have been titled 'Betty Meets the Lesbians'" captures the self-evident quality of the episode's queer content but not its multiple signifying possibilities.[47] Marc's analysis hinges on a politics-of-respectability approach propelled by the assumption that marginalized people are insulted by depictions of us as deviation from white normativity and decorum. In keeping with this approach, Marc's analysis overlooks the episode's use of irony, irony clearly indicated by the title "Betty, the Track Star" and the sly use of "Elvia" as a good-witch corollary of the unspoken proxy "Elvira." Beyond the Anderson family home, Elvia is the track star. Betty "saves the day" just by showing up. The episode proposes no one hero. After several scenes composed of one and two shots in medium close-up, the climax scene uses long shots of the school locker room to show Betty and Elvia engulfed by a swarm of track team extras that help the characters make it, in eight minutes, from one competition to the next, when it usually takes Betty an hour to get dressed.

The story world of this episode refracts and extends the already-notably-gender-queer world of *Father Knows Best*.[48] According to Marc's feminist work, Gloria (Fintan Meyler), one of the other spotlighted track team members, "talks like a tough guy." But that character is styled as femme. Femme is a queer form of gender that is often interpreted as stereotypical femininity. In this case, queer gender is misread, interpreted against sex assignment as "female masculinity." Meyler's performance does convey strength, but strength is not the exclusive province of "tough guys." The details of Meyler's vocal delivery in a minimal one-off role may seem minor, but considering them makes a big difference in the context of trans gender queer history. In this way, Marc's account registers, alongside the cisnormativity of 1990s television studies, the value of queer gender in "tough girl" roles, femme and butch gender, and gender variance, as well as the reach and power of queer gender in spite of such ongoing limitations.

Camp was assimilated faster and more meticulously as the 1960s proceeded. Sitcoms continued to trade in queer gender, flipping the social codes of gender and sexuality. As it had in the 1950s, this created moments of textual complexity and trans gender queer camp. This content is camp in that, as Ann Pellegrini writes in "After Sontag," it is "refusing to refuse" stereotypes and thereby "converting" the "sting" of stereotype "into the sharp wit of social commentary."[49] Local stations, the network structure, and structures of affect and embodiment continued to solidify in tandem with television sitcom consumption and related consumer practices in everyday life. The camp TV archive, as a sum total of self-reflexive sitcom inference, was already an immersive intertextual world of queer gender then.

Who Made Room for White Domestics?

Having transformed mixed vernacular into nonethnic ethnicity across the 1950s, the industry's sitcom production continued to tap subcultural slang in the 1960s, creating another round of white middle-class sanitization on display. Mary Grace Canfield, one of many other artists in league with Ann B. Davis, Nancy Kulp, and Rose Marie, played housekeepers, one of the few character types partially available to black actors. Canfield also landed parts as teachers and briefly replaced Alice Pearce in *Bewitched* in the role of Abner Kravitz's sibling and Gladys's (Pearce's) in-law. Canfield's Amanda Allison worked as a white maid for a white LA couple on *The Hathaways*, a 1961–62 Ezra Stone–produced Screen Gems sitcom that cast the Marquis Chimpanzees as adopted relatives Charlie, Enoch, and Candy Chimp. Canfield played Ralph Monroe of the Monroe carpentry team in *Green Acres* (CBS, 1965–71). The role embarrassed Canfield only because it "was so easy and undemanding," even though the coding is nonstop heteromisogynistic ridicule.[50] Critics, however, have had other concerns. Steven Capsuto writes of Ralph's "undeniably gay vibe" but bars Ralph—and Jane Hathaway, Uncle Arthur (Paul Lynde, *Bewitched*), and Zachary Smith (Jonathan Harris, *Lost in Space*)—from *Alternate Channels: The Uncensored Story of Gay and Lesbian Images on Radio and Television 1930s to the Present*.[51] For Capsuto, queer gender is stereotype and Ralph's ceaseless pursuit of Hank Kimball, a cute and awkward bureaucrat who speaks in spirals of prevarication, is a strike against. Christopher Castiglia and Christopher Reed, in *If Memory Serves*, call Ralph "a fashion-crazy . . . carpenter" with a "tool belt fully loaded."[52] However, they misconstrue genderqueer passion and interaction within a cis frame in labeling Ralph "female" and a "drag-wannabe." Give Ralph some room, and drop the "wannabe," and look for the art in the acting.

The style of coupling, supposedly "opposite-sex," is trans gender queer, as indicated by a *Los Angeles Times* obituary citing "a memorable 1963 episode of *The Andy Griffith Show*" in which Canfield queerly coupled with Jim Nabors's Gomer Pyle when, after meeting for the first time on a date, "the two socially awkward, lovable bumpkins defied everyone's expectations and had a wonderful time."[53] They were jitterbugging, that is, doing a dance that Maxine Leeds Craig shows was "recast from black cultural creation to race-less product of US youth"—easily recast as white because of "its compatibility with gender conventions."[54] These conventions, in turn, were repeated as camp (even in *Andy Griffith*) through the partnering of gender nonconforming performers, the matching of which multiplies queer gender in the sitcom context.[55] Like Marah Eakin of *The A.V. Club*, author Steve Chawkins identifies Canfield's main type as a "love-crazy spinster," cisgendering Ralph as "a down-home gal in bib overalls and a white painter's cap worn backward, a funny, plain-spoken woman doing 'man's work' before feminism made the term quaint."[56] If feminism has made a term quaint, stop using it. Why call Ralph and characters like them, even the crushed-out character of the unsold 1962 pilot "Archie and his Electric Cupid," "spinsters"?[57] Why write "female," "woman," "girl" again and again (while the so-called opposites remain unmarked)? Why the indefinite alien subcategory "working women"?[58]

This pro forma move indicates a limited feminism, one tantamount to vectors of discrimination along lines of class, race, and ability usually considered separate but intertwined in the television industry, which at this time corresponded "in a casual, effortless way to the housing and real estate restrictions so prevalent in the burgeoning LA County and metropolitan areas."[59] *Hazel*, one of Screen Gems' big sitcoms of the 1960s, indicates in its production history the ways in which the racist cissexism encapsulated in the "working women" classification prompts specialty and mass overlooking of trans gender queer camp. In *Hazel*, star Shirley Booth deadpanned an unselfconscious domestic worker character. According to the rote bifurcation, the character lands in the "female" category. As a consequence of gendered and classed connotations, Booth's Hazel, despite characterization as an *everyman*, is presumed to be unconnected to minority history and distant from insider industry perspectives. Southern California is where many camp TV producers lived and worked while conjuring East Coast suburban scenes; in the case of *Hazel*, producers considered moving the characters closer to home halfway through.

"Hazel in Hollywood" was an idea for a revamp of *Hazel* that Screen Gems worked on in 1964 and 1965, in anticipation of the sitcom's fifth season. A camp production model is evident in the proposal for the change, in the form of the producers' conviction that "Hollywood itself will be most fertile ground for Hazel."[60] Harry Ackerman writes, "Hazel is going to Love Hollywood" and "millions . . . are going to love [Hazel] being in Hollywood," in part because Hazel would be paired up with a playboy character, a "swinging young bachelor" with a "pool-side home up in the Hollywood Hills."[61] "Hazel in Hollywood" articulates the benefit of the new setting in terms of "Hazel's foils" for the reboot and in terms of Hollywood-specific situations, predicaments that involve parody. New characters include Samuel P. Egret, the production head of a major studio, and Jerry Brigham, an unmarried talent agent whose Hollywood Hills home hosts a stream of aspiring movie stars. The writers give Brigham a playboy reputation. In the proposal, Hazel, a less knowing version of Alice from *The Brady Bunch*, gives advice to producers bringing a Jesus movie to a fickle film audience; comedy along the lines of the "priest, rabbi, and a minister" set piece based on old jokes that later appears in *Hail, Caesar* (2016) ensues.

In another extended bit scripted for this revamp-that-wasn't, Hazel enters deadpan drag mode, playing a parody of a Cinderella role. Hazel finds the footprints of Wallace Beery in front of Grauman's Chinese Theater on Sunset Boulevard to be a perfect fit. The intertextuality sourced from the camp situations and settings such as this, which Hazel's relocation to Hollywood inspired, are Hollywood white, ethnic-nonethnic. Hazel melts upon seeing Victor Mature, a classic beefcake star and camp icon. Hazel is wrong, however, and it's not Mature but rather a nonactor who takes Hazel to lunch, trying to pass as Mature. Hazel literally stands on the street corner trying to spot stars, in a class-mixing conceit that could have been perpetually restaged. However, the twist was scrapped in favor of a suburban family setting more consistent with the first four seasons, when the production moved from NBC to CBS. In this context, the relocation-that-wasn't represents the industry's iterative intensification of self-reflexive camp productive of queer gender, and its ingrained reproduction of white normativity during the rise of civil rights.

Whitened Slapstick, Race, and Ethnicity

Appraising unexpected trans gender queer camp onscreen amid the discarded queer gender production in evidence in TV archives shows a kind of slapstick, or broad physical comedy, filtered into trans gender queer posturing and wordplay across the assimilation period. Ackerman couldn't sell a *Paul Lynde Show* until the 1970s,[62] but there was plenty of queer gender in the decades before, even without programs such as "Do or Die," one of several series pitched for Lynde (or Donald O'Connor, or Vic Damone, or Dwayne Hickman, or another, depending on who was available and fit the type).[63] In the 1960s, marriage, marriages of convenience, and single (lack of) status took on even more prominence, as evident in the world that Donna Douglas as Elly Mae; Max Bodine, Jr., as Jethro; and Kulp as Jane create in *The Beverly Hillbillies* (CBS, 1962–71). While all episodes of this series, and of *Hazel*, are relevant—indispensable—to the study of camp TV, programs of particular interest with respect to investigations of white-supremacist Hollywood include "Manhattan Hillbillies," "The Clampetts Play Cupid," "Elly in the Movies," "Love Finds Jane Hathaway," "Jane Finds Elly a Man," "Elly, the Working Girl," "A Bride for Jed," "Jethro Proposes," "Jethro Returns," and "Lib and Let Lib." Also essential are "Jethro's Pad," in which Jethro discovers a stack of *Swinger* magazines in Mr. Drysdale's garage; "War of the Roses," in which Kulp's Hathaway plays Queen Elizabeth I; "Granny Goes to Hooterville," in which Granny suspects Jed and Jane of marrying; and "Jethro Proposes," also about Jane staying single. Coupling and sexism are camp points of focus and focal points for camp—as in "Dash Riprock, You Cad" and the nine other episodes featuring Riprock, a movie star character played by Larry Pennell, one of which, "The Bird Watchers," also guest stars Wally Cox's professor, a double for Kulp's Hathaway that points to a longer history of the coding (and self-coding) of Cox and Kulp as "nature boy" types, such as in *Love That Bob*.

Nancy Kulp's comic performances and structuring role as Jane Hathaway are, while far from the only source of queer gender, routinely crucial to the trans gender queer camp accessible in *Beverly Hillbillies*. Art imitates life ironically, especially around Hathaway. Kulp didn't work the week they made "Elly Becomes a Secretary," so Hathaway is, in the fictional context, also a no-show. Still, Kulp's character is central to the conception of the episode, and Kulp, along with Hathaway, appears as a local offscreen presence conveyed through prerecorded audio. Kulp's Hathaway is instrumental to this episode even though Kulp need not act. Jane's audiovisual characterization is partly through the term "sick benefits," a bureaucratic term for paid leave from work that the writers have the characters Granny, Jethro, Elly, and Jed quote often, creating comedy through the repetition because it is these actors' performances that provide the punch line, in that they convey the characters' assumptions that "sick benefits" is a virus like "sick stomach," a miscommunication that motivates fish-out-of-water shenanigans at the Commerce Bank of Beverly Hills and continued reference to Hathaway playing hooky.[64] (Not a chance, for this meticulously diligent, hypercommitted character; a doctor is there when Drysdale calls Jane at home.) In episodes such as "The Clampetts Entertain," Kulp has two costume changes, two dance partners, and a runway moment with Jim Backus as Marty Van Ransohoff, who Jane inexplicably sets up to take Jed, Granny, Elly, and Jethro's behavior not straight but rather as parody poignant camp.[65]

Camp TV took over even more in the 1960s, yet long-standing camp-producing troupes such as the Three Stooges had a hard time getting work. The Stooges's recut films (mostly from the 1930s, sometimes censored and sometimes not) were widely syndicated, and merchandising continued, making money for Columbia via Screen Gems. Their existing deal with the film studio at the time they started working in TV ruled out running a new series, but they kept making pilots. Trans gender queer representation is everywhere in the Stooges's nonethnic-ethnic Jewish oeuvre. Moe Howard's trademark bang-centric bowl-cut is an indirect tribute to the long hair that Jennie Gorovitz Horwitz, Moe's parent, loved to curl and couldn't bear to cut. Circulating still, the hairstyle continues to mourn the abuse Moe dealt with for ten-inch curls, which Moe calls "the battle of my school career."[66] Moe's Wikipedia entry rehearses the story minus the many tears Moe and Jennie cry the day Moe is finally pushed, in a racially charged erotic exchange, to lop off the long locks.

Yet, again, the censorship of queer gender becomes acute in the 1960s.

According to David Hogan, the scene in the Stooges's 1936 short *Movie Maniacs* in which "Moe dragoons three starlets . . . to demonstrate the proper way to give and receive a kiss," is "a cute, innocuous sequence that," after having played in theaters, "was occasionally axed by local TV stations."[67] In this context terms such as "cute" and "innocuous," considering status quo sexual harassment, signal trans gender queer sexual representation. The Stooges, a group that consisted of a rotating cast over the decades, consistently played the parts of women as well as their own parents, partners, and kids. We see this queer gender jettisoned even as it intersects with camp TV in terms of workers and work history, such as with Joe Besser, one member of the Stooges, who landed a recurring sitcom role in *The Joey Bishop Show* as an eccentric manager.[68] The contract situation of the Stooges exemplifies the continued assimilation of comedy associated with vaudeville-oriented Broadway, which is where the Stooges got their jump-start. While one-off episodes such as "Baby Fat" (*Dick Van Dyke*) located the theater in a special place within the imagined world of sitcom episodes, Broadway sitcom series were few and far between. *Where's Raymond?* with Ray Bolger lasted two years, with a rebranding and story overhaul in between seasons. A *Just off Broadway* pilot with Rose Marie wasn't picked up, and *My Sister Eileen* (CBS, 1960–61), in which Rose Marie played a Broadway type, wasn't renewed for a second season.[69]

Camp production continued to skyrocket, however, even as the most straightforward ethnic vernacular was expunged from scripts and sitcom concepts. *Car 54, Where Are You?* (NBC, 1961–63), which was made and set in New York in the 1960s, was in frequent conversation with Broadway. This series fulfilled expectations of the sitcom set by its predecessors and peers while poking fun at the theater and "theater people." At this stage studio sitcom production standardizes, operating in an industrial, streamlined mode producing light comedy fare across the early 1960s, a time of the uneven coming of color broadcasts. Dialogue and music brought color (as discourse and present absence) into black-and-white shows, through wordplay, scores, and performance, including in ads and interstitial material. In *Car 54, Where Are You?*, cops dished about Joan Crawford, already an established camp icon in the period,[70] and provided critiques, in mixed Bronx dialect, of Shakespeare in the park.

Car 54 queerly couples Francis Muldoon (Fred Gwynne) and Gunther Toody (Joe E. Ross). Like many sitcoms of the 1960s, *Car 54* imagined social relations that celebrated queer gender when it was shunned, ridiculed, and vilified in the broader imagination. As plenty of other shows did then in real time, *Car 54* demonstrates the continuity of camp discourse in vaudeo and sitcoms, through scripted wordplay, performance, and their combination in characters such as Silvia Schnauser (whose last name is a big-nose-and-small-dog reference), formerly Sylvia Schwarzcock (whose last name replaces the Yiddish "schnoz" with a more sexualized organ), played by Charlotte Rae, a sitcom icon whose camp acting is well known if not well documented or studied.[71] *Car 54* production materials housed at the Wisconsin Center for Film and Theater Research relate a provisional title for this landmark series of "Snow Whites," a slang term for cop cars (with white roofs). The change of the title is indicative of the context. Sponsors considered "Snow Whites" too obscure, too difficult. This jettisoned title is appropriate in terms of the structural racism of US TV and the way police officers are, despite records of brutality and discrimination, depicted as pure, innocent, and good-hearted in popular media. *Car 54* questioned this depiction of cops. It also cast and intermittently showcased momentarily actors of color, including Nipsey Russell. Sitcoms were emblematic of what Judith Smith in *Becoming Belafonte* calls "TV's Snow White Land."[72]

The camp of TV shows such as *Car 54* explores questions of class, taste, art, economics, ethics, and medium specificity in ways that resonate beyond the capitalism that occasioned all this racism and surface ridicule of gender nonconformity. In the case of Crawford-obsessed *Car 54* episode "That's Show Business," for example, backstage narratives, media maker guest characters, and a self-reflexive ending characterize the economic imperatives of the media industries as absurd. The working-class precinct's financial backing of what the posh producer Mr. Sinclair Fenwick calls the "brilliant first play" *Waiting for Wednesday*—and which another investor, referencing a potential "movie sale," calls "the surest thing since *My Fair Lady*"—ultimately leads to writer Robin Stewart revamping *Wednesday*, a "straight play" denouncing police brutality, transforming it into *Copper's Capers*, a musical about "a whole precinct that invests in a Broadway play." The performance of the resolution critiques the conditions of *Car 54*'s own success. The writers' light treatment of routine gender policing in relation to media genres and the episode's nonethnic-ethnic version of the theater world includes critical trans gender queer camp takes on sexual assault and harassment while also suggesting a condemnation of corrupt law enforcement.

He & She, and They

The critique of camp TV was often even more dispersed through the parodic signifiers of the young marrieds fare of the late 1960s, which overlaps with the camp sex farce cycle of popular film production in the period in unpredictable ways. By the 1970s, camp TV producers had consolidated formerly sprawling queer gender signifiers in standardized white gay types less capacious in their implication of a specifically sexual deviance. The show *He & She* illustrates this change and the continued industry move away from ethnic heterogeneity in sitcoms. Writers scripted Paula (Paula Prentiss) and Dick (Richard Benjamin) Hollister as sophisticates in a Manhattan high-rise. These characters are fully ensconced in the queer decadence Pamela Robertson Wojcik describes as part of apartment plotting. The producers relied heavily on the character Oscar North (Jack Cassidy). The couple premise constructs this Oscar character as second banana and third wheel. North is the live-action superhero Jetman in the animated children's television show that Dick, a cartoonist, draws. Paula and Dick emerge as hip, based in part on the knowingness they display in response to North's camp behavior— within the story world of the *Jetman* program and behind the scenes, in the office of the production house where they work and in the apartment building where they all live.

North specializes in expressions and styles of gender that question, critique, deny, avoid, or otherwise show no interest in upholding common sex, gender, and sexuality categories, in the tradition of a wide range of performers. Producers relied on tropes evident in related camp material such as the disparagement of specific employees in the case of Richard Deacon's Mel in *Dick Van Dyke* and Nancy Kulp's Jane in *Beverly Hillbillies*. In *He & She*, Oscar's coworkers disparage Oscar's performance mode and style of self-expression, which comes off like acting in everyday life. This is one definition of camp, which aestheticizes the everyday in the process of performativity. Specifically the coworkers and Oscar's neighbors tease Oscar for being a TV actor, and for starring in a program that is animated and addressed to children. Resilient, Oscar took the craft and the kids seriously, constantly self-lampooning in defense, in classic camp elaboration of queer gender.

In *He & She*, queer gender ran rampant, in the office environment as in the apartment complex setting. Oscar acted the prima donna, prancing into Dick's studio wearing the superhero suit or dropping in on Dick and Paula during off-hours, in street clothes coded as excessive. Yet while more isolated in an individual character, queer gender remains an ensemble production. In one scene, Dick, for example, performs the trademark voiceover from the crime series *Naked City* in a moment of intertextual parody humor, consistent with the sensibility Oscar displays when delivering, upon exiting the soundstage, the line: "You just missed my big dramatic scene. Fortunately it lives forever on film." This comment epitomizes camp TV as an industry sensibility and "live" mode of production. In the backstage spaces of *He & She*, Oscar displays queer composure, including incongruously, to comic effect, during intermittent pauses midtantrum. In Cassidy's affected performance of precise leg-crossings, and other such mannerisms differing from the queer gender of the Jetman character portrayal. Cassidy and the others who contribute to the characterization present a regionally and historically specific reflection on the industry. Writers created Oscar in Los Angeles, projecting ideas about ways of relating to the media industries onto a posh advertising scene in the Madison Avenue offices of a New York City Studio, remapping dynamics at play between Broadway and the Bronx borough in *Car 54*.

He & She's metatextual framing devices also play up the homophobia and gender normativity of racism in the industry. Censorship intensified in the 1960s, as ABC, for example, in constant court hearings, gradually standardized to the National Association of Broadcasters Code. Hal Humphrey reported, upon Ernie Kovacs's death in 1962, that censorship of trans gender queer representation in TV had intensified.[73] Percy, a camp poet character continuous across Kovacs's series and specials, had been censored by "some brain at ABC . . . [who] thought Percy too effeminate . . . even though Ernie had been doing Percy for 11 years on TV and elsewhere."[74] According to Humphrey, Kovacs replied, "I can't believe it. It's the first time anyone has put this interpretation on Percy."[75] This put-on of a blank response, here a translation of camp TV deadpan to print, is fake surprise and dry sarcasm. Yes, they have been getting away with something, something—queer gender— that stumps Capsuto in *Alternate Channels*, a "gay and lesbian" compendium that calls this Kovacs character asexual, based on the mix of gender markers, despite how often Kovacs-as-Percy voiced awkward devotion to Norman, a camera operator, in monologues.[76]

A regular guest on *Bewitched* and a veteran of *I Love Lucy* and *The Garry Moore Show*, Cassidy, in *He & She*, stops the show.[77] Paula asking Oscar how long each make-up session takes before taping the show sets up a hyperbolic inversion: "It takes them an hour just to tone down my teeth." In one episode, titled "The Old Man and the She," Oscar makes a big entrance, hands conspicuously aflutter, playing even bigger than usual, testing out new trademark Jetman moves dictated by some in-house department.[78] Dick, Jetman's creator, responds alongside a visiting lawyer. Do they consider the new gestures a successful interpretation of Dick and Oscar's shared character? Both raise their eyebrows instead of answering.

The entire scene is oriented around queer gender. Dick is about to break the news to Oscar that *Jetman* is getting a sidekick; in typical stage queen fashion, Oscar does not want to share the spotlight. Characterization by queer gender involves media industry code words, in the following: pictures, gallery, publicity, preview, and fall fashions. Dick's dialogue cues Oscar's entrance: "Mondays are the day he takes pictures at the gallery for publicity. Brace yourself. You're about to see a preview of the fall fashions."[79] Despite this, Dick and the lawyer are flummoxed by the camp outspokenness, clearly of a world apart, and do not know how to respond. The producers hand the dialogue back to Cassidy. Oscar, in a distinctly camp move of self-absorption, of irrepressible self-sustenance, recounts, as if for self-amusement or the amusement of an audience that might share in the pleasure of defying dominant norms, reactions already received in passing, taking the similar responses of office workers as good early reviews: "I tried it out in the hall just now—I can't tell you the people who stopped and stared." This is, tellingly, a point of pride, and, as such, trans gender queer camp.

He & She's producers use Oscar to highlight the unspoken norms and limits of hip straight couples. Characters question Oscar's gender expression, and the *Jetman* program positions Oscar as always on the verge of being fired for queer gender, as Sheila Kuehl, Alan Rafkin, and others, out of those spared some other kind of blacklisting, actually were.[80] Oscar enjoys life despite the danger and sometimes because of it. Like *The Bob Cummings Show*'s Pamela Livingstone, whose deviations instantiated a context of interpretation beyond hetero norms, Oscar is ironically celebrated while characterized in contradistinction to conformity and offered as an alternative. *He & She* and such 1960s sitcoms demonstrate consolidations in the heterosexism and cissexism that camp TV sets in disarray. As camp proliferated, many sitcoms began to assert a more direct connection between gender nonconformity and gay codes. The industry repurposed diffuse camp discourse as a white-centric gay stereotype, in a move whose full effects would not be seen until the 1970s. The stereotype solidified within dominant discourse, divorcing queer from trans representation in white-centering moves toward normalcy. Classification categories related to relationships, social norms for policing nonconformity, and industry methods of typing and casting all ironically contributed to trans gender queer representation.

Marriage and Two Single People

In programming presumed heterocentric, in that it is expected to be all about wholesome marriage and devoid of queer life, there is ambiguity and contradiction of the kind ideologically construed as distinctive of trans people. Jack Halberstam's *In a Queer Time and Place* argues that dominant media culture typically characterizes gender nonconformity as duplicitous, pathetic, and deceptive, as if trans experience were a deficit, and "as if other lives—gender-normative lives—were not odd, not duplicitous, not doubled and contradictory at every turn."[81] Sitcoms elaborate and invert rigid typing. Sitcoms show the refraction of taste and class as a trans gender queer media phenomenon. In terms of taste and class, gender is construed against a rigid system of typing, which sitcoms mimic parodically as part of the repetitive white-centric schema of the format. This is evident in *Occasional Wife*, an NBC program broadcast in color that debuted with a glaring lack of people of color in the fall of 1966, the TV season following the circular conclusion of *Dick Van Dyke*.

Occasional Wife offers thirty episodes of high-concept marital camp: A wife? Occasionally. Greta (Patricia Hardy) is a hat-check girl, another trans gender queer profession, but a hat-check-girl-no-more, a self-reliant New Yorker turned life-partner-for-hire. Greta meets Peter Christopher (Michael Callen) while working at a club as an employee who stores coats and personal belongings for tips. The premise is a pickup. Greta, chatting, explains that a wedding ring keeps the on-the-job harassment rates down. Inspired by the idea, Peter decides to pose as married to mitigate the discrimination at a desk job in advertising for Brahms Baby Food. Peter's boss at the company, the retrograde Mr. Brahms, represents a system that will not hire or promote women at the executive level, and Brahms, whom the promotional material calls "paternalistic," makes a strong preference for married employees clear.[82] This nearly unavoidable—but not quite—requirement makes prejudice part of the ongoing gag. Brahms will not give Peter a raise on hetero principle. Greta helps Peter get ahead, theatricalizing the role of "beard," a figure of speech for a chosen companion offering wearable privilege. In typical sitcom fashion, the promotion so desired remains elusive, and getting ahead happens only at the expense of others. No one wins. Nothing changes. Deception is thus the primary theme. In NBC's promotional pamphlet, Peter's plan is "wily" and his wife is "counterfeit."

This sham marriage positions the program in a space of camp performance. In a visual refrain evoking the experience of conditional passing privilege, Peter calls on Greta to attend company events and be on call in case Brahms unexpectedly visits. As part of the comic premise, Peter rents a high-rise apartment for Greta two floors below his flat, and they use the fire escape, rather than the front hallway, to travel between apartments. Many of the series' jokes consist of the characters voicing traditional complaints about their marriage, which does not actually exist, a contradiction the writers used to fuel double entendre about dating and sex. Despite many sexist and conservative elements, *Occasional Wife* contributed to trans gender queer representation through industry-generated camp. Peter, "a sophisticated bachelor in glamorous New York, the playboy's paradise of luxurious parties and beautiful women," is perpetually misunderstood. LA Dodger announcer Vin Scully narrates the situation in voiceover, paraphrasing daily discrimination in cheeky radio sportscaster-style play-by-play, transposing the vocabulary of athletics to dating scenarios at the opening of each episode.[83] Press relations for *Occasional Wife* mined a rhetoric of supplementarity, inauthenticity, and suspicion of the kind projected onto trans people and people of color, especially queer people, women, and other minorities. The series thus tangled with the demonization of and desire for effeminacies of the kind in which sitcoms and character actors specialize, setting ambiguously gendered behavior in the context of Upper East Side, New York City, and Connecticut cultures of conventional business sexism, defined by racism and appropriative depictions of absurdly intersecting otherness. This whole repertoire of comedy tropes, all rife with queer content and conceptual and contextual resonance, can be thought of as closet parody, a defining feature of TV accentuated in the critical inversions of 1960s sitcoms.[84]

The plots of *Occasional Wife* episodes emphasize differences between the single-and-dating main characters and their married counterparts. They deploy stock elements of domestic scenes while incorporating subcultural spaces. The stage again served as a relay point for camp production and trans gender queer representation, as did film and other media arts. In "No Talent Scouts" (1966), Sally Field guest stars as Nancy Zogerdorfer, an aspiring actor with an "eccentric," ethnic-nonethnic moniker. Zogerdorfer is cast in the role of someone who, *Metamorphosis*-style, turns into a grapefruit over the course of the five-and-a-half hour performance piece. When Peter and Greta are pressured to introduce Field's character, an aspiring no-talent actor from Ohio, to the New York theater scene, they enlist their director friend Martin Martin (Severn Darden) to undercut Zogerdorfer's artistic ambitions. This big bearded nonconformist happily auditions the character for the nine-act off-off-Broadway play *Sunflowers and Sadism*, a work that is "impossible to understand" and calls for the newcomer from the Midwest to "retreat from society."

Such farcical scenarios launched multiple registers of double meaning in relation to differences between being married and acting married. What seems like evidence of a marriage—Greta's to Peter—in the perception of Peter's boss (a fictitious construction of Jack Collins's) is actually witty banter about the drawbacks of marriage in general. When Peter and Greta lash out at one another while in the presence of people who think they are a couple, those people invariably interpret their bickering about their business arrangement as quintessential newlywed behavior. It is a sitcom, so these are revealing moments in terms of class and taste hierarchies. Raced signifiers of gender and sexuality proliferate as Greta and Peter spoof marriage for their own amusement, in scenes throughout which other characters remain oblivious.[85] To start, the characters voice their own unique aversions to settling down in the context of acting married. Then, as they pretend to be married, they learn even more things about marriage that they loathe.[86] From sly digs at the other's faults as an "occasional" spouse to sarcastic commentary about their secret lives as single people, this running commentary plays up the double consciousness involved in a double life.[87] While this resonates in terms of sexuality, trans experience is also a queer point of contact, constructed across multiple pop culture venues contributing to tropes of playing two roles with one embodied being.[88]

Under the demands of performing marriage, Peter and Greta increasingly voice their distaste for conventional relationships. This creates camp through recurring genderqueer themes related to masculine and feminine norms, sexual mores, the division of labor, and issues deemed domestic. In *Occasional Wife*'s pilot episode, Peter and Greta prepare to host a dinner party, at which Peter plans to introduce Greta to his coworkers as his new wife. Greta and Peter, along with recurring episode star Chris Noel (Marilyn) pass Marilyn off as Greta's sibling instead of Peter's lover. The faux couple fights about the food presentation and apartment décor, judging their efforts against the pictures in "a sophisticated home-type magazine" key to the "Bride's First Meal" genre of popular print, a post-honeymoon suite trope prompting marriage advice repeated in various patriarchal capitalistic forms throughout mass culture. The type "wife," in other words, is a particular performance involving food and (typically) uncompensated labor.[89]

The Jell-O mold, now a central retro signifier of the era, is one visual punch line. In the *Occasional Wife* context of appropriating norms, parody makes plain the hypocrisy of the sex/gender/sexuality system. The comedy consistently points to financial arrangements and class hierarchies, with the literal contract and the contract metaphor mimicking romance myths, highlighting the economic dimensions of marriage. Negotiation is a situation corollary to the series premise. For example, Peter agrees to provide Greta with room and board and money for art lessons and contact lenses, a joke related to an implied ambiguity around indulgence and necessity in the context of ableism, lookism, and the undervaluing of craft and self-expression. Their contract, which is precisely not a conventional marriage contract, generates trans gender queer camp. From the outset of the series' conception and in the increasingly baroque convolutions of its later episodes, this camp occurs according to sitcoms' style of real time. In this odd, repetitious present tense, the deal is done, meaning the leads are committed to one another and their fraudulent relationship, but the contract is broken, because the Greta character can demand more compensation (requiring Peter to solicit a raise, which is one way the writers of episodes set up new situations). Initially reluctant to take on the everyday performance of "wife," Greta quickly catches on to the camp act of passing privilege, displaying hetero mechanics self-reflexively, from the perspective of the disenfranchised gaining marginal leverage. Early in the series, Greta begins focusing on fashion design. The prime topics are gender discrimination and sexual harassment, and Greta and Peter's nonmarital marital interactions are about blackmail, labor, and disparity in pay and career opportunities.

As the characters negotiate, bargain with, and bribe one another in order to reach agreements, the series implies that it is common knowledge that people with husbands should receive much more from their spouses than they do in order to make marriage worthwhile. With this premise, the series offers a picture of prejudice against Peter that emphasizes the frequency of other forms of discrimination. As Peter's references to "Mrs. Christopher" win favor, *Occasional Wife* invites a now-knowing audience to consider at whose expense. Identifying Peter as "the single man fighting the entire system," the opening monologue explains that society is, overall, hostile to Peter for transgressing the boundaries of a dominant culture in which family symbolism is sacred. With the series focalized around Peter's perspective on the most reactionary boss in Madison Avenue's "culture of cool," *Occasional Wife* highlights heterosexism and cis norms.[90] The camp sensibility manifests in the wordplay of character names, episode titles, and actors cast.

In *Wife*, Peter and Greta's social worlds are white-centric but characterized as diverse, especially in relation to the social life of the Brahms couple, which accords with a caricatured ideal of marriage in corporate New England. The world depicted in *Wife* includes eccentricity and formulaic eccentrics tied to Greta and Peter and motivated by their ongoing paramarital situation. The pair participate in a New York City social sphere that includes a range of different kinds of artists from a variety of cultural realms. By incorporating Greta's daily life as an aspiring fashion designer, the series manufactured characters reminiscent of Sally Rogers's fallback fellas dished about at the office. In addition the Herman Glimscher–style recurring standby date Bernie (Stuart Margolin as Bernard J. Kramer), Greta sees artists, a model, and a design instructor. Peter and Greta also turn to countercultural types for help in implementing and keeping up their charade. In an episode that repurposes a plot from an ABC TV movie called *In Name Only*, Peter and Greta audition actors to play a minister at their wedding. They hire Frank Maston (John Astin) in a purported second ceremony for the benefit of Peter's parent. In another, they ask Peter's sibling, a Greenwich Village painter, to pose as a "normal" sibling, describing that type of performance as enjoyable. In episode ten, Peter's uncle Harry, a Bohemian artist, impersonates a marriage counselor. Harry and Frank, like culture makers in later episodes, help the couple keep up appearances with a notable lack of scrutiny toward the unorthodox proceedings. Portrayed as interesting and trustworthy, these characters clearly inhabit a world apart from the Brahms crowd where people are uninhibited by the bourgeois norms of Peter's coworkers. These counterculture types do not expect people to marry and do not value marriage. In rare moments when the supposed importance of marriage registers with them, it turns them off. Playwrights, painters, actors, casting agents, criminals, socialites, professors, gossip columnists, fashion designers, aspiring clothiers, activists, interior decorators, psychoanalysts, and group therapy members appear as friends, family members, contacts, and acquaintances.

Like *Gilligan's Island* (which included Ida Lupino–directed episodes—channeling Lupino's history with the sitcom *Mr. Adams and Eve*—one guest-starring Hans Conried as Wrongway Feldman) and like sitcoms in general,

Wife is "ultimately . . . about dressing up and playing make-believe."[91] The *Gilligan's Island* episode "The Sound of Quacking" is a *Gunsmoke* send-up, according to IMDb, for example, and in "St. Gilligan and the Dragon," the Professor character appears as "a teen idol in the mold of Frank Sinatra" and "does Tony Curtis doing Cary Grant," as in *Some Like It Hot*.[92] In a *Gilligan's Island* episode featuring The Mosquitoes, the stranded crew of regular characters participate in the bob shag or "long-hair"—actually mid-length—trend, in sequences dressed in rock star costuming. After their music industry muses The Mosquitoes have departed the island, the castaways retain an LP, an ironic, supernatural/absurdist documentation of their pop alter egos. According to Kevin Olzak's review of the episode "St. Gilligan and the Dragon," titled "First Bonafide Classic Episode," the dream sequence device, a common sitcom trope Morreale discusses in "Dreams and Disruption in the Fifties Sitcom," was a favorite of the cast. Dream sequences often doubled as drag devices. The use of costumes and props in general in shows such as *Gilligan's Island, Mr. Ed, The Addams Family, My Favorite Martian, The Beverly Hillbillies*, and *Green Acres*, some of the most seen sitcoms of the 1960s, are, along with forgotten programs such as *Occasional Wife*, examples of trans gender queer camp. There is a sorting and resorting of gender formulaic in the sitcom mode of telegraphing social difference through taste distinction.

By contrasting ways of life within ironically hierarchized systems of signification, *Occasional Wife*'s writers showcase the open-mindedness of many cultural producers and position their approach as an antidote to the normative suspicion of the straight world of work. *Occasional Wife* often depicted independent and sexually adventurous characters managing sexual assault and harassment situations in a manner reminiscent of *The Bob Cummings Show*'s camp shenanigans.[93] As Greta maneuvers around predatory seducers, *Occasional Wife* renders gender and sexuality interesting. The Hungarian count doing modeling wants to marry instead of working (unlike Denver on *Gillis*, who avoids both). A famous French fashion designer grows perversely more interested in Greta after learning of the (fake) marriage to Peter and meeting Peter.

With a playful "freeze-frame" technique, partly mod and primarily formulaic, producers accentuated Greta's and Peter's inevitably queer gender. The visual style amplifies performativity in sitcom characterization in relation to norms. During a regular Friday night dinner date, the parent character asks if Peter is "eccentric," one of those euphemisms for queers that undermines the viability of the nonnormative while constructing its power in context. Peter storms off upset, embodying the parental charge of eccentricity visually, through queer gender, by accidentally grabbing a nearby purse instead of the character's trademark accessory, a briefcase. The editors pause the image on a frame in which Peter's mannerisms are particularly camp—in other words, particularly trans gender queer.

The effect is even more compelling in written form. As an early draft had it, Peter's parent "screws up" the courage to inquire into the details of Peter's life only after much consternation, suggesting the familiar laments of elders mourning defective children. Writing in the euphemism of "eccentricity" for gender and sexual nonconformity, the producers use the parent to broach the subject and linger in the confusion of changing times. This first script instructed the actor to trail off and speak "with difficulty" before grabbing the purse instead of the "attaché case."[94] Peter responds, in a "fury," "Am I what?? Eccentric?! I don't believe it!" and "That does it!" In this version, part of the trans gender queer camp comedy is that feminized "male" emotions cause the distraction and subsequent loaded choice. In the write-up, Peter reacts to the inquiry while holding the purse, continuing to shout defensively, "To think that!!! My own mother!" Then, there is an added punch line, fueled by complex gender performance. Peter returns to exchange bags, saying angrily, "I made a mistake!" This is the literalization of social code from queer gender to gay stereotype, but from a formulaic distance, in advance of the explicit solidification of the discourse. Is the mistake the carrying case, the rage, or the source of the collective anxiety?

There does not appear to have been any direct censorship in play here, but the bit is downplayed in the shooting script that follows. Peter's reaction changes to set aside the treatment of insult at stigmatization. Still, stage directions let Callen and the crew take the Peter character's reaction in this and other trans gender queer directions. Between the two versions, the scene shifted in many ways. The first version included three players. One parent uses innuendo to probe for reassurance about conformity from their offspring, for the benefit of the internal audience, their spouse. It is yet more intimate in the revision, a two-person scene in which Peter's parent "looks aghast at Peter" and calls out the name "Peter!" (presumably, within the story world, a name assigned by them and/or the no-longer-present spouse) to warn and reprimand. Rewritten for the single-parent context, the final script reads, "[Peter] storms out as his mother looks after him, apprehensively. In an instant, Peter returns." In the telefilm version, in contrast, Peter's chagrin is about the process of mediating gendered perception outside the home, beyond parental assessment. Callen's performance highlights a social context hostile to single people, to people who have lost nuclear family privilege and are gender nonconforming in their navigation of social norms. The trans dimensions of this register especially in the prop visual play with the handbag, which implies that the only thing keeping Peter from carrying a purse is mindless convention. The implication in interpreting this joke in the context of the decision making behind the scenes is that, if showbiz ways were to ever win out over the representational limits dictated by the bottom line—in other words, by the imperative to straighten out gender based on market and profit calculations—people like Peter would carry purses. This implied imagined space of more gender freedom is a consistent camp refrain in sitcoms.

Straightening Up San Francisco

Queer gender can appear novel in the 1960s, specifically in the later, color-TV era 1960s, after the resettling of industry interests following Newton Minow's storied 1961 "Vast Wasteland" speech, when independent producers such as Ackerman took surprisingly schlocky projects on in order to play the TV game. A more overt camp sensibility may seem to appear, but that camp was just as shockingly bright the decade before. Overall, the repertoire of camp TV expanded in the 1960s, even under the onslaught of white normalization, in particular through the incorporation (appropriation and transformation) of subcultures with counterconfigurations of looks norms. As in the 1950s, camp modes of production hinged on standardized industry practices rather than on specific auteurs. Patterns at play in characterization, casting, performance, and the construction of intertextual story worlds created an infrastructure for camp. With ironic timing well suited to sitcoms, TV production made use of subcultural sensibilities and iconographies as they reached the mainstream.

The history of the ABC program *Love on a Rooftop*, which debuted the year before *He & She*, 1966, demonstrates how unpredictable the television production process is with respect to normative forces and trans gender queer representation. Methods of censoring nonconformity from TV screens can actually produce trans gender queer representation. In the sitcom context, assimilated versions of subcultures serve as raw material for queer gender. Subcultural types provide fodder for backstage comedy in programs that are not principally set in the media industries. *Rooftop* focused on Julie, a kooky free spirit with wealthy parents willing to support life in San Francisco. The city is prominent in the series. The sweeping crane shot and panoramic tracking sequence of the opening credits establishes the setting by showcasing the Bay Area—historically a thriving site of art, counterculture, and LGBTQ+ life—as offering a world of possibilities. After Julie marries Dave, an architect, the couple survives on the small salary of an apprentice.

This ABC series underwent significant revision during preproduction to moderate potentially controversial subject matter. Initial discussion sought to define just how independent their independent lead character, Julie, could be. Writers refined cast relations as the show developed. Julie is peculiar in contrast to her husband Dave, who is rational and straight-laced. The series' premise called for a range of figures from the local San Francisco media arts scene as minor characters and in cameo roles, which it positioned as secondary to the main couple's marital situation. To render Julie's eccentricity palatable, *Rooftop*'s producers used the supporting characters Stan (Rich Little) and Carol Parker (Barbara Bostock), the neighbor couple, as both a model for married life and as an indication of extremes in relation to which the Julie character could appear unconventional, but not too unconventional. *Rooftop* is a strong sign of the industry's continued attempts, across the 1960s, to funnel eccentricities typically associated with trans gender queer media producers into talked-about programs featuring otherwise conventionally gendered married couples. The Julie character's plots and the fashions that Carne modeled in advertisements linked to the series, which featured a fashion line generated as program merchandise, suggest that the kookiness *Rooftop* cultivated produced a version of San Francisco counterculture from which queer gender as comportment and everyday queer influence had been swept, or seized and transformed even as it continued, in the mode of sitcom camp, to ambiguously recirculate trans gender queer references and postures. This is a critically queer observation embedded in the broadcast text as well as a backstage insight.

The series that eventually became *Love on a Rooftop* was first pitched as "Just Married," with the alternative title "The Happy Couple." This 1958 prospectus, written by John Whedon, whose other color projects include *That Girl* and *Walt Disney's Wonderful World of Color*, criticized several "unnecessarily limiting" sitcom conventions.[95] Whedon, grandparent of screenwriters Joss, Zach, and Jed Whedon, complains that most sitcoms are about married couples and feature restrained husband and wife characters in stories confined "to their direct relations with each other," whether quarreling or sugarcoated.[96] The author, who wrote for *Donna Reed*, *Dick Van Dyke*, *Leave It to Beaver*, and *The Great Gildersleeve*, among other series, finds it especially annoying that, when couples were parents, situations nearly always concern the characters' "joint interest in the children." Whedon's *Just Married*, in contrast, would explore the husband and wife's "existence as separate individuals." Outlining an idea for a show following "the daytime activities of the husband one week, with the other mate coming in perhaps only incidentally," Whedon challenges Screen Gems to develop a sitcom about a married couple that "recognizes that husbands and wives do have separate lives." In its first incarnation, the series explored situations with a husband and wife arising "during the forty hours a week that they are not together." During a meeting in January 1959 discussing Whedon's original proposal, two executives, Alvin Cooperman, who began his career at NBC, along with Ackerman, agreed with Whedon that both partners should hold jobs "because of economic pressure as well as inclination."[97] Classic sitcom characters such as Lucy Ricardo, Gracie Allen, and Vicki Angel were unable to secure serial employment because of their partners. They are circumscribed by gender, as were actors such as Paul Lynde and Kulp, at the bottom of the top of a white pecking order. The premise for the series, which actually started as a spy situation, was an equal relationship.

Whedon's 1958 prospectus is barely recognizable in the aired version of *Rooftop*, which wouldn't be broadcast until the mid-1960s, when, in consultation with ABC, Screen Gems producers transformed Whedon's idea into a series in which the unconventional Julie sometimes looked for work but never landed a job. The revamped concept devised a working-class couple with high social and cultural capital. Using the financial situation as a source of conflict inseparable from conservative gender roles, writers refigured the wife's desire to work as one of necessity rather than "inclination." During development, the wife's activities away from the husband, which Whedon envisioned in the public sphere, came to resemble the wifely duties of archetypal family sitcoms. Julie's situations usually materialized at home while Dave is away for the day. According to the workers who developed *Rooftop* from Whedon's original prospectus, Julie, a former model, wants to be a clothing designer, a "fashion artist" like Greta. Producers briefly considered having this lead character work in advertising. Overall, the creative team relied on the connotations of queer gender to characterize Julie as independent as they attempted to locate her in proximity to the art and culture of San Francisco.

However, two main factors, the series' narrative space and its emphasis on wide appeal, limited the prominence of these elements. After the rooftop apartment from which the series took its title, the offices of the architectural firm where Dave apprentices provided *Rooftop*'s second regular set. In one episode, Julie visits the San Francisco Art Student League building, but such landmark locations were relatively rare. Without an established setting for local color, artists usually visit Julie at home. The series played it on the safe side with wholesome domestic scenes and sanitized allusions to race, ethnicity, capitalism, sexuality, and gender. Rich Little's white male underdog Stan was sometimes as close as *Rooftop* came to representing the counterculture. For *Rooftop*, executives first sought a block of viewers who would tune in to see a free spirit. Then, they imagined that audience appreciating a character defined by kooky independence but happy to give up a career for a throwback home life. In both cases, this character's nontraditional self-expression was the attraction. Despite its early goals, the series' cast, characters, and premise were transformed over the course of *Rooftop*'s development, to the point where the program mimicked earlier sitcom assimilation. In this way, there is considerable evidence that its relative prominence in popular memory stems from the active assimilation of its countercultural affinities, particularly the camp skepticism of traditional marriage that distinguished the show when it was first pitched.

More specifically, a range of wacky screwball scenarios and backstage situations that would have emerged in the first version were curtailed through the focus on the main characters' marriage rather than their independent lives. The production company's decision to showcase Julie's eccentric characteristics within marriage represents the networks' measured attempts to adopt new camp styles. This choice initiated a process of assimilation in which the character's cultural differences played out in a familiar combination of domestic family sitcom-style scenarios and the hegemonic incorporation of eccentricity through secondary characters. This new-type-of-wife role channeled "odd" and "artistic." However, Julie was neither as odd nor as artistic as were the struggling-comedian-cum-restaurant-menu-writer neighbor or the artists and agents stopping by the apartment to tempt Julie to re-enter San Francisco's creative class.

In general, sitcom production crews suited wardrobe to the light comic treatments of class, subculture, regional difference, and taste distinctions. These patterns were well established as the basis of sitcom characterization by the 1960s. Within this episodic guest-star system, abstracted fringe fashion consistently indicates the truncated legacy of counterculture expression. Camp costuming is a hallmark of the format, through which producers created icons of defiant social deviance. A good example is Bob Denver's antagonist to the social order, Maynard G. Krebs, who was, like Sheila Kuehl's Zelda, an eccentric centerpiece of *The Many Loves of Dobie Gillis*. The jazz-loving Maynard has not a beard but something "like a beard," facial hair approximating a referent, meaning the way in which the character speaks (as well as how they dress and groom, or don't) interrupts cis logics naturalizing gender and its production processes; the iconic goatee "is, like, a beard," meaning that the insertion of seemingly empty slang marks gender as a process of signification and queer gender expression as a camp riff on standard concepts of "sex characteristics."[98] In 140+ episodes of *Dobie*, Krebs, in flattering tatters, came to life alongside Warren Beatty's Milton Armitage, Steve Franken's Chatsworth Osborne, Jr. (who appears as Winthrop Van Money VIII, in a fantasy sequence in Franken's second of thirty appearances), and Doris Packer as the obscenely demonstratively rich, old money parents of both.[99] Chatsworth was Yale spoofed from the inside, wearing V-neck sweaters, ascots, sport coats, and wailing about "my little blue sports car . . . my forty-foot white cabin cruiser . . . [and] my blue blazer with the solid gold buttons and the Osborne crest on all the pockets . . . [and] suits with narrow lapels."[100]

The context of camp fixation on themes of class and coupling that such moments of queer gender production convey is, on the surface, hyperracialized. Characters such as Maynard and Dwayne Hickman's Dobie, a sedated version of Hickman's Chuck from *Love That Bob*, are industrially refined for mass consumption within cis-heterosexism to the point of pure self-parody. The blank deadpan mode obviously and ironically suited to the white-centric context, identified in histories of the sitcom as naturalizing, draws attention to itself and to market calculations behind the scenes. *Dobie Gillis*, which reran extensively, was only occasionally somewhat integrated in terms of guest stars and extras, and only in the context of racist colorblind casting. Camp orientalism is an episodic feature (such as in the high-school-hang-out setting of Wong's snack shop), as it is in 1960s sitcoms in general.

Like *Dobie*, *Love on a Rooftop* showcases struggling white middle- and upper-class characters while focusing on intersecting issues of age (generation) and gender (norms in marriage). *Rooftop* represents the way ABC and Screen Gems attempted to balance their colorful youth culture appropriations with sober depictions of benevolent white patriarchal authority. Multiple meanings and modes of address are possible even in severely compromised market-driven programming. This later camp TV high-concept "teen marrieds" pitch for family audiences stuck for two seasons and is relatively available. Backstage conversations translated to the depiction of backstage conversations in the series. The comedy relates to the near complete white normativizing and full "censored" displacement of minority representation onto a generalized eccentricity.

Rooftop and shows like it—sitcoms, in general—offer repeated and prevalent insight into standard industry procedures for representing queer culture through media producer characters and media production references, in particular. Reshaping television history around camp TV indicates that queer gender incubated within the industry, resisting prevalent discursive pressures to solidify a monolithic gay type. The recognizably-effeminate-but-not-too-feminine, butchesque, straight-acting-lite, overwhelmingly white, often sexist and racist character in this category, is either on the model of or generally less inventive than the not "out" predecessors. Some are classic guest star parts for character actors, juggling multiple queer codes of eccentricity and excess, unassimilable to respectable LGBT community today. Others circulate more seamlessly in support of simplistic classification systems tied to since-conventionalized visibility (i.e., positive representation, respectability, and neoliberal) politics. Ultimately, the queer gender of camp TV challenges us to think beyond familiar constructions of sexuality and one-to-one queer coding. The accumulated riffs on all manner of taste cultures embedded trans gender queer contexts within sitcoms, on the side of questioning white male privilege, indirectly but continuously.

4

Trans Camp TV

METHODS FOR *GIRL* HISTORY

An October 1967 column in *The Los Angeles Times*, "Where Is Wife Once He Wed?," instructs partners in the best ways to investigate their mates to confirm they're not communists.[1] This is a deadpan piece riffing on norms of spousal selection, a first-person account of scrutinizing a companion for signs of nonconformity in order to preserve both of your standings as good citizens. It mimics Cold War scare tactics of surveillance and white obsession with "otherness" in the manner of Bob Dylan's "Talkin' John Birch Paranoid Blues," a song Dylan was set to perform on *The Ed Sullivan Show* in 1962 before CBS, afraid of backlash, rescinded the opportunity to transmit it.[2] Doubly referential, "Where Is Wife Once He Wed?" relays a *Newsweek* report about an article in *American Opinion*, a publication of the white supremacist John Birch Society, the racist organization cited in Dylan's song. The author of the article, Jack Smith (not the filmmaker of the same name persecuted at the time for the now classic trans gender queer *Flaming Creatures*), adopts anticommunist rhetoric to excess: total scrutiny, taken to comical lengths, is compulsory to the point of absurdity. This marriage situation comedy in print lists the "certain telltale tastes and associations" of "unfit wives and mothers," instructing people to avoid "Vassar grads, members of the League of Women Voters, hippies, mods and 'contemporary revolutionists.'" The column, which makes plain the prevalence of queer gender in cultures of consumption, hinges on the pop icon Twiggy, a British model who culture critic Marshall McLuhan at the time argued transcended categories and proliferated identificatory pleasures indicative of new media and generational tensions. These threads of social change were synonymous with the threat of queer contamination from within.

At the time of Smith's writing, Twiggy had been prominent in the United States for three years, and increasingly saturated newsstands during that time. In this column, Twiggy is an agent of corruption, effectively queering every marriage in America. Smith argues comically that any awareness of Twiggy is an alarming sign of susceptibility to communist corruption, in the same category as a taste for vodka, canned grasshoppers, and queer poet Allen Ginsberg. According to Smith, Twiggy, who is associated with mod fashion, is "too skinny" and looks "like . . . an adolescent schoolboy." Smith's wife disagrees and, in doing so, channels McLuhan's media theory, dryly delivering Twiggy's mass deconstruction of gender: "'I kind of like her,' . . . '[Twiggy] has a gamin quality. [Twiggy] isn't supposed to be a real woman. Just a symbol.'" The punch line is the appeal: "I couldn't believe that liking Twiggy would be a dangerous symptom in an otherwise blameless" spouse. This is a critically queer moment in media production of the kind I assemble in this chapter in order to examine trans textuality, the contours and dynamics of transgender representation, through a study of trans camp textuality in New Hollywood, by way of *The Ugliest Girl in Town*, a short-lived musical sitcom from 1968 that was inspired by Twiggy.

The producers of this backstage series about international fashion modeling, which I refer to as *Girl* to avoid assaulting you repeatedly with the show's transmisogynist title, confronted a variety of pressures to dampen exactly the countercultural content the network, ABC, would seem to have been attempting to appropriate for profit in developing the program. With *Girl*, the camp TV archive orchestrates its own put-on with camp TV implicitly media theorizing the late 1960s production context. I treat *Girl* as a feminist text over and against the transmisogyny that conditions its existence, initial circulation, and afterlife.[3] I use *Girl* to demonstrate a more equitable distribution of creative credit for queer trans content across the industry and the subcultures it commodified in the 1960s. The archives of executive producer Harry Ackerman document an important space of trans textuality, and, within that space, a queer trans protagonist created through the impersonal industrial operations of sitcom production and promotion. I invoke Timothy, another name for Tim and Timmy, *Girl*'s Twiggy-inspired lead, as a gender outlaw, in order to show how complex queer gender is and how indispensable trans insights are to media studies. I present this character as queer and trans as opposed to queer because they are trans.[4] Ultimately, I use the written record to recount a version of history in which transgender practices are *mad* as in *mod* and *mad* as in power movements but not construed as crazy in support of the class distinctions of white cis privilege. Building on production documents, I re-create the trans gender queer texture of everyday entertainment media in the last years leading up to the 1970s.

Girl is a complicated text, and writing about it as both queer and trans is a complicated endeavor. Regarded as a turkey, an inferior product, *Girl* is rarely mentioned by media historians and yet also is regularly misreported.[5] My rendition of *Girl* centers a feminist perspective on archives. I reconstruct behind-the-scenes visions through queer and trans interpretations of print culture in order to emphasize that *Girl* is a product of the work of many people. Sitcoms follow a process designed to maximize potential appeal to different markets. In television's characteristic mode of polysemic address, *Girl* captures both the means of gender regulation and detachment from it. The history of the program provides a snapshot of the experience of gender embodiment and of presenting and being perceived as many genders.[6]

Trans History and the Development of *Girl*

Girl, a weekly, episodic series, rewrites ugly as attractive. *Girl*, like other sitcoms, establishes as "the defining feature of [a] microcosm of characters... that they performed for one another."[7] This program presents swinging late 1960s London as the setting, imagined as one of many epicenters of mod fashion.[8] The show is high concept, and the premise is plot intensive.[9] Julie Renfield (Patricia Brake), a British actress filming a gorilla pic in Hollywood, meets Timothy Blair (Peter Kastner), a stylish Los Angeleno who runs errands for Harper Talent Agency in Beverly Hills, taking lunch orders in a spiffily lined three-piece suit. On their first date, Tim[10] acts like a big shot for laughs and tips the waitstaff with his wristwatch. Julie, like Kulp's

Jane Hathaway, has a flashy convertible in LA, and makes the first move. Sequential zooms in and out from three different locations break conventional continuity editing patterns to signal the intensity of their kiss through an aesthetic simultaneously cliché and innovative in context.[11] In a crucial moment of courtship, Tim interrupts a live commercial for a car dealership on TV. Hotel doorframes and other frames, like the frame of the television set, aestheticize the genderqueerness of the courtship.

Timothy, who is always going on and on about love and romance, is about to borrow money (in ongoing parody of the male provider role) for another date with Julie from his roommate and sibling, fashion photographer Gene (Gary Marshal—not Garry Marshall,[12] both camp TV), when Gene (Noel Prince on *That Girl*) by chance overexposes commissioned film recently shot for a feature in the works on youth culture. Gene, who is implied to generously hand out cash to Tim under ordinary circumstances, asks Timothy to re-create a profiled flower child in a reshoot in exchange for twenty dollars. Taking time to remember the amateur model, Gene describes this "beautiful kook"[13] without using many gendered pronouns. This "character" made the whole series, tying everything together like *Citizen Kane*'s "Rosebud" or the rug in *The Big Lebowski* (ironically). Tim happily models for the replacement prints. In a musical montage of the shoot, Tim wears beads, fur, tassels, and a wig.

The backstory is extensive. First, the photos cross the Atlantic, and David Courtney (Nicholas Parsons), of Courtney Modeling Agency, decides to make Tim the next big fashion sensation, in the tradition of Jean Shrimpton. Courtney, a stock English person, proper yet lascivious and expectantly fey, reads the model as female and starts throwing money at the siblings. They head east, taking their chances through airport security, with Tim presenting as Timmy (a name Gene chooses), a takeoff of the persona that emerged during the photo shoot and the type of model that Courtney and Sally Whittaker (Rose Alba), the editor of *Glance* magazine, might be expecting, or not. The last name? "She dropped it for publicity reasons." Publicity work, a focus of the program from the earliest planning stages, begins immediately, on an airport runway, where Timmy encounters Julie, kisses her for the camera, and learns that they are booked for a photo shoot together the next day. Julie promptly recognizes her lover, and the pair scamper queerly to the park loo (the bathroom, a possible site of seduction and discrimination for trans gender queer people). As Gene, a genderqueer character by name and narrative positioning, quips of the series, from within, "Isn't that the put-on to end all put-ons?"

The program went into production in April 1968 and debuted in September 1968. ABC canceled it with twenty episodes in the can. As it continued airing, into January 1969, there was an opportunity to watch knowing the show was officially over, which characterized trans possibilities through Timmy as surviving beyond conceptual death. In every episode, *Girl* reclaims "ugly" straightaway, and over and again, with a feel-good, advertiser-friendly theme song.[14] A carefree melody recontextualizes the term *ugly* in articulating Timmy's charm. Timmy's clothes "are setting the pace." She has a "fabulous face." The catchy tune assures viewers, "You don't have to be a Mia [Farrow] or Sophia [Loren]."

Girl's put-on was metafictional, simulacral. The premise amplified purported real-life fads in flat chests, short haircuts, and mod wigs. *Girl* parodied a plethora of popular reports on "twiggyness," an adjective turned mononym turned generic (white) look.[15] Ambiguous in terms of artistic legitimacy, Twiggy was an "international merchandising triumph" and a flashpoint in taste wars around compulsory differentiation and gender and sexual spectrums.[16] In a *Chicago Tribune* review of the Farrar, Straus and Giroux book *Twiggy and Justin* (1968) discussing the model and manager as a duo, a queer couple, Reed College anthropology professor Gail Kelly wrote, "In an age of manufactured mass memorabilia, the March 1967 arrival of Twiggy in America may serve as the very pattern for the creation and marketing of the pseudo-event."[17] "Pseudoevent" implies pseudoperson. In response to the widespread mockery of Twiggy's body, the denial of authenticity to nonnormative self-presentation, and the dismissal of the importance of the mod phenomenon in the press, Timmy-flat rivals Twiggy-flat as a fashion statement within the world of *Girl*. In the broader social context of stars and size, this further revised 1950s revisions of media taboos, which had prompted attention to sudden tolerance of explicit discussion of a consumer trend for bigger breasts. The reported source of the flat-chested Twiggy fad was Twiggy's boyfriend and manager, Justin de Villeneuve, a camp self-inventor described as having two different voices.[18]

In taking inspiration from this scene, *Girl* became one of many ephemeral indications of simultaneously queer and trans representation in the new media moment of the late 1960s. At the same time, queer trans representation is a routine facet of television programming connected to the industry's history, dating to the 1940s, if not before. The culture industries, seemingly collectively, branded Twiggy the capital-C "Cockney kid," mobilizing a foreign white working-class culture in a displaced interrogation of urban geography, everyday prejudice, and collective identity.[19]

Twiggy media took these issues up in addressing everything from sit-ins to psychedelic drugs. With *Girl*, ABC tapped the genderqueer current of diverse 1960s subcultures. In an ironic turn of events, the major Hollywood studios were investing in television following a drop in revenue from theater ownership and film distribution. *Girl* was tentpole kitsch from an established content provider. It sparked the production and consumption of ancillary pop objects within a televisual landscape oriented toward constant novelty on supermarket shelves. The property can be traced to various intertexts concerned with looks, accents, assimilation, and upward mobility, such as *My Fair Lady* (1964), so it is telling that the production lore around *Girl* cites Twiggy as inspiration, not artist-model Donyale Luna, Andy Warhol superstar Mario Montez, electro-folk sensation Norma Tanega, or comedian musicians Tiny Tim or Timmie Rogers, possible inspirations for similar adaptation projects had whiteness not been the presumed default at the time in the industry practices of conceiving, casting, and scripting sitcoms.

Girl's very premise conflicted with basic social mores. Screen Gems, the production company, worked with Yardley of London, a health and beauty aids company, and the ad agency Young & Rubicam. Screen Gems, a trendsetting subsidiary of Columbia Pictures,[20] oversaw the negotiation of cis norms, in effect encouraging employees to think about gender variance in pursuit of a successful series. Scholars usually presume that sitcom producers are the proponents of ideological beliefs, but the makers of *Girl* resisted as well as purveyed heterosexism, as they used euphemism, subtlety, and intertextual reference to communicate through taboo. As they attempted to render the concept appealing to a broad set of viewers, they faced pressure to simplify women and femininity, roughen Tim's masculinity, and dampen the chemistry between Timmy and Julie. *Girl*'s producers confronted "homosexuality"-dominated discourse about gender variance and presentation internally at the studio and in attempting to publicize the series.[21] This was a time of transformation, Gavin Butt notes, in "the terms of the cultural field through which homosexuality is habitually lived and understood," a rearrangement of cultural notions constructing bodies, embodiment, and meaning following the pansy craze of the 1920s and the "transformation in the semiotics of queerness" that Steven Cohan charts from the 1930s and 1940s.[22] Such discursive changes contributed to possibilities in self-conception for trans people, as scholars such as Joanne Meyerowitz have detailed.[23] The ephemeral records that preserve this extensive and uneven transformation showcase the kind of queer gender that Jay Prosser argues queer scholars have a history of violently appropriating from trans people whose identities they undermine and obscure.[24]

Trans history deserves more recognition. Jack Halberstam describes the "paradoxical... but necessary" project of producing transgender history, advocating writing trans histories based on material records that preserve "only a bare trace of a life lived in defiance of gender norms."[25] Such traces have a history of being commandeered for the purposes of queer theory, as Prosser demonstrates in "Judith Butler." Prosser argues that queer theory has relied on "the figure of transgender" as a liminal icon perpetually crossing "both the boundaries between gender, sex, and sexuality and the boundary that structures each as a binary category."[26] As Prosser explains, queer criticism often evaporates trans agency as it appropriates trans dynamics for a queer charge, profiting conceptually, in terms of queer cachet, from gender crossing, ambiguity, and nonconformity. Julia Serano has called specifically for an end to commentary equating "transgender" with gender transgression. She directs our efforts to "the intersection of multiple forms of gender-based prejudice," such as prejudice against (especially nonwhite) femaleness, femininity, and feminization (to which the term "transmisogyny" refers).[27] Texts such as *Girl* can help us to devise new methods for attending to queer gender without undercutting trans possibilities, including for "visible transsexuals" of the kind Sandy Stone outlines in "The *Empire* Strikes Back: A Posttranssexual Manifesto" and reiterates in "Guerrilla."[28]

Girl's camp mode of production is evident across drafts of proposals, outlines, story ideas, and scripts, and in records documenting meetings, conversations, audience testing, advertising, merchandising, publicity, and cultural commentary. The creative process of sitcom production is difficult to reconstruct, and "bare traces" of it, to use Halberstam's phrase about lives lived in gender defiance, are preserved in official archives. Queer questions of authorship abound. Many people contributed to *Girl*. Many changes simultaneously normalized the program and cultivated camp.

Girl involved sponsors as well as commercial segments. Screen Gems collaborated with Yardley, Young & Rubicam, ABC, and others, including ASI Entertainment, a Screen Gems offshoot specializing in audience testing. The paper trail is partially preserved by way of Harry Ackerman, vice president of West Coast operations at Screen Gems from 1953 until 1973. Ackerman worked on *Girl* as a pet project, during a career high, one of many. After contributing to series including *I Love Lucy* (CBS, 1951–57), *Our Miss Brooks* (CBS, 1952–56), *Bewitched* (ABC, 1964–72), and *Gidget* (ABC, 1965–66), Ackerman championed *Girl* through its production process. After snatching up a pitch from Robert Kaufman, who had written for *The Betty Hutton Show* (CBS, 1959–60) and the first *Bob Newhart Show* (NBC, 1961–62), Ackerman debated *Girl's* structure with Bernard Slade—the author of *Same Time, Next Year* (1975) and *Romantic Comedy* (1979), who went on to create *The Partridge Family* (ABC, 1970–74)[29]—and coproducer-writer Jerry Davis, who had just finished *Bewitched* and *That Girl* (ABC, 1966–71) and would go on to make *Funny Face* (CBS, 1971) and *The Odd Couple* (ABC, 1970–75). Davis went to London to manage the production.[30] Davis, who called Ackerman every Friday night in May 1968, instructed the crew to move the camera more often and in more creative ways.[31] These new wave techniques attest to the experimentation requisite in the new media landscape of the late 1960s. Many of the style markers of oppositional subcultures had been quickly commodified, raising questions about the politics of representation. ABC was distinguishing itself from competitors CBS and NBC by "seeking ways to keep pace with the sexual revolution."[32] Screen Gems, a classic Hollywood independent, was pushing the envelope, leveraging the success it brought to NBC with *The Monkees* (1966–68), one of the more notorious sitcom put-ons at that point, about a made-for-TV band that included some cast members who were just learning to play their instruments.

Girl fit the Screen Gems brand of sitcoms, which came with the powerful alibi that they were inclusive of kids, if not developed explicitly for children. Much-publicized "merchandisers of the mod look" mass-produced attention to Twiggy's body as a new "type," along with her working-class vernacular and disregard for gender conventions, in the form of witty slang terms and consumer products.[33] Julie Byrne published articles about Twiggy in the *Los Angeles Times* on April 9, 25, and 28.[34] All of this audiovisual stimulation was source material for sitcoms at Screen Gems, especially for *Girl*, a camp take immersed in the genderqueer style of late 1960s mod culture that was broadcast in color. Twiggy's paparazzi-attended landing at New York City's JFK Airport in 1967, a camp version of the so-called British invasion of the Beatles and other musical groups in 1964, instigated photo shoots, cultural criticism, and TV specials.[35] *Girl* rhetorically turned on that recent, ongoing history, referring to "Anglo-American relations" at the outset of every episode.

Girl testifies to Ackerman's innovations, but also to Twiggy's, and to the impact of a broader scene of participants in street-level queer trans culture. Twiggy appeared on the cover of *Harper's Bazaar*, a magazine that *New York Times* critic Russell Baker likened to "poor man's LSD" because it presented "portraits of a life so outrageously chic, so gay, so fey, so exclusive that ten minutes' exposure to it often produces a fatal giddiness."[36] At the time, media scholar McLuhan, a public intellectual working the college circuit, theorized Twiggy as, variously, an X-ray, an icon, a form of abstract art, and a performance artist in the tradition of Mae West, another "visual pun," who was not performing conventional femininity but rather "was impersonating a female impersonator."[37] I remember Ackerman's desk files housed at Dartmouth including popular commentary on West, a performer Pamela Robertson Wojcik calls a "deliberate anachronism" and one who continues to inspire explanations of trans gender queer camp that self-undercut by virtue of their binary formulations.[38]

Ackerman's research is a telling reminder of how efficiently US media industries absorb into their products anonymous street-level queer and trans culture reaching across time and national borders. I also remember newspaper features on celebrity fashion and a profile of the Beatles' manager Brian Epstein, a publicity expert now understood to have been out at that time and who can be credited with orchestrating the longhair look associated with the Beatles prominence. Included in the background research for Screen Gems productions including *Girl* were mainstream magazine weeklies with images covering people of varied gender presentations wearing homemade clothes and sometimes elaborate costuming. In the space of these print publications, clothing continued to differentiate, but not always reliably so according to gender. From the *New York Times Magazine* came "The 'Hashbury' Is the Capital of the Hippies," an article by new journalism icon Hunter S. Thompson emphasizing the comprehensive extrication of the Haight-Ashbury scene in San Francisco. In this feature, representation inseparably queer and trans appears as a self-evident part of the counterculture's community food, housing, consciousness raising, and art projects. A clipping from *Look* on "The Future of Sex," cowritten by McLuhan and correspondent George B. Leonard, begins with an anecdote about gender perception from Michael Murphy, a cofounder of the Esalen Institute in Big Sur, California.[39] Murphy writes, "Members of the younger generation are making it clear—in dress and music, deeds and words—just how unequivocally they reject their elders' sexual world."[40] The article concludes, "The future holds out infinite variety, diversity." "The search for a new sexuality is," they say, "a search for a new selfhood, a new way of relating. This search already is well under way. What it turns up will surprise us all."

Girl incorporated countercultural source material of this sort through a camp mode. The production itself, in terms of the written record it left, seems camp, in that it seems to take, as Cohan puts it, "queer pleasure in perceiving if not causing category dissonance."[41] Publicity documents characterize the program's protagonist as a sitcom heroine akin to Samantha Stevens (Elizabeth Montgomery, *Bewitched*) and Sister Bertrill (Sally Field, *The Flying Nun*), feminist icons in two other ABC–Screen Gems series at that time—in their fifth and second seasons, respectively—who were loved despite, and precisely for, regularly defying social convention passed off as natural law. Timmy's superpowers were witty sexual innuendo, chutzpah emblematized by curly red hair, vinyl miniskirts, and signature knee-high black leather boots, a style evocative of liberation-era subcultures and the special knowledge—especially of sexual dynamics—that comes with living not as female or as male, or as female and male, or male and female consecutively, but as someone beyond that distinction. The perspective came from formulaic situation comedy amid the commercial mod newness and musical score.

Trans-Testing the Television Market

ABC ran *Girl* at 7:30 PM on Thursdays. This was a campy, kid-friendly, innuendo-laden, merchandise-friendly time slot designed to both generate excitement about weekend programming and stoke demand for color TV sets amid network consolidation.[42] A saturated décor of bright hues replaced earlier references to color in camp TV, such as to shades of pink (shocking and surprise). *Girl* was in one of *Batman*'s former time slots, a gateway to the Thursday evening schedule and weekend programming. On twice a week in 1966, *Batman* episodes were also color saturated, translating to broadcast the comics' "garish hues of turquoise, cerise and emerald" and images such as those of "the riddler in [a] lime green costume spinning madly against a shocking pink background."[43] It was the former hour of ABC's *Flintstones*, camp TV that ran in the 1963 and 1964 seasons, with its own flashy color scheme. *Girl* appeared opposite a new *Blondie* adaptation on CBS featuring Jim Backus and Bryan O'Byrne, people who are major camp figures if you get deep enough into this TV history. *Daniel Boone*, an hour-long program, began at the same time on NBC. Now you could watch both if you wanted to, with a Digital Video Recorder, but at that time it would have been one or the other.

Amid trends in gender variance, *Girl* brought to prime time and to people's fingertips a story of gender experimentation.[44] How was the comic timing? How countercultural were the tie-ins, product placements, publicity events, and press coverage? Television was in some ways in synch with mod culture, with both typed scandalous, obscene, diseased, addictive, consumable, pleasurable, beautiful, and sex-laced. The ambiguity of the relation of TV and mod itself resonates as camp. Music critic Lillian Roxon reported in late 1969 that the "ruffled, flowery Carnaby Street look" and "the military look"—two of Timmy's protoglam looks deemed acceptable for network television—were "definitely out . . . because the old people took them up."[45] Was *Girl* a symptom of this appropriation or a snide commentary on it? While a Twiggy clothing line could be turned around in two months, television production had to work within the strict cycles the networks had standardized for prime time series programming, debuting new shows every fall followed by midseason replacements in the new year. On which side of the genderqueer trend, in constant fashion, was *Los Angeles Times* critic Cynthia Lowry, in calling Twiggy a "1967 phenomenon" in January 1968?[46] Weren't still queerer things to come?

In the case of *Girl*, as Screen Gems adapted recent history for the small screen, test audience influence confined workers preoccupied with comedy to less fun trans and queer camp farce. Young & Rubicam, the program's advertising client, is integral to broadcast history, with the company's history highlighting *Girl* as a medium for advertising. Contributing to the creative process entailed indirect communication about gender and sexual perception, as the sponsors acted as consultants to network executives, requesting revisions based on story outlines and scripts, amid waning (residual and resurgent) influence. Writers, script doctors, copy editors, designers, directors, and performers refined *Girl*'s aesthetics and storytelling techniques as they drafted documents, prepared to shoot episodes, and circulated publicity. This is representative of the thinking about gender and sexual expression that sitcom production initiates. Sitcoms can be in constant development for a year or several years, or in some cases many years, or remade. *Girl*'s mod signature changed in combination with conception, casting, marketing, and production. There were many people involved. Networks of *Girl*'s producers negotiated pressures to sideline Timmy—to reduce her to a token or a prop. Timmy, however, remained central. People at the network, at ad agencies, in publicity, and at sponsoring and market research firms negotiated the limits of acceptable content, merchandising, and design.

Transphobia, cissexism, and heterosexism shaped the production process for television sitcoms in the 1950s and 1960s. In-house documents detailing ABC execs' ideas about *Girl* suggest that while the network was going for a cutting-edge youth market and excited by the prospect of tapping into other emerging markets, which they thought they could reach, the audience they imagined did not encompass an antiestablishment ethos of the kind that made mod a distinct subculture. The stalemate over hippie wear meant that the signifiers of fashion and gender affiliation would remain vague. With the premise initiated, the creative process generated scenarios inflected by signifiers of gender and sexuality. Programmers continued to develop content according to dominant generic conventions, hinging on patterns of ethnic othering, with multiple authors penning scripts based on collectively generated story ideas and outlines. As time went on, ABC argued that Tim should detest Timmy, be seen as Timmy infrequently, and be motivated to appear as Timmy for the sole reason of being near Julie. The network instituted firm guidelines requiring the show's writers to stick to a more conservative model. They based many of these policies on audience research. Surveying target viewers who brought their own ideas of hippie and mod culture to the table, Screen Gems used pointed questions to gauge its success in selling the Timmy character. Polling three sets of adult viewers on consecutive days, then children, and then teens, the company's audience testing outfit, ASI (Audience Studies Incorporated) Entertainment, found that "many viewers did not like the idea of a man dressed as a girl."[47] This limited imagination negates the reality of trans lives while reproducing queer gender.

Audience Studies Incorporated emphasized viewer complaints about wardrobe. A sample of teenage viewers "generally felt that Timmy should wear 'hippie' rather than mod attire."[48] This category of viewer was an emerging target market, especially for ABC. Overall, the polled viewers responded favorably to hippie fashion, particularly its genderqueer elements, and less favorably to mod looks, but *Girl*'s producers had already decided to distance their characters from hippie aesthetics in favor of what they described as "high fashion mod."[49] As ASI put it, "Some viewers questioned Timmy's change from hippie to mod," a change described in terms of a transition to clothing understood, within the mainstream, as more visibly gendered. In the context of white middle-class heteromasculine norms, femininity stands out. In an outline Kaufman submitted for the series, in contrast, Tim immediately turns to mod fashion. After Gene (here Jean, a roommate of no family relation) overexposes the photos of the "wild looking wierdo [sic]" who writes "blank verse poetry, love prayers, [and] whacky philosophy," Tim "flings open the closet and slips on a super mod jacket and black outfit Jean's sister bought last year when . . . visiting from Des Moines and then didn't have the guts to take home to Mother and the P.T.A."[50] Another idea was for the modeling session to feature the clothes Tim usually wore. In that version, Courtney and Whittaker would perceive Tim as female based on everyday attire, not on Tim's imitation of someone with a different sensibility. In the final premise, Tim cannot usually pass as a hippie but rather plays hippie for a day.

The consumer landscape that cultivates queer gender is generally inhospitable to it. Decisions proceed from programmers' mandate to protect advertiser dollars. In the case of *Girl*, costuming encapsulates this antagonism. Timmy's footwear is, on paper, not just any black leather boots but "the high black leather boots of Motorcycle Cop Jack Davis."[51] Economic constraints produce a shadow text, out of buried intertexts and ideas set aside. Queer gender remains at the foundation of *Girl*, though, just as it remained a source of celebrity and high and low fashion revenue in 1968. Still, even with unisex clothing design on the rise, manufacturers labeled dress as men's or women's. Sitcoms, with their formulaic reliance on trans gender queer eccentricity—even in protagonists, even into the late 1960s—break down this binary discourse. To establish the premise, the producers have Tim request a shorter wig for the shoot in the pilot episode, only so that Gene can brush off Tim's concerns about not looking like a guy. Hair and other supposed secondary sex characteristics are, the character implies, in this moment and others, artificial, unreliable, and not of primary concern.

ABC attempted to assess possible reactions to this nonbinary content. The consulting company ASI solicited detailed feedback on the pilot episode from people categorized as adults, teens, and children. This audience study highlights an outsourcing of labor within the product-testing rubric. "Most felt Timmy would be funnier in hippie dress where sex is not easily distinguished" than in mod outfits. This data provided a readymade strategy for countering "negative comments . . . deal[ing] with the 'high fashion' clothing worn by Timmy," but it was not picked up. Although demographic research seemed to call for the original "longhair" premise that Kaufman had pitched (whether in terms of a "Beatle wig" or a mop top protagonist), ABC preferred the mod style. Censors were as concerned with hippie hallmarks as they were with the execution of the drag premise. The network warned Screen Gems to distance the show from dropout culture and avoid "emasculating" Tim, a discourse of lost or stolen masculinity signaling the dominant valuing of the "respectable" over femme gender.[52]

Following audience testing, the mechanisms of mass sitcom production directed executives to invest in transphobia and cissexism. According to ASI, "Because many viewers did not like the idea of a man dressed as a girl, many felt that Timmy should feel more conflict and reluctance to don the Timmy attire."[53] According to the people processing the test audience survey, "A number of viewers felt it would be more realistic if Tim would have circumstances that made it necessary for him to be Timmy and was thus forced into the role."[54] ABC could have pulled the series based on potential viewers' problems with the basic concept. Instead, after initial audience testing, the network reconceived *Girl* as a show in which Timmy would appear "only when essential to the story and necessary and *natural* to the development of a plotline."[55]

ABC had not prevented Screen Gems from establishing Timmy as the show's protagonist and as Kastner's starring role in advance publicity, which described *Girl* as an answer to the question "What if Twiggy is really a boy?" Later, though, they demanded that Timmy appear less often and only as a last resort. The network's Standards and Practices Department screened scripts according to the presumption that, for their target markets, charisma required gender conformity. Martin Starger wrote to Screen Gems just over a month before the series premier to reiterate the network's "understanding of future . . . episodes: use Kastner 'less as Timmy (the girl) and more . . . as Tim.'"[56] However, backstage norms for naming and gendering characters could be screwy. In the manner of Starger's memo, an earlier letter from one Screen Gems exec to another attempted to "confirm [an] understanding" that even those two parties do not seem to have shared. Ironically, Jerry Hyams, in trying to smooth relations between ABC and Screen Gems, complicates things by referring to *Timmy* as "a very virile young man," writing, "We will endeavor to insert into as many . . . scripts as possible a feeling of warmth and a true love affair between Timmy and Julie . . . while Timmy is playing himself."[57]

The network was set on rescripting the series, but Screen Gems had already devised its ensemble, assembled a cast, and commissioned a brand of mod psychedelia tied to gender rebellion and the rejection of any obvious distinction between boys and girls. In spite of ABC's resistance, producers continued to conceive of romance on the modeling circuit as *Girl*'s main situation. The mod wardrobe remained prominent. At a loss as to how to perpetuate the series without Timmy—or with Tim on some bad trip about Timmy, the other option offered—the people on the ground at Screen Gems ignored ABC's instructions. The network may have already considered *Girl* a loss at that point anyway.

One site of compromise was the use of first-person monologue sequences shot in direct address. In the prototype for these monologues, the protagonist casts freedom as adaptability, identifying as "no intellectual" and also as "not a grown up Holden Caulfield" (even though a likeness to the *Catcher in the Rye* rebel drew producers to Kastner).[58] Tim "digs... life [and] girls" and Tim's "square" and "establishment oriented" parents. As if accused, the character denies being "detached, alienated, angry, or turned off," announcing, "The Haight Ashbury drop-out syndrome bores me to tears."[59] Dropping out was, as Gretchen Lemke-Santangelo argues, "above all, an opportunity to escape suburban domesticity, the sexual double standard, and the limits imposed on female creative self-expression and physical autonomy."[60] Refiguring dropping in as hipper than dropping out while denaturalizing female status diverted the feminist resonance of the trope. This produced trans textuality in dispersing dissatisfaction with sexism across the ensemble of the sitcom and its guest stars.

While appropriating the counterculture in producing *Girl*, Screen Gems came up against cis and hetero norms, including through pressure, evident in Aniko Bodroghkozy's account of 1960s TV, to depict the social mores and political stances of beats, hippies, and dropouts as ridiculous.[61] Free love seldom appeared in any favorable light in news programming, and many sitcom projects inspired by the counterculture remained dormant into the 1970s. Yet producers were drawn to the queer and trans representation that defined *Girl*. Still, Kaufman reports having been laughed out of offices before reaching Ackerman, whose reaction was anomalous. Screen Gems had been setting trends, and attempted to do so, in this case, by following them, such that the notion of *Girl* as satire spotlights all the camp surrounding it.

Trans Textuality

Material records documenting the assimilation of *Girl*'s aesthetics and the program's queer trans backstory record the gender multiplicity within mod pop culture, something not otherwise understood to be encompassed by television archives. In the mid-1960s, street styles evolved rapidly. Queer gender was an indelible aspect of the popular landscape. Tapping this energy, *Girl* combined established narrative formulas and obliquely topical humor. The production company drew on the classic genre formula Chris Straayer critiques in *Deviant Eyes, Deviant Bodies*, in which drag is by definition temporary and "for [the] purpose of necessary disguise."[62] Producers routinely marshal excuses in justification of Timmy and her continued modeling career. These include Julie's job, Tim's relative poverty, and a gambling debt Gene racks up when they first arrive in London. At the same time, in staying true to established tropes, the details of the program undermine coercion and economics as motivating forces and the whole idea of disguise.

In the episodic sitcom context, *Girl* highlights the trans dimension to what Lynne Joyrich has theorized as the "peculiar logic of knowing (or not knowing) sexuality" in sitcoms, a logic enmeshed with definitional uncertainty around gender distinction.[63] As Eve Sedgwick writes, in the domain of sexuality, "residues, markers, tracks, signs referring to that diacritical frontier between genders are everywhere, as well, internal to and determinative of the experience of gender."[64] As part of the TV industry's routine production process, in other words, *Girl* rendered the instability of identity broadly appealing. In the climax of the fast-paced montage sequence that follows the opening monologue of later episodes, the agent Courtney announces, "I want that girl." What does Courtney mean? Quick cuts, slow zooms, eye-catching visual effects, and a range of new wave techniques glamourize knowing *and* not knowing along with a host of subcultural sensibilities and queer trans practices. Transitions, travel scenes, media production settings, and music video sequences of photo shoots offer glimpses of lived culture that include trans gender queer people and fashions.

Trans modes of recognition proliferate in the social context of the series' story world. With the multiplicity of Tim's gender, the text cultivates, in a contemporary context, a camp attitude toward dominant gender perceptions. Tim is accepted as a trans person by savvy friends as well as by incidental characters. As part of the situation, queer gender emerges through images, in sequences that canvass onlookers for reactions. In *Girl*, extras represent fringe communities and visually articulate questions of gender perception, identity construction, and social norms. One noteworthy segment in the pilot episode is a quick scene at a mod nightspot filled with frilly and flowery extras dancing with Brake and Kastner. The final cut of the scene presents Julie and Tim equitably, but not entirely similarly, constructing a view on the proceedings that triangulates the perspective of the characters to foreground Julie's gaze at Tim, who go-go dances in a cage suspended above Julie and at a distance.

Fashion is key to these dynamics. Timmy's own style is represented as campy mod in contrast to the classic preppy professional look, which remains safely within the brown, black, blue, maroon, tan, and sometimes green color schemes orchestrated to type Tim as a "very masculine young man."[65] As part of its mod sensibility, *Girl* shows the ambiguous responses of other characters to Timmy and her wardrobe. Behavior within the story world indicates shifts in gender perception that accompany the production of new gender possibilities. Encounters with some characters suggest a discerned "secret" while others suggest that Tim's self-identity is public knowledge, not something to objectify through exposure. Timmy was just another high femme making the London scene among a range of "Frankly Beautiful New Young Gentlemen."[66] A mix of reactions on the part of a wide range of characters creates the sense of a queer reception context in which many people are in on camp performance. Not everyone has preconceived notions about other people's bodies.

Kastner and Ackerman's commentary at the Mexico City press conference articulates trans subjectivity through camp banter. While deflecting insinuations about sexual deviance, Kastner jokes with reporters about plots in which "some very short-sighted garbage men fall in love with me."[67] The actor's flip comments about working-class mores denaturalizes the "opposite-sex" presumption of sexual object choice within hetero norms. It draws attention to the importance of perception in constituting and revising norms. In interviews, Ackerman maintains that Timmy's flirtations with men are not "homosexual," a position productive of trans possibilities (in that sexual attraction transpires apart from gender assignment).[68] Kastner, in focusing on the importance of playing Timmy "frenetic" rather than "limp," emphasizes personal energy in excess of gender and sex distinctions. The introduction of a limp/frenetic dichotomy allows Kastner to reference his own identity: "I'm really not naturally too limp. I have no limpness to bring to the role. The way I play it, I'm always fixing my hair and fooling with my face, in a nervous way."[69] Ackerman's defense ("there isn't going to be anything offensive, you can believe me") and Kastner's commentary on gender presentation drew attention to perception and camp self-defense.

Queer gender permeates the print documents that different writers used to generate the series' audiovisual story world. A series of press releases peppered with snappy dialogue and cultural references evocative of London locations report that Kastner is "masquerading" around London "as Timmy," in a context where the "masquerade" has as much to do with camp practices of seeing and being seen as it does with cis norms and transmisogyny. One publicity announcement introduces a specified character reminiscent of the nonethnic-ethnicity that continued to "diversify" whiteness amid racism in television sitcoms including *Girl*, as it describes how Timmy, out and about in London, was confused with two people for whom only names and no explanations are given: "There were some square looks from the crowd at Wimbledon dog track this week when a sharp looking red head bowled into the enclosure. 'Is that Phyllis Diller, Hermione Gingold or something off the moon?' said a bookmaker."[70] Intertextual signifiers strung together through the mode of camp excess make up this publicity passage, produced by people at the London agency Townshend Bryer Associates Ltd. The copy suggests that frenetic girl energy is attractive from multiple viewing positions, which is a genderqueer concept. To consider Timmy's mod identity as an alibi for gender and sexual transgression misses the fact that the genderqueer concept articulates as part of the trademark aesthetic of the series. Writers consistently drew attention to sexism, sexual harassment, the malleability of gender presentation, and possibilities for transgender perception within a field of celebrity, romance, fashion, and comedy referents. As becomes evident when examining Nancy Kulp's work across *The Bob Cummings Show*, *The Gale Storm Show*, and *The Beverly Hillbillies*, Hollywood itself, as a site of the production of excess excessive signifiers, contributes to critique circulating through the formulas that constitute sitcom form. In the *Beverly Hillbillies* episode "Hedda Hopper's Hollywood," for example, notable for its citational title and comic silent-film western parody within, Nancy Kulp's Jane Hathaway character—a Twiggy and *Girl* prototype—emotes camp effeminacy through idiosyncratic performance of posturing, holding a cool prop of sunglasses. Later in this episode from October 14, 1964, Jane does racialized "vamp" drag as a famous Juanita structurally reminiscent of Timmy's "earthiness" and the ethnic-nonethnic exoticized mods populating the hip world of *Girl*.

The textual dynamics that emerge within *Girl*'s industrial context offer insight into the possibilities of queer trans representations within standardized TV formats. In a general sense, *Girl* offers a backstage view of what life was like in a climate in which a person's style and their ability to move and shake within the media industries superseded gender difference, or where flouting gender conventions could help your social climbing. Theorizing the roles of Screen Gems' unwitting producers of genderqueer TV culture shows that queer trans possibilities are coextensive with feminism. As the foundational feminist media histories of scholars such as Patricia Mellencamp and Julie D'Acci show, women characters in sitcoms were complicatedly pushed to the margins and increasingly sexualized in the 1960s.[71] *Girl*'s characters had access to public space, despite backlash, and scored a slot on the Thursday night TV schedule. Overall, agency was drastically skewed toward white men and middle-class masculinity, but *Girl*'s attention to mod camp mores occasioned femme gendering. Author Burt Hirschfeld's novelization makes the trans gender queer camp of the Timmy franchise obvious within the assimilation. One character tells another they would "glare like a piece of chipped glass in a tray of diamonds."[72]

Girl built camp momentum through merchandising and advertising (e.g., the tie-in book) in the months leading up to its debut. Trans gender queer textual moments continued even after ABC began adamantly bifurcating Timmy from Tim, insisting that *Girl* was a story in which "Tim . . . does everything . . . to keep [Timmy] as little a part of . . . life as possible."[73] In terms of the backstage plot, tensions built toward a stalemate: the network demanded that Screen Gems write Timmy out of the series. The producers kept her in the picture. Ackerman described the series' cancellation as a "tragedy of sorts" based on scheduling factors and market research, or what Ackerman called "the odd fact that—if one believes the Nielsen studies—about sixty or seventy per cent of the audience never even tuned in to see what we were all about."[74] So, had the public spoken? Had Ackerman "flipped his wig," as Ackerman, who had just that season broken a record in landing three series—*Girl*, *The Flying Nun*, and *Bewitched*—back to back on one night (Thursday), said "Madison Avenue" stated he had when they first fielded the *Girl* pitch?[75]

Ackerman's reference to the square reactions of "Madison Avenue" and "the people in New York" to *Girl* implicates management within the Screen Gems office as well as executives and researchers at the sponsors, networks, and advertisers.[76] It was Yardley of London that was reported to "control 95 per cent of the teen-age market with their cosmetics and other products."[77] It was Marvin Korman, vice president in charge of the East Coast Advertising and Public Relations Division at Screen Gems, who clamped down

FIGURES 4.1–4.4. Nancy Kulp with Irene Ryan and Raymond Bailey in the *Beverly Hillbillies* episode "Hedda Hopper's Hollywood," October 14, 1964.

on a scene with "the girl . . . and Patricia Brake" because "the entire ['13-second I.D.'] spot revolves around . . . kissing Patricia."[78] In a classic institutional move, Korman attributed concerns about queer trans representation to other people, who Korman imagined would automatically reject trans and lesbian love and gender variance as corrupting influences. Explaining the executive viewers' anxiety about using the scene without the entire narrative frame of the series' conceit, Korman declared, "By itself, it can be very misleading and might give some people the wrong idea and a queasy feeling about the show."[79] Without naming the issue, Korman censored *Girl*'s queer trans representation, committing the company to diminishing Timmy on the dotted line. Established industry formulas for sitcoms, however, made it impossible for other producers to follow through, propagating "femme."

Trans Camp

From the perspective of the present, *Girl* undercuts all attempts to assign progressive value to a television sitcom. At the same time, the text also questions its own participation in tenacious regimes of hetero and cis normativity. The UCLA sweatshirt Timothy wears briefly for a camp moment in a confessional-style monologue performance medley in the series' pilot episode identifies the specificity of the production culture from which *Girl* emerges. In the manner of this nod to the inescapability of the media-military-industrial complex, reminiscent of *My Living Doll*, *Girl* mobilized a camp treatment of gender norms across individual episodes, promotions, and publicity materials. Gender and sexual nonconformity are par for the course in sitcom production and promotion. In this case, the documented work it took to get the *Girl* project off the ground overflows with ambiguous references to potentially compelling historical actors such as Nigel Terry, Jacques D. Belasco, Tommy Dawson, Miss Millie Gusse, Renee Valente, Justin de Villeneuve, Timm (or Jimm?) Rummell, Burton D. Metcalfe, Donna Brainard, Jacqui Brandwynne, Lil Firestone, Barry Lategan, Jean Shrimpton, and Twiggy.

All might seem incidental within the reams of paperwork produced as part of collaboration and conflict among Screen Gems, ABC, the sponsoring brand Yardley, and Young & Rubicam (where Ackerman had worked in radio broadcasting from 1936 to 1948, before moving, while at CBS, to Southern California, at the height of the expansion of television programming in the pre-cable era). Yet, the details of production supply a reservoir of camp resonance within *Girl* as a historicized sitcom text. Meaningfully so with respect to queer history, the program made media fashions productive of trans camp textuality across racial, ethnic, and national borders amid mainstreaming. Through conventional sitcom practices, Screen Gems contributed to queer culture in the course of manufacturing comedy.

Camp suffused the television schedules in the late 1960s through queer attention to production, consumption, and showbiz history in both longstanding sitcoms such as *Bewitched* and shorter-lived "failures" such as *Girl*. Despite censorship, network economics allowed the subtly absurd character-driven story worlds of sitcoms to incubate queer, genderqueer, and transgender representation. With capitalist competition and countercultural influences encouraging experimentation with repetition, camp TV contributed to the success of local stations, the network structure, and the overall consumer culture that the national pastime of TV fortified in an era of protest. Analyzing programs such as *Girl* alongside the history of their production and their historical context shows resistance to social convention and facility with social conventions in the service of resistance to be a principal link between the television industry and the queer and trans cultures forged in the 1950s and 1960s.

Girl manufactured the mass interchange of multiple forms of gender and a brand of gender and sexual defiance that links queer and trans culture. *Girl* shows that this connection points up mod culture as another related link. Fashion journalist Marylin Bender wrote in *The Beautiful People* (1968) about the envelope-pushing dress of the day (which Bender dubbed "the Mod revolt"): "Today the alienated hippie spits in the eye of the world and then [s]he is invited to help launch a department store promotion."[80] *Girl* reverses this situation, using department store promotions to stage rebellion. In 1968, Timmy visited Yardley's cosmetics counters on a "Beauty Bash" tour,[81] took viewers to London through the domestic medium of TV, and then nearly vanished.

This is the case with so many trans gender queer icons of camp TV, such as Jethrine Bodine, a drag collaboration of Linda Henning, Max Baer, Jr. and the writers, sound designers, and the rest of the crew on *The Beverly Hillbillies*. Linda Henning, offspring of Paul Henning and witty spouse Ruth Henning, whose name had been lent to a character at the margins of *The Bob Cummings Show*, provided a vocal track for Jethrine's speech, which was processed with special effects. Baer, who more often played Jethro, Jethrine's cousin, appeared in Southern frills against a backdrop of hillbilly kitsch, a big woman in the white US heartland whose aesthetic distance from black mod culture in comparison with Tim's world only begins to suggest the vast range of queer gender that late 1960s sitcoms circulate, including all over the Internet today.[82]

Conclusion. Around-the-Clock Queer Gender
DIGITAL CAMP TV

This book has sourced camp, a style of queer critique, from network television programming—from the material records of situation comedy production found in collections at places such as the American Heritage Center, Brigham Young University, and Dartmouth College; from the University of Southern California, the archive of the Writers Guild, and the University of California, Los Angeles; and from the widely accessible store of vintage programming online, which shifted drastically during the course of my research. I set sitcom history within a mixed race genealogy of performance and popular entertainment that demonstrates, within the overall racism and sexism of sitcom production, consecutive purges of nonconforming workers from the medium. Twice in this period, and overall, a spike in sitcom camp corresponds with stricter limits on explicit representation. The air at the time of the lavender scare was thin, and getting thinner, in that government policies artificially narrowed the broadband spectrum for private interests and the stated "public good," understood in terms of white cis heteronormativity.¹ Queer gender, however, was in abundance. Given this, my queer trans critique has been oblique, indirect, and displaced, designed to mirror my objects of study, in that, in the purist historical sense, there are no objects at all, but rather the question of what is possible in transmitting images and sound over airwaves, and through print.

Getting work in the industry means signing on to further a racist system. This is the condition of camp TV as expressed in the United States in the 1950s and 1960s. As a part of this system, camp critique and queer gender continue to happen all of the time, twenty-four hours a day, seven days a week, including in the sitcoms from the 1950s and 1960s that continue to run half-hourly on cable and satellite TV, stream from websites, and circulate in a variety of formats, on DVDs and thumb drives, lunch boxes and pajamas. You may have thought this programming was 100 percent heterosexual. Nothing is 100 percent heterosexual.²

Sitcoms rely on industrialized labor. They produce representation that transcends current distinctions between queer and genderqueer identities, through a camp mode that exceeds individual intention and agency. But sitcom history is written and rewritten according to the aims of those narrating it, who typically attribute significance to TV programs of the past based on their popularity, longevity, and quality. People rarely factor camp in, even though it was clearly part of the cultures of production of situation comedy in the foundational decades of commercial broadcasting. A quick scenelet in the rapid-fire comic ending credit sequence to the final *Ernie Kovacs Special* (#8), for example, depicts a writer suddenly returning to work on the program interrupting a make out session to lunge for pen and paper, suggesting in a camp manner that, behind the scenes, along with the copious queer gender, white women contribute to TV production and can call the shots physically.³

This discrepancy between camp as lived history in the period and ongoing perceptions of sitcoms of the time as antithetical to camp (in line with reconstructions of history in general as without camp) is significant, because camp circulates through 1950s and 1960s sitcoms indicative of what else was on the dial. Andy Warhol, addressing middle America, guessed that "your favorite TV police show" was probably even "gayer" than Congress and the Factory, the studio that made recognized camp classics such as Warhol's *Gold Marilyn Monroe*, *Empire*, and *Warhol's Fifteen Minutes*. Kelly Cresap's *Pop Trickster Fool* interprets Warhol's claim that police procedurals were not only gay but gayer than the House of Representatives and the groups at the Factory, which is a self set-up for an intertextual punch line, as a homophobic and closeted comment. Warhol wrote, "Naturally the Factory had fags." Warhol wrote, "We were in the entertainment business and—That's Entertainment!"[4]

This statement, characterized by Cresap as hostile and heteronormative, deadpans the everyday reality of queer workers, which is important to continue to do, because imagining queer workers prepping crime scenes for telefilm shoots has historical value in the present for the project of disrupting cis norms—for historicizing the possibility of the question of camp producers prior to the mid-1960s. There is historical value to Warhol's statement precisely because it is kept purely speculative, when it is hardly beyond belief that Warhol and the people Warhol knew did know prop masters, actors, assistants, and others on *Felony Squad*, and on other legal dramas, such as *Perry Mason*. Warhol is precisely not referring to any one person or set of people. Within camp such specificity, or "denotative" directness, is not necessary. What is offered is a camp impression of camp as replete, as pervasive, and as readily apparent within pop culture, at the level of connotation as a form of critique. The joke is not an indictment or distancing of "fag" as an identity, even if it seems exactly this when taken simply and straightforwardly.

Camp does not require corroboration, but there is evidence for Warhol's claim, which, like Warhol's insight, takes the form of comic displacement. Raymond Burr, for example, the lead performer in (nearly five hundred episodes of) *Perry Mason* (CBS, 1957–66) and *Ironside* (NBC, 1967–75), hour-long legal dramas set in Los Angeles and San Francisco,[5] worked with a mostly behind-the-scenes partner, Bob Benevides.[6] Elsewhere in the network television schedules at the time—either a few hours later, or across the dial—comedians such as Jerry Lewis and Ernie Kovacs professed feelings for specific crew members on air; producers, including executives and assistants, made cameos; and fleeting, focalized programming followed technician-extras across disintegrating fourth walls.[7] Why perceive as camp only the most obvious, "campy" versions of camp? There is this; and there is so much more.

Trans representation is in the middle of all of it, in successive hostile climates of erasure and misconstrual, despite the routine dehumanizing instrumentality. It is part of the record of Burr's career, for example, as indicated by a Turner Classic Movies.com review of Michael Seth Starr's Burr biography, *Hiding in Plain Sight*. Writer Steve Ryfle reports that Burr effectively avoided personal exposure of his sexual nonconformity in the early 1960s, when the "scandal sheet" *Confidential* "sanitized" an article about Burr's "one night stand with a female impersonator" by making "it appear that Burr

FIGURES CONC.1–CONC.4. Joe Mikolas and Margaret Styne credit Mary Anne Hooper in *Ernie Kovacs Special* #8, January 23, 1962, in a fleeting skit flanked by trans gender queer representation.

had been fooled."[8] As with commentary on the now-out Richard Deacon, Jim Nabors, and Dick York, Burr's story is recounted as one of a homo/hetero closet incompatible with trans identity and agency; Starr's subtitle is *The Secret Life of Raymond Burr*. But you can see through the purported straightness requiring secrecy supposedly overpowering and irresistible at the time. You can see through the cisnormativity used to establish white gay identity (in accord with the reproductive futurism of media industrial ideology). Seeing through all of this, or rather sensing the undercurrent and singing a different tune, is part of a project of perceiving and pushing beyond the power relations of the present that uphold cis norms in periods prior to their articulation. Burr and Benevides bought an island in the South Pacific for cattle and coconut farming. They bonded about orchid cultivation and built a winery together. If they represent minority workers in TV in the 1950s and 1960s, they also indicate the ongoing histories of exploitation interwoven into Hollywood television and media culture, as a tangible, collective social hypocrisy, and to all individual success and celebrity. They expose the hierarchical reliance on "same-sex" constructions of white gayness that continue to marginalize trans people.

Across the 1950s and 1960s, TV producers remediated racialized hierarchies of class, gender, sexuality, and ability, hierarchies still playing out in contemporary unwillingness to recognize trans queer of color culture. Television production distilled and reproliferated the dispersal of roles (namely gendered secondary, guest, and extra roles) in radio, film, and other arts, creating queer legacies of racist, ableist heterocissexist typecasting and cultural appropriation. The media system skewed further in favor of white privilege during a period of presumed improvement in civil rights. Queer gender spotlights, within this context, the fascinating craft of sitcom writing and all of the labor that goes into creating, scripting, editing, selling, and executing sitcoms, as well as sometimes into keeping them going. Queer gender is created, often at the time of a television series' conception, and it is scripted, casted, and performed, as well as marketed, postproduced, and publicized.

Those involved in the industry helped establish the world of constantly updating technology and rapidly shifting taste cultures we now inhabit. Intertwined racism and gender norms meant work distributed disproportionately according to privilege, among mostly white celebrities, and especially among men whose images were hetero-oriented. In the adjustment period when advertising shifted from full program sponsorship to split commercial time slots during ad breaks, camp settled down slightly, while continuing to brew in late night and talk blocks of television variety entertainment and bouncing back in sitcoms. Overall, across the two decades, networks and stations voided fast-paced camp imported from radio, recordings, and performance culture, as actors of color lost and then regained important but still very limited access to TV. While continuing to change, industry practices in the 1960s solidified many traditions established in the 1950s. Many sitcoms in the 1960s appear more polished than those in the 1950s, however schlock only expanded in the 1960s. In addition, the incoming wave of Hollywood film camp meant that some sex comedy–styled sitcoms, such as those Screen Gems offered, had relatively high production values, and in this way resembled series of the 1950s geared toward kids and sophisticates.

During this time, the networks' synchronized yearly schedules, competing against and copying each other with new sitcom offerings, especially domestic family series, and, increasingly across the mid- to late 1960s, with an influx of hybrid sci-fi/fantasy situation comedies. *Mr. Ed*, a series about a talking horse, partnered the animal, an insubordinate wisecracker, with the architect Wilbur, who works from home in the barn where Ed resides. *My Favorite Martian* had a similar fantastic-secret story structure. That series featured Ray Walston and Bill Bixby as cohabiting characters passing as relatives. Combined with other series of over fifty or one hundred episodes, namely *The Addams Family, Bachelor Father, Bewitched, The Bob Cummings Show, The Dick Van Dyke Show,* and *The Beverly Hillbillies* (which has nearly three hundred episodes), these programs constitute a backdrop of camp TV against which to assess particular episodes, comedy routines, cultural references, and trans gender queer codes in these series, other series, and elsewhere. This includes unaired material, such as the proposed revision that tried to send *Hazel* to Hollywood, which would have added regular and one-off media producer types to what had been mostly a family- and neighborhood-based ensemble. Instead the series stayed in suburban New York State for another season and ended with classic sitcom camp orientalist conceit, with the couple moving to generic Arabia for business. With leads as dispensable as this, secondary casts were stars. The queer gender production of character actors isn't the fifteen-minutes-of-fame model; this is about a career of continuous employment, relative job security, industry accolades, and comparative anonymity.

This book is the result of a long obsession with series linked through their unspecified producers' obsession with displaced dialogue about dating, desire, and commercial art. I traced queer gender through the backstage byways of the more marginal US-produced television texts made by the less prominent character actors and more likely to be forgotten TV personalities of light comedy. I found queer gender in the shows deemed turkeys, considered the worst shows in the history of television, and in the most acclaimed, the *I Love Lucys*. Series from *The Jack Benny Program* to *Accidental Family* to *The Monkees* featured characters and television celebrities doing stand-up, singing, dancing, and sometimes interacting with fans and audiences. In live performance, film features, and other productions of the day, including advertising and publicity texts, framing devices and self-reflexive transitional and promotional moments invigorated by the new medium of TV encouraged representation considered taboo. I have gathered this material to draw attention to the patterns of production portraying the sexual harassment of women as a characteristic of effeminate playboys and to the ways in which those characters that are feminist are devalued as "spinsters" and also kept from the category of "cad" due to cissexism.

A lot of the camp TV of the 1950s and 1960s is (or was) available through digital distribution, but not much, speaking relative to what aired in the period, remains, in spite of how much still circulates. This camp TV is prevalent today: there are late-night *Lucy* marathons on the Hallmark cable channel and *Our Miss Brooks* episodes uploaded in blocks of three and four to YouTube. Even in abundance, however, relatively little is preserved and accessible. With regard to this paradoxically plentiful and lost archive, people are generally reluctant to permit the possibilities of queer and trans dimensions, even when they recognize the multiplicity of meaning involved. Queer gender circulated for profit, in first-run broadcasts, ads, merchandise, and syndication, and yet it is as if none of this ever was. Systems of media production both inaugurate queer and trans representation and banish it from history, by way of contextual discourses construing trans gender queer representation as novel, new, and now, while concurrently ahead of its time, and/or dated, as if incompatible with the present. People with the best of intentions ruthlessly discard from the mainstream of the medium's history peripheral concentrations of trans gender queer icons that have been central to the success of TV, especially through the sitcom. The industry is always superficially self-reinventing, tying people to the rhythms, norms, and inequities of consumer capitalism, by way of the texture of everyday life, through TV-based interpersonal relationships, planned and perceived obsolescence cycles, and the melodrama of idealized straight white gender roles.[9] As part of this process, the industry mines its own archives for profit. My research notes include references to Internet Movie Database user reviews of *Hank*, for instance, a mid-1960s program with at least one impersonation routine every episode, that leap from "Unfortunately Warner [Bros.] has this show so buried that I bet even they couldn't find it if they wanted to" (in 2008) to "Now out on DVD! Buy it on Amazon!" (as of 2015).

The air is still thin, or rather the people who appropriate the ether exclude. At the same time, those who fill the airtime from which investors profit foster queer gender in flesh and text. Rampant myths about the significance of a cultural category of "biological sex" and the threat of its disturbance are ironized in abundance everywhere thanks to camp TV, in archives such as Mary and Bob Cummings's and through rentals, cable, YouTube, DVD, file-sharing platforms, and other formats twenty-four hours a day, seven days a week. Sitcom writers continue to repurpose their own conceits and those of others.[10] Series previously unavailable legally are newly distributed all the time, bopping from one conglomerate to another across bootleg cultures and release formats. Despite cis archival drift and institutionalized amnesia, a relative safe space of sitcom ridicule and queer gender celebration persists, including in ongoing popular historiography, expanding and interlacing, more hospitable often than real life even when viciously misogynous and punishing of gender variance.[11]

With *Camp TV* I have documented queer gender in media texts typically considered straight, doing so in order to show how transgender representation enhances queer history. Queer culture is grounded in gender rebellion, yet many assume representations of gender nonconformity made for straight cis people to laugh at are insulting and repressive. Recognizing the trans gender queer value of these representations presents a corrective to the recent minoritizing of trans identity. Riki Wilchins explains, in an introduction to the anthology *Genderqueer: Voices from beyond the Sexual Binary*, "While it's hard not to cheer the emergence of transgender as an important queer cause, confining the dialogue on gender to one identity has had the curious side effect of relieving the rest of society—gay and straight—from examining its own history of transcending gender norms."[12] This expansive but specificity-invested study of camp TV unspecified to individual LGBT+ producers begins to show just how vast the overlap of cis history and trans history is, in the form of trans gender queer cultural production.

Camp TV is a web of eccentric, or queer, gender. Public and professional eccentricity is a privilege. It is also part of a powerful "ceiling" on comedy performance, in terms of top industry prospects, the kind Ed Wynn, Bob

Cummings, and others up to today anomalously transcend, along with less famous and for the most part popularly unrecognized character actors. Eccentricity is classed and raced, including by ethnicity, authenticity, and intelligence, within Hollywood's white-dominated and segregated occupational system. In sitcom contexts, and the typically all-white slots for lead parts and most supporting parts, the traditions of "character actors" and comic character acting produce queer gender across a spectrum of intersectional privilege that effeminacy and various queer gender representations question when considered together. Comedy emerges in relation to constructions of education and race, as well as gender, sexuality, class, and ability. Racist casting practices define the period of camp TV discussed here. When taking into account the broader context of exploitation and tokenization,[13] bit actors, extras, and those continually typecast are important media producers. They were important in the 1950s and 1960s, but more importantly they are crucial now, for present attempts to revise television history away from the transphobic self-perpetuation of the media industries.

Notes

INTRODUCTION

1 R. Becker, *Gay TV and Straight America*, 3. For scholarship considering series prior to the 1990s, see Wlodarz, "'We're Not All So Obvious'"; and Villarejo, *Ethereal Queer*.
2 Leibman, *Living Room Lectures*, 8. Leibman lists *The Bob Cummings Show*, *The Phil Silvers Show*, and *The Gale Storm Show* as examples.
3 For a discussion of "queer gender" in binary terms see Villarejo, *Ethereal Queer*, 61–65.
4 On "gawking at the gawkers," surviving scorn, and valuing queer trans work history as critical praxis, see Clare, "Gawking, Gaping, Staring" (259–60). This analysis "flirts" back, as in Clare's account, as a project of queer temporality (Freeman, "Introduction"). It gravitates "backward," discarding narratives of progress toward "modern Homosexuality" (Ferguson, "Sissies at the Picnic," 193–95). I follow a trail of presumed ugliness and undesirability preserving of trans history through the network system of "economic and institutional consensus" with sponsors and advertisers; "a 'success-versus-failure' model of gay television obscures more than it reveals" (McCarthy, "Ellen," 596).
5 Torres, *Living Color*, 1–2; Spigel, *Welcome to the Dreamhouse*; Schwoch, *Global TV*.
6 On the overlap and antiracist feminist methods, see Brettschneider, "Critical Attention to Race." On the black dandy and these popular entertainment traditions, see M. Miller, *Slaves to Fashion*, 6, 101; Glick, "Harlem's Queer Dandy"; Wojcik, "Mae West's Maids," 288–89; Chude-Sokei, *The Last "Darky,"* 98–99, 200–203; Mizejewski, *Ziegfeld Girl*, 105–7; Stark, *Men in Blackface*, 71; Rogin, *Blackface, White Noise*, 103–5; Lott, *Love and Theft*, 159–66; Toll, *Blacking Up*, 76–77, 122–24, 139–45, 273–74; and Snorton, *Black on Both Sides*, 4. A full consideration of the specificity of this debt that US sitcoms, and the dominant media matrix of consumer culture overall, owe to queer and trans of color culture—here by way of the complex appropriations involved in a long view of intermingling production cultures—is regrettably beyond

the scope of this study. Villarejo identifies Eve Arden as a TV dandy (*Ethereal Queer*, 63), and the connection is evident also in the blackface performances, in particular Harry von Zell's rendition of Eddie Cantor's signature trans gender queer number "If You Knew Susie," in the *Burns and Allen* episode "A Night of Vaudeville," April 9, 1956, https://www.youtube.com/watch?v=b3uJH_SJPt4.

7 Hall, "Encoding, Decoding."
8 Halberstam, *In a Queer Time and Place*, 45.
9 See Kodat, "Making Camp."
10 Hal Humphrey writes in 1967 that Steve Allen's ten-year-old comment in *Bigger Than a Breadbox*, on the increased scrutiny comedians were facing, remains relevant: "The comedians who continue to function despite the trend are subject to increasingly heavy attacks from critics, audiences, rating services, and from the vaguely defined spirit of the times." Hal Humphrey, "Good TV Comedy in Short Supply," *Toledo Blade*, August 22, 1967. On censorship in this period, see Litvak, *The Un-Americans*.
11 I use "trans gender queer" and "genderqueer" as historicized critical terms, meaning I am assessing queer positionality in relation to the discursive system of gender, sexuality, class, and race in operation at the time. At the same time, as Stryker, Currah, and Moore explain in "Trans-, Trans, or Transgender," "Territorializing and deterritorializing 'trans-' and its suffixes . . . as well as the movements between temporalizing and spatializing them, is an improvisational, creative, and essentially poetic practice through which radically new possibilities for being in the world can start to emerge" (14). It is in keeping with this practice that I use "genderqueer" and "trans gender queer" to counter the conviction in camp studies as articulated by Katrin Horn that "a critique in mainstream culture will inevitably be less radical in terms of gender variance and intersectionality than its articulation in less commercially oriented discourses and media might be" (*Women, Camp, and Popular Culture*, 5).
12 In *Having a Good Cry*, Robyn Warhol explains effeminacy as a nonbinary gender enterprise produced in tandem with a binary gender system (9).
13 Salamon, *Assuming a Body*, 71.
14 Judith Butler, *Gender Trouble*, 155. All gender is queer gender in trans gender queer camp. You never know how others are reading you or who you are for sure. Max Wolf Valerio, an author who describes trans experience as one of "uncovering and displaying nature's hidden cacophony, its subtext of sabotage and dissolution," explains, "You never know whom you are talking to. You never know what you will do someday, what you are capable of" (*The Testosterone Files*, 2).
15 Straayer, *Deviant Eyes, Deviant Bodies*, 2.
16 Booth, "*Campe-toi!*," 69.
17 Gilbert Seldes, *Writing for Television*, 179. Hainley's chapter on Paul Lynde in "How to Proceed in Everything I Can Think Of" (47–85) explores this "guest-star system." See P. White, *Uninvited*; Roof, *All about Thelma and Eve*; and McCarthy, "Ellen."

18 Butler, *Gender Trouble*, 155.
19 Character actors, commonly defined as those who may be widely familiar based on appearance and performance but whose names circulate only among aficionados, are not stars in the classic Hollywood sense of conventional beauty or popular name recognition. See Wojcik, "Typecasting"; Leff, "Becoming Clifton Webb." These sources, especially Wojcik's attention to theater traditions, indicate the broad accounting of classification my research has entailed. On my terms, even Clifton Webb, who stuck to features, was a camp TV producer, in the moment of appearing on *The Ed Sullivan Show* in 1954. On eccentricity and character acting, see Ruth and Paul Henning, interview by David Marc, September 9, 1996, Steven H. Scheuer, *Television History Interviews*, Box 22: 20–22, Syracuse University. See also *The Life of Reilly*, by Barry Polterman, Frank Anderson, and Charles Nelson Reilly, Civilian Pictures (2007) and *I Knew It Was You: Rediscovering John Cazele*, by Richard Shepard, Oscilloscope (2010). Thanks to Chris Finley for the Cazele reference.
20 Jack Major, "Richard Deacon: He Played the Cards He Was Dealt and Came Out a Winner," *Akron Beacon Journal*, September 6, 1964 (accessed May 14, 2018), http://major-smolinski.com/NAMES/DEACON.html.
21 Jeremy Butler, *Television*, 70.
22 See Tartaglia, "Perfect Queer Appositeness"; and McDonald, *Cruising the Movies* ("When Louise Beavers Awakens Jean Harlow," 222–23).
23 Major, "Richard Deacon."
24 Promoting the release of *How I Lost 10 Pounds in 53 Years*, Ballard recounts growing up as a "very strange child" obsessed with movie stars: "No matter what I was doing I was impersonating whoever I saw on the screen." A YouTube video advertisement and comedy routine includes Ballard's performance of a younger Ballard washing dishes as Bette-Davis-dubbed-in-Italian. Moschroi, "The Unbelievable Kaye Ballard," September 10, 2009, https://www.youtube.com/watch?v=PwU6-wmAvoM.
25 Another of Ballard's recurring roles indicative of imbrication in industrial camp production is Angie Pallucci (*The Doris Day Show*, CBS, 1968–73).
26 Elements of camp characterization include hair and makeup, décor, costuming, and performance, specifically brash eye shadow, faux sideburns, and a sculpted crop cut uncommon for men and women at the time; wall hangings signifying femme production, iconic cosmopolitan taste, and the authority connoted by specialized degrees on display; ornate earrings and a half-sleeve black-on-white jacket paired with its inverse—white pearls contrasting with a black shirt; all in the context of Ballard's expressive posture, projected confidence, and steeled expression. These elements combine with vocal delivery and other aspects of acting and intertextuality to constitute queer gender. The eponymous Patty Duke participates in camp performance, coproducing queer gender and pointing up the irony involved in norms and the establishment of norms.
27 On parody and the importance of parody in 1950s TV, see Thompson, *Parody*

and Taste. On mimicry as "an *ironic* compromise," see Bhabha, *Location of Culture*, 122.

28 *Transparent*, "They Is on the Way." Written by Bridget Bedard. Amazon. September 21, 2017.

29 See Griffin's multiplatform study *Tinker Belles and Evil Queens* (143), a discussion of studio authorship in the context of camp, fantasy, animation, drag, realism, and "fabulously false femininity" and masculinity (72).

30 See Rose Marie, *Hold the Roses*; and Rose Marie, "'Dick Van Dyke' Star Rose Marie: What Happened When I Publicly Shamed My Sexual Harasser," *Hollywood Reporter*, December 7, 2017, (accessed May 14, 2018), https://www.hollywoodreporter.com/news/dick-van-dyke-star-rose-marie-what-happened-i-publicly-shamed-my-harasser-guest-column-1063597.

31 Each of the *Stevie Parsons* episodes frames Sal's television appearances through the eyes of Rob and Laura, who witness Sal's everyday desperate-to-marry antics momentarily reach an audience beyond friends by way of the fictionalized broadcasts—which resemble Rose Marie's stints on celebrity game shows, talk shows, and in other venues. These episodes exemplify the mise en abyme structure of sitcom textuality as a whole, articulated through repetitive casting and intertext-intensive characterization. A stage kiss Sal stands triumphantly in the midst of at sign-off—an overplayed performance of sexual assertion reversing conventional gender norms—indicates not only Rose Marie's self-branding within typecasting but also some of Nancy Kulp's roles and parts in countless series suited to still other camp sitcom actors' malleable recurring personas, where what may seem like excessive heterosexuality and sexism works as trans gender queer representation.

32 See Q. Miller, "*Bob Cummings Show*"; and Miller and Rand, "Hot for TV."

33 See P. White, *Uninvited*, 173–74.

34 On Arden, see P. White, *Uninvited*; Roof, *All about Thelma and Eve*; and Villarejo, *Ethereal Queer*.

35 Tinkcom, *Working Like a Homosexual*, 24.

36 Feuer, "Genre Study and Television," 146; R. Williams, *Television*, 77.

37 M. White, "Crossing Wavelengths," 51.

38 Spigel and Curtin, *The Revolution Wasn't Televised*, 4. Sconce, "What If?," 94, 101.

39 Seldes, *Writing for Television*, 180.

40 The "astonishing variety of jobs" Dana's character performed "served to emphasize . . . otherness and social irrelevance" in trans gender queer fashion (Avila-Saavedra, "Ethnic Otherness," 276).

41 See Villarejo, *Ethereal Queer*, on the type of sitcom exchange that "remakes desire into identification" (62–63).

42 Zsa Zsa Gershick, "Estate of Entertainer George Burns Gives 1M to School of Theater," September 22, 1997, news.usc.edu.

43 Villarejo, *Ethereal Queer*, 8.

44 Vaudeville overlaps with blackface minstrelsy and informs these histories,

which structure segregation in public performance and consist of the routine white appropriation of black art, specifically queer and trans of color cultural production and performance. See M. Miller, *Slaves to Fashion*, 310n17. On the freak show, another influence, as opportunity amid exploitation, see Clare, "Gawking, Gaping, Staring," 257.

45 Seldes, *Writing for Television*, 177.
46 Bratten shows that the success of Dinah Shore, a white popular singer and variety show host who did comedy in the 1950s and 1960s, entailed the manipulation of markers of nonwhiteness and whiteness, and the diminishment of Jewish history ("Nothin' Could Be Finah"). In *Dance and the Hollywood Latina*, Priscilla Peña Ovalle details such reracialization as a dynamic of casting and characterizing "in-betweenness" through the "careful manipulation—and simultaneous semiotic representation—of whiteness and nonwhiteness" (20). On whiteness as "a fiction created by elites who wished to protect their own class position of extreme wealth," see Bashi Treitler, *Ethnic Project*, 54.
47 Avila-Saavedra, "Ethnic Otherness," 274.
48 The presumptions involved in this line of thinking understand gender only in terms of assigned sex. Queer gender eludes coercive assignment, at birth and after, through what Roderick Ferguson calls "terrains of the imagination ... that offer what official narratives withhold." Ferguson, "Sissies at the Picnic," 194.
49 Judith Butler, "Politics, Power and Ethics," 9.
50 For Tab Hunter and *The Tab Hunter Show*, see Tab Hunter, *Tab Hunter Confidential*. On Kaye, see Bayless, "Danny Kaye"; and Cohan, "Manic Bodies of Danny Kaye," 22. Halberstam's *In a Queer Time and Place* and several essays in *Enfant Terrible!* speak to queer gender in the work of Jerry Lewis, a prominent postwar TV comedian. In a review raving about the pairing of Ezio Pinza with Martha Raye in an episode of *All-Star Revue*, "a rare streak of genius" on KNBH, Walter Ames used trans gender queer comedy referencing Lewis's queer gender to explain what made the episode, and specifically the "combo" of Raye and Pinza, "one of the funniest shows to come out of this series," writing, "On first thought viewers will probably want to label Martha a 'female Jerry Lewis.' But Martha has been giving out with this type of comedy for many years. So I guess we'll have to call Jerry a 'female Martha Raye.' I'm only kidding, Jerry." Walter Ames, "Keighley Urges Host Emcees for Dramatic TV Shows; SC-Cal Films on KTTV," *Los Angeles Times*, October 23, 1951, 22.
51 Bronski, *Culture Clash*, 43.
52 Bronski, *Culture Clash*, 43; D. Johnson, *Lavender Scare*.
53 Ross, *No Respect*, 162.
54 O'Reilly, in *Bewitched Again*, ix.
55 Doty, "I Love Shari."
56 Green, *Becoming a Visible Man*, 11–12.
57 Green, *Becoming a Visible Man*, 11–12.

58 Sedgwick, *Epistemology of the Closet*, 22.
59 Feinberg, *Transgender Warriors*, 4.
60 Mary Ellen Cohane, personal conversation with the author, October 14, 2009, Five Colleges Women's Studies Research Center.
61 Nealon, *Foundlings*; Villarejo, *Lesbian Rule*.
62 Sedgwick, *Epistemology of the Closet*, 63. Again, see P. White, *Uninvited*, 173–74.
63 *Red Channels*, 183–84.
64 Krefting, *All Joking Aside*, 24–25.
65 *Television Genre Book*, "Advertising," 94.
66 *Television Genre Book*, "Advertising," 94.
67 For a camp accounting of sitcom tropes, see Jacobs and Jones, *Beaver Papers*.
68 *Television Genre Book*, "Situation Comedy, Part 2," 69–70.
69 My framework brings together work in feminist queer of color media criticism, such as Eve Tuck and C. Ree's "Glossary of Haunting" and Celine Parreñas Shimizu's *The Hypersexuality of Race*. See also Nash, *Black Body in Ecstasy*; and Miller-Young, *Taste for Brown Sugar*.
70 The adjective "ethnic-nonethnic" is a reversal of "nonethnic ethnic," a phrase I take from Phil Rosenthal's *You're Lucky You're Funny* (85) and also reproduce, in reference to network mandates for sitcom success, as "nonethnic-ethnic." This is a way of speaking of inside-outsider dynamics, in a context where "race's eroticism is often linked to its hyperbolic absurdity, and . . . racial fictions can be . . . comical even as they are also painful" (Nash, 127).

1. SITCOM HISTORY

1 *The Martha Raye Show*, NBC, September 28, 1954, written and directed by Ed Simmons and Norman Lear, UCLA Film and Television Archive.
2 Alvey, "Independents," 141, 145.
3 Scott, "From Blackface to *Beulah*."
4 *Yoo-Hoo, Mrs. Goldberg*, by Aviva Kempner and Judith Herbert, Ciesla Foundation (2009).
5 Lipsitz, *Time Passages*, chapter 3; Spigel, *Make Room for TV*, 147. Joy Elizabeth Hayes, building on Michelle Hilmes's research, shows that a similar and related assimilation cycle had played out already in radio as program production moved to Hollywood (99).
6 Gilbert had previously starred alongside Phillip Reed in the five-minutes, five-nights-a-week, single-camera, split-screen sitcom titled *Ruthie on the Telephone*, written by Goodman Ace, CBS, August–November, 1949.
7 *My Friend Irma*, January 29, 1952, CBS, UCLA Film and Television Archive.
8 On the ideological construction of supposed firsts, see McCarthy, "Ellen."
9 I adopt the term "nonethnic-ethnic" from Rosenthal's *You're Lucky You're Funny*, a memoir including an explanation of how, in the case of *Everybody Loves Raymond*, a 1996–2005 sitcom, Italian identity and Jewish identity that

existed on paper in pre-production, which the network wanted less explicit, became recognizable after casting in the performance style of an Irish actor (85).
10   Karlyn, *Unruly Women*; Koestenbaum, *Anatomy of Harpo Marx*.
11   S. Murray, *Hitch Your Antenna to the Stars*, 71.
12   S. Murray, *Hitch Your Antenna to the Stars*, 71.
13   Brook, *Something Ain't Kosher Here*, 45.
14   Spigel, *Make Room for TV*, 151.
15   Tahmahkera, *Tribal Television*, 186n57, 187n72.
16   Virtually but not entirely. Mellencamp, *Logics of Television*, 4.
17   Newcomb, *TV*, 27. This is true even though the TV sitcom was partially retooled from radio, an ongoing partner-competitor in broadcasting, intricately interwoven in Hollywood conglomeration.
18   See D'Emilio, *Sexual Politics, Sexual Communities*.
19   Spigel, *Make Room for TV*, 137.
20   "Television Backs a Code of Ethics," *New York Times*, October 20, 1951, 28.
21   Cassidy, "Touch, Taste, Breath," 37.
22   "Television Backs a Code of Ethics," 28.
23   Spigel, *Make Room for TV*.
24   See Metz's work with Lipsitz's *Time Passages* in Metz, *Bewitched*, 25.
25   Marc, *Comic Visions*, 64. Gitlin, *Inside Prime Time*, 4, 225.
26   "Television Backs a Code of Ethics." See Anderson, *Hollywood TV*.
27   "Television Backs a Code of Ethics."
28   For an indication of the discursive overlap of femininity and TV at this time, see discussions of Philip Wylie in Wojcik, *Apartment Plot*, 93; Reumann, *American Sexual Character*; and Terry, "Momism." Wylie, whose work is notoriously homophobic, was a television—perhaps a camp TV—producer, of *Crunch and Des*, an action-adventure buddy drama about two professional fisherpeople.
29   Browne, "Political Economy," 178.
30   "Miss Rose Marie—Is a Big Girl Now!," Bud Lewis and Associates, 4, Hal Humphrey Collection, Box 14, USC Cinematic Arts Library.
31   *The Dinah Shore Chevy Show*, September 6, 1959, NBC, UCLA Film and Television Archive.
32   Rose Marie, *Hold the Roses*, 73–74, 5, 29–32, 67, 99, 111, 115–16, 120, 149. See also *Wait for Your Laugh*, written by Christina Tucker and Jason Wise (2017; Culver City, California: Samuel Goldwyn Films, 2018), DVD.
33   *The Jimmy Durante Show*, "All Star Revue," April 11, 1953, UCLA Film and Television Archive.
34   *The George Jessel Show*, written by George Jessel and Sam Carlton, ABC, February 7, 1954, UCLA Film and Television Archive.
35   Billy Barty, another iconic character actor, also did Liberace, on the *Colgate Comedy Hour* in 1955 and, with Spike Jones and the City Slickers, on tour and on TV, but "dressed in a silver wig, tails and high-top tennis shoes . . . while playing a miniature piano as shaving cream bubbled from a candelabra." Jon

Thurber, "Billy Barty; Diminutive Entertainer," *Los Angeles Times*, December 24, 2000.

36 Doty, *Making Things Perfectly Queer*, xii.

37 de Villiers, *Opacity and the Closet*.

38 Another version of this *Mister Peepers* joke had appeared previously in an episode of *The Jack Benny Program*. Coming on for the opening unexpectedly wearing spectacles and deploying them as a prop, Benny, whose self-deprecation, Doty argues, signifies as queer, explains in comic monologue that the show's producer insisted on Benny wearing glasses because it would help them achieve better ratings (i.e., "it wouldn't hurt") if Benny's audience thought that instead of watching Jack they were watching Mister Peepers. This punch line implies a queer framework ironically coextensive with mainstream tastes: in the case of *Mr. Peepers*'s popularity and in many other possible comparisons across the dial, higher TV ratings went to the less conventionally masculine, despite the fact that generally most people are rewarded for subscribing to norms, not celebrated for deviating from them, as these comedians are within the camp discourse. MrPrivateShow, "Jack Benny and Rochester," October 12, 2010, https://www.youtube.com/watch?v=QALv6bwZi9E.

39 Browne, "Political Economy," 178.

40 Lipsitz, *Time Passages*, chapter 3; Spigel, *Make Room for TV*, chapter 5; Bratten, "Nothin' Could be Finah."

41 On *The Morey Amsterdam Show*, see Weinstein, *Forgotten Network*, 99–107.

42 This joke, which endorses pleasure over conventional wisdom, may seem frivolous, but the approach to the sexist "has-been" concept that it outlines is productive in terms of the access the dialogue provides to camp. The logic of this slang, which refers to a person past their prime, presents motion picture casting practices in relief and a view of the career cycles of lead actors in terms of faded silver screen masculinity. The performers repetitively run through three examples of icons a potential actor might be paired with in a kind of verbal montage of the fade-to-black kiss climaxes of classic Hollywood love scenes. In the wordplay, the "where" in "where you has been" is both a spatial reference pointing to Hollywood production cultures and slang for sexual adventure, and is metaphorically explicit as regards the body. The way in which in camp TV queer representation doubles as trans representation is evident here in converging senses of "sex," as simultaneously sexual behavior, bodily narrative, and sexualized gender performance. *The Ed Wynn Show*, October 6, 1949, script, Seaman Jacobs Scripts, 1946–1992, Syracuse University Special Collections.

43 C. Becker, *It's the Pictures*. Desjardins begins *Recycled Stars* by examining how a guest appearing on *The Beverly Hillbillies* gives Gloria Swanson an opportunity to reject misogyny and sexist ageism. *Recycled Stars* also demonstrates connections between the queer 1990s and the history of television situation comedy in chapters on experimental film and video.

44 Douglas, *Listening In*, 194.

45 *The Ed Wynn Show*, Seaman Jacobs Scripts, Syracuse University Special Collections. Jacobs worked with many collaborators and is notable for adapting the *How to Marry a Millionaire* concept to television (see Berke, "Bad Feminists") and writing episodes of *The Betty White Show*, *My Favorite Martian*, *Grindl*, and *The Addams Family*, among other camp TV highlights, including episodes of *Bachelor Father*, *The Mothers-in-Law*, *The Red Skelton Show*, *Here's Lucy*, and *The Love Boat*. An obituary published by the Writers Guild of America noted Jacobs was an "in-demand comedy writer" often solicited for monologue material. Jacobs is an example of one of many cases in which you can focus in on a writer and see a unique slice of camp TV history that brings many other new old camp TV icons into focus.
46 On camp orientalism, see Argadé (*Jungle Boys*); Muñoz (*Disidentifications*, ix); and Mark Williams ("Entertaining 'Difference,'" 22).
47 Moore, one of Cassidy's many "charm boys," "prospered in the daytime sphere of women and paradoxically succeeded in validating masculine control" (Cassidy, *What Women Watched*, 84). Moore's work as a host, guest personality, and sometime comedian is marked by the broader white normalization of the TV industry and by queer gender, camp, and trans gender queer representation. Cassidy writes, "Moore's brand of masculine charm . . . featured 'feminine' qualities": Moore was small, appeared at times in costumes socially sanctioned only for women, and presented a "solicitous attitude toward housewives," a group Moore spoke of wanting to rename in order to convey dignity (*What Women Watched*, 82).
48 The name Edwina is an example of the use of names within camp TV as ambiguous intertextual references citing unspecified, likely queer cultural paratexts, such as, in this case, Edwina Mountbatten and the newspaper cartoonist Edwina.
49 This style of gag is also evident in the comedy of Jackie Gleason, who is of interest for a playboy character, Reginald Van Gleason III, and trans gender queer catchphrases ("It's a Dan-Dan-Dandy!"). Sterritt (*The Honeymooners*) and Weinstein (*Forgotten Network*, 99, 132) note Gleason's familiarity with Jewish comedians. For Gleason's endorsement of a new "dan-dan-dandy" CBS-Columbia TV set available at Barker Brothers on Seventh Street, Flower and Figueroa, see *The Los Angeles Mirror*, October 8, 1952, 29; this advertisement appears below a plug for Imogene Coca's "Bashful Ballerina" episode of *Comedy Cameos* (KTTV), in which Coca "portrays the ugly duckling in a ballet troupe and climaxes [the] bunglings with a cultured strip tease." "Coca in Ballet Satire," Hal Humphrey Collection, Box G, "George Burns and Gracie Allen," USC Cinematic Arts Library.
50 Hogan, *Three Stooges FAQ*, 183.
51 See Balcerzak, *Buffoon Men*, especially on Mae West and Jack Benny.
52 Shandley, *Hogan's Heroes*, 16.
53 Si Rose and Seaman Jacobs, "Aunt Lydia Comes to Town," final draft, September 16, 1958, Seaman Jacobs Scripts, Syracuse University.

54 C. Becker, *It's the Pictures*, 73.

55 "Come on to Mars' House," written by Sol Saks, about a period piece starring Eve and Howard called *The Glory That Was Rome*, emphasizes what is queer about media producers. They may or may not be in positions of power, and they may or may not know how power works or how to work that power to their advantage. Three potential extras are recognizably queer. Almost immediately after they enter the office of the studio boss Hafter, they are sent away, rejected for on-screen roles. *Mr. Adams and Eve*, "Come on to Mars' House," February 11, 1958, UCLA Film and Television Archive.

2. HOLLYWOOD CAMP TV

1 They called another company Gemini—Bob's sun sign; MEC is a Scorpio. They invested in oil and a rice farm in Australia, as well as the vitamin supplement sales firm Nutri-Bio, television production, and program syndication.

2 In "Bad Feminists," Annie Berke indicatively refers to Schultzy not by name but as "the unattractive, desperate spinster-secretary character in *The Bob Cummings Show* . . . not to be confused with the *other* desperate spinster-secretary character," indicating *Berle*'s Max, as if there were only two in all of TV at that time (168). Kulp's *Cummings* character, portrayed within the dominant discourse as less attractive than Davis's, is—again, in a pattern defining well-intentioned feminist television studies scholarship—absent from the discussion.

3 The title refers ironically to Bob's Beanblossom character. "Hero" more accurately describes the character played by Julie Bishop (Julie Marshall), who regularly saves the day for Beanblossom, who is shy and easily embarrassed.

4 On vocal pitch, modulation, and gendering, see the work of Shana Goldin-Perschbacher; and Art Blake, "Finding My Voice While Listening to John Cage," *Sounding Out!* February 23, 2015, https://soundstudiesblog.com/2015/02/23/finding-my-voice-while-listening-to-john-cage/.

5 Bob would have passed on *12 Angry Men*, for example, probably the most critically acclaimed of any piece in which Bob performed, but MEC "got hold of the script. 'It's good. . . . It could be great. You've got to do it.'" Bud Goode, "A Family to Cherish," *Radio-TV Mirror*, July–December 1955, L. Tom Perry Special Collections, Harold B. Lee Library, Cummings Papers, Brigham Young University (hereafter given as Cummings Papers, BYU).

6 "Return to B'dwy? Perish Thought, Says Bob Cummings," in the March 14, 1959, *Lima Ohio Citizen*, and "Back to Broadway? Cummings Says No Thanks," a similar article that ran in the *Cincinnati Post and Time Star*, cite Actor's Equity contract conditions and union rules as deterrents from working on Broadway. Cummings Papers, BYU.

7 "College boy" was a gay look. Cole, *"Don We Now."* It was also the phrase Bob used to describe early development of *The Many Loves of Dobie Gillis*. Rex

Polier, "Bob Cummings Here; Plans Multiple Show," *Sunday Bulletin*, January 27, 1957, 4, Box 82, Folder 2, Cummings Papers, BYU. See *How to Be Very, Very Popular*, 1955, directed by Nunnally Johnson, writer of the *How to Marry a Millionaire* TV series (1959).

8   Rick Du Brow, *Toronto Telegram*, "In the Stars: TV's Bachelor Usually Selects Employes [*sic*] through Their Horoscope," January 17, 1959. Robert Cummings File, Collection T Pho B., Performing Arts Research Collections—Theater, Performing Arts Library at Lincoln Center, New York Public Library.

9   Marc, *Demographic Vistas*, xv.

10 Norman Lear, for example, *the* sitcom auteur of the network era, adapted *All in the Family* from *Till Death Us Do Part* and took the idea for *The Jeffersons* from Black Panthers who came to Lear's office to protest *Good Times* (Lear, *Even This*, 267). Lear garners widespread endorsement as having invented TV satire after the point in time that Sontag writes of camp as having supplanted satire. See Lear, *Even This*, 131–32; and Sontag, "Notes on Camp," 62.

11 Marc, *Demographic Vistas*, xv.

12 Raymond Williams, *Television*. See also the work of Laurie Ouellette.

13 Mellen, *Big Bad Wolves*, 193.

14 "What TV Is Doing to the Movie Industry," *US News and World Report*, February 7, 1958, 88–90, Box 63, Folder "Paid T.V.," Cummings Papers, BYU. The article is in a sizable folder of materials on Pay TV, in a camp subcategory, "Pay TV and Industry Doldrums." This report privileges the perspective of "media men" as the heartbroken but confident center of attention.

15 This abusive framing is ironic because it was a charge from the government to keep violence off of television that razed broadcast comedy. The Vast Wasteland rhetoric rallied to protect children and families and provide programming for the public good while supporting American imperialism and continued segregation, discrimination, and injustice.

16 Conner and Johnson, "Starlit Screens." On discrimination, segregation, and suburbia, see Kruse, *White Flight*; and Tongson, *Relocations*.

17 Raymond Williams, *Television*.

18 Hainley, "How to Proceed in Everything," 2.

19 On intertextuality and genre in the years since, see Gray, *Watching with the Simpsons*, 30.

20 Meyerowitz, *How Sex Changed*, 89.

21 Sontag, "Notes on Camp," 54. D. A. Miller criticizes Sontag's work, describing "Notes on Camp" as a "wish for a Camp theoretically detachable—and therefore already detached—from gay men," in which the author "justified [the] phobic de-homosexualization of Camp as the necessary condition for any intelligent discourse on the subject" ("Sontag's Urbanity," 213).

22 Sontag, "Notes on Camp," 63. See Monica Miller, *Slaves to Fashion*, 17.

23 Coward's popular queer work appeared on UK TV beginning in the 1930s and 1940s, and Coward moved into US TV production spaces by the 1950s.

24 This is presumably in reference to the white dress norms applied to cis people

without disabilities and thus in reference to scrutiny even more viciously directed at people of color, people with disabilities, and trans people. Harry Belafonte notably challenged dress norms, as did Cummings and Faye Emerson (See Smith, *Becoming Belafonte*; and C. Becker, *It's the Pictures*). According to Cecil Beaton, an actor and friend of Coward's whom Faderman and Timmons interviewed for *Gay L.A.*, Coward advised Beaton, an aspiring photographer at the time, to carefully monitor wardrobe (specifically tight shirt sleeves), and to change vocal pitch and inflection (which Coward thought "too high and precise") when interviewing for media industry jobs. Explaining, "I take ruthless stock of myself in the mirror before going out," Coward urged Beaton to do the same (56).

25 Cohan, "Queering the Deal," 41.
26 Cole, "Don We Now," 61.
27 Leonard Spigelgass, quoted in Faderman and Timmons, *Gay L.A.*, 56.
28 Camp "breathes new life into old situations." Muñoz, *Disidentifications*, 128.
29 Martínez, *On Making Sense*, 139.
30 Muñoz, *Disidentifications*, 128. The use of "his or her" in the original signals the need for an identity framework broader than binary gender.
31 Tinkcom, "Labor Camp." My accent on *person* here plays off of the ubiquitous designation of "queer men" throughout *Working Like a Homosexual*.
32 Tinkcom, *Working Like a Homosexual*, 27; Newitz, *Pretend We're Dead*, 2.
33 Evelyn Hooker, "The Psychologist—Dr. Evelyn Hooker," quoted in Minturn, *Departing from Deviance*, 220.
34 Van Doren, *Playing the Field*, 54.
35 For references to California conservatives, see Ross's *Hollywood Left and Right*, Frost's *Hedda Hopper's Hollywood*, and Critchlow's *When Hollywood Was Right*. Critchlow tellingly mistitles *Love That Bob* as *I Love Bob* and notably identifies Randolph Scott—a "staunch conservative"—as a cowboy star and a western star but not as Cary Grant's partner (130).
36 Louella Parsons, *Los Angeles Examiner*, July 11, 1960, Cummings Papers, BYU.
37 Freeman, "Introduction," 159.
38 Cole, *"Don We Now,"* 61.
39 Nealon, *Foundlings*, 12. This foundling discourse is a formulaic feature of sitcoms' homoerratic inside-outsider humor. This UCLA Film and Television Archive episode of *The Aldrich Family* queerly couples Henry, who is "drooling over someone who's ten years older," with Sandra Watson, who compels Henry, intent on an impromptu hair touchup, to use the back of a pan as a mirror (while wearing a "cute" apron). *The Aldrich Family*, 1949–1953 [1950–51], UCLA Film and TV Archive. In the episode, when people suggest donating the green Tyrolean, Henry calls it "just about the most dashing hat I've ever worn" and "the most valuable thing Homer ever gave to me." Homer needs no introduction because sitcom characterization, especially of eccentrics, is instant. Marking the transgression of this accessory, and potentially the source of the gift, Henry's parent tells Henry, "You'll be doing a nice thing for yourself,

not to mention your family and mankind in general" when wearing it, as if the taste would contaminate. This unidentified episode, from between 1950 and 1951, was written by Norman Tokar and Ed Jurist and produced and directed by Lester Vail. Tokar wrote for *The Tab Hunter Show*, penned the "Eleven Angry Women" episode of *The Bob Cummings Show*, and made the TV movie "My Sister Hank" (1972), with Jodie Foster as Hank. Jurist worked on *The Patty Duke Show, Grindl, The Flying Nun, The Paul Lynde Show*, and more camp TV. The Paley Center has preserved an additional episode of *The Aldrich Family*, that one written by Bud Grossman, a notable camp TV writer. *The Aldrich Family*, written by Bud Grossman, NBC, March 19, 1953, the Paley Center.

40 Freeman, "Introduction," 159.
41 John Maynard, "Don't Envy the Wife of a TV 'Glamour Boy: Bob Cummings' Harried Spouse Drove Herself to the Hospital to Keep a Date with Mr. Stork,'" *Milwaukee Sentinel*, July 3, 1955, Cummings Papers, BYU.
42 Maynard, "Don't Envy the Wife," Cummings Papers, BYU.
43 Bud Goode, "A Family to Cherish," *Radio-TV Mirror*, July–December 1955.
44 *The Bob Cummings Show* was still running in syndication in 1971—in eighty-six countries besides the United States—and had by that time grossed $5.5 million, according to a pamphlet from 1971 announcing Bob's new gig as a goodwill ambassador for Holiday Magic, a cosmetics company pyramid scheme William Penn Patrick started in San Rafael, California, in 1964 that was later linked to Mind Dynamics, a self-help school investigated by the State of California. Holiday Magic promotional pamphlet, square yellow paper, 1971, Cummings Papers, BYU. David Marc's biography of Bob for *American National Biography* identifies Bob as a vice president at Holiday Magic.
45 Irvin, *George Burns Television Productions*, 73, 65. Irvin notes that "Cummings' character would infrequently make asides directly to the audience as Burns did" on *Burns and Allen*, but Schultzy was more often the one to break the fourth wall. Irvin writes, "*The Bob Cummings Show* was as subversive of marriage as *The Burns and Allen Show* was to logic," but this analogy obscures *Burns and Allen*'s own subversions of marriage via its married characters (64). Nevertheless, as Irvin attests, *Cummings*' "main theme" involved "attacking marriage" (81).
46 Michael Warner, *Trouble with Normal*, 11.
47 In this episode from October 13, 1956, advertising Nestlé products and young adult fashion from the Midwest, Helga, who is ethnically marked as within whiteness, by name, costuming, and dialogue, weeps in an initial appearance, gesturing effeminately. As Kulp melodramatically bemoans being single, Gale Storm's Susanna character self-reflexivity indicates a trademark desire to meddle, speaking as if directly to the viewer, as is common in *Cummings, Burns and Allen*, and other sitcoms showcasing camp. Zasu Pitts's Nugey is, like Kulp's Helga, unmarried and derided, but Nugey criticizes Peterson's usual appearance in favor of a still-whiter glamour ideal, an image reminiscent, in Kulp's new visage, of *The Bob Cummings Show*'s signature models. Helga, whose voice is

suddenly sexy immediately following Nugey's makeover, declines a request to "be yourself again," saying, as the mistaken identity drama of the plot escalates, that there is "not a chance" of a return to old form. "You're fascinating, whoever you are," Kulp tells Helga's reflection in the mirror, one of many camp lines of dialogue. Later in the episode, Nugey and the new Helga patronize Le Chat Mort, a hyperxenophobically depicted underground club that Susanna's tour group mistakes for the sheltered establishment on their itinerary. After being seated by one of the many actors and extras costumed to represent decadent Tangier, Nugey draws attention to Helga's jewelry and Kulp's physique, as in a scene where Helga, suddenly popular, receives a cigarette light from one of several suitors, and the blocking and camera angle highlight both the offer, a parody of scripted gender roles, and Kulp's body, framed against an out-of-character glamour gown consistent with others of Kulp's tight-fitting, "uncharacteristic" sitcom costumes. Sunglasses, a mirror, and profile shots also contribute to queer gender production, suggesting that Kulp's usual type is deliberate, enjoyable—and profitable in the sitcom context—because unconventional.

48 "Photo Gratis," from John Scott Fones and Benjamin Sonnenberg, *My Hero* shoot, 1952, Box 60, "My Hero—Publicity" Folder, Cummings Papers, BYU. On camp orientalism, see Tartaglia, "Perfect Queer Appositeness." On whiteness as a bad habit, see Ahmed, *Queer Phenomenology*, 121, 129.

49 Hal Landers, "Reviews of the New TV Shows: *The Bob Cummings Show* ("The Sheik"), *Hollywood Reporter*, January 3, 1956, Box 86, Folder "Reviews & Ratings—Bob Cummings Show," Cummings Papers, BYU.

50 Other western spoofs include an Elvis Presley appearance on *The Steve Allen Show*, Rob Petrie's solitary antics at playing cowboy in *Dick Van Dyke*'s "A Farewell to Writing," and a *Gunsmoke* parody on *Gilligan's Island* involving Alan Hale, Russell Johnson, and Bob Denver. See also *Your Show of Shows*, *Jack Benny*, and *Garry Moore*.

51 Hal Landers, "Reviews of the New TV Shows: *The Bob Cummings Show* ("The Sheik"), *Hollywood Reporter*, January 3, 1956, Box 86, Folder "Reviews & Ratings—Bob Cummings Show," Cummings Papers, BYU.

52 Eddie Beloin and others worked on sound, aiming for a relatively muted, minimalist experience of the laugh track, losing most of the recorded laughter in the studio, in favor of the sound of a few people chuckling in a room together.

53 Hal Horn, "Television Review: *Love That Bob*—"The Sheik," *The Horn Section*, June 14, 2014 (accessed May 14, 2018), http://hornsection.blogspot.com/2014/06/television-review-love-that-bob-sheik.html.

54 In a setup emblematic of the makeover and matchmaker tropes littering sitcoms and *Love That Bob*, in particular, the primary plot line, in Landers's account, "concerned Cummings' efforts to marriage-match a country couple, Nancy Kulp and Bob Easton," a narrative device foreshadowing Kulp's Hathaway character in *The Beverly Hillbillies*, a Henning-produced LA-set white cast

sitcom that began investigating class and taste politics in 1962, in which Kulp's character, as Attallah points out, eludes the otherwise stark division between hillbilly and cultural (usually LA industry) insider. On the commercial success of this series, see Staiger, *Blockbuster TV*.
55 Reid-Pharr, *Archives of Flesh*, 11.
56 *TV Guide*, "Program of the Week," n.d., Cummings Papers, BYU.
57 In moving from NBC to CBS, the series shifted time slots, from 10:30 PM to 8:00 PM, "so more teenagers could view it." Irvin, *George Burns Television Productions*, 69. "Davis Signed," *Chicago Tribune*, December 14, 1958, SW19.
58 Ruth and Paul Henning, interview by David Marc, September 9, 1996, Box 22, Steven H. Scheuer Television History Interviews, Special Collections Research Center, Syracuse University Libraries. Marc refers to the contract issue as an "unfortunate muddle," after Henning states, "[MEC] was the sweetest.... But... posed many problems."
59 C. Becker, *It's the Pictures*, 158.
60 On metronormativity, see Halberstam, *Queer Time and Place*; Herring, *Another Country*; and Tongson, *Relocations*. On sophistication, taste, and space, see Litvak, *Strange Gourmets*; and Herring, *Queering the Underworld*.
61 Harriet Van Horne, "Robert Cummings, a Very Funny Man," *New York World-Telegram and Sun*, January 13, 1955, Box 86, Folder 1, Cummings Papers, BYU.
62 "Happy New Year! It's Loaded with Talent," *New York World-Telegram and Sun*, December 31, 1954, Box 86, Folder 1, Cummings Papers, BYU.
63 *The Jack Paar Show*, November 17, 1960, NBC, Paley Center, New York.
64 Irvin, *George Burns Television Productions*, 76.
65 Marc, *Comic Visions*, 80.
66 Attallah, "Unworthy Discourse," 113.
67 *The Bob Cummings Show*, "Choosing Miss Coffee Break," written by Paul Henning and Bill Manhoff, guest starring Benny Rubin, May 1, 1955, UCLA Film and Television Archive.
68 "'The Bob Cummings Show' (Emergency Script)," Box 59, "Henning, Paul" folder, Cummings Papers, BYU.
69 "'The Bob Cummings Show' (Emergency Script)," 1.
70 "'The Bob Cummings Show' (Emergency Script)," 4.
71 "'The Bob Cummings Show' (Emergency Script)," 3.
72 "'The Bob Cummings Show' (Emergency Script)," 2.
73 "'The Bob Cummings Show' (Emergency Script)," 2–3.
74 "'The Bob Cummings Show' (Emergency Script)," 4–5.
75 The Cummings Papers at BYU register support (monetary and rhetorical) for Goldwater and Nixon among other Republican politicians, countering any simplistic idea that the people producing queer gender in television were on the left.
76 Wilson, *Noel, Tallulah, Cole, and Me*, 153. "Judy Garland in MGM's *Meet Me in St. Louis*," *The Judy Room* (accessed May 14, 2018), http://www.thejudyroom.com/louis.html.

77 McHugh, *Alan Jay Lerner*, 47. McHugh's characterization is based on Hugh Fordin's book on the Freed Unit, *MGM's Greatest Musicals* (1975). Kendall, *Runaway Bride*, 161–62; Keefe, *Casual Affairs*, 313; Edwards, *Katherine Hepburn*, 78; Higham, *Kate*, 22.

78 See Box 57, "National Broadcasting Co—David Levy" Folder, Cummings Papers, BYU.

79 On the Freed Unit and camp production, see Tinkcom, *Working Like a Homosexual*; and Cohan, *Incongruous Entertainment*.

80 Fordin's account demonstrates the sexist framework of the industry and its historians, even, in this case, of a historian inclined to interrupt the Scheherazade mythology that references *One Thousand and One Nights*. Messinger told Fordin, "If Arthur [Freed] wanted Mr. Mayer to like a story he asked [Messinger] to tell it to him." Fordin writes that this "could possibly conjure up the picture of a contemporary Scheherazade, young, seductive, spinning [a] tale. But Lillie Messinger was just a middle-aged, soft spoken, knowledgeable lady." *MGM's Greatest Musicals*, 93. See Erin Hill's *Never Done* for an account of feminization (a form of queer gender production) in Hollywood labor, 14–15.

81 Baer, *I Don't Drop Names*, 62.

82 Fordin, *MGM's Greatest Musicals*, 545.

83 Letter from Messinger to Bob, April 12, 1960, Box 57, "National Broadcasting Company" Folder, Cummings Papers, BYU.

84 "Bob Meets Mamie Van Doren," February 3, 1959, UCLA Film and TV Archive. The episode establishes Van Doren as a friend of Schultzy's from an earlier time when they each rented a room at the Hollywood Studio Club, a real-life women's dormitory run by the YWCA in Los Angeles. It housed actors ranging from Marilyn Monroe to JoAnne Worley throughout the 1950s and 1960s.

85 Hope's joke is part of a monologue in a 1958 NBC special episode of *The Steve Allen Show*, preserved at the UCLA Film and TV Archive, which also included a charged skit with Bob Cummings and an actor standing in for Mary Cummings, as well as a routine about network hypocrisy from George Gobel. Hope riffs on *The Gay Caballero*, a 1932 feature in the Cisco Kid franchise—starring Caesar Romero, a camp TV icon—and one of at least six movies in less than a decade with "Gay" (*Defender, Diplomat, Bride, Divorce, Desperado*) in the title. Hope lisps the term "surprise pink" and mugs, with trademark morphologically ambiguous profile, miming carrying a surprise pink purse in brownface drag over black-and-white airwave feed. The queer gender and the trans gender queer implications of the situation can be reduced to simplistic stereotype, but why? The collaboration among producers on screen and off circulates camp traditions and plays up competing vernacular uses of gay slang. See Cohan, "Queering the Deal." According to a *Variety* review of the broadcast, this moment in the network's showcase for its new fall lineup made some in-studio viewers of the live performance "scream at [the] questionable line." "CBS & NBC's 'This Is Our Best' in Sullivan, Allen Talent Parades,"

Variety, September 24, 1958, B2, USC Cinematic Arts Library. While the Cummings skit indicates pointedly the ways in which sexist and queer concepts intertwine, Gobel's routine called NBC executives "not really crooked, but a little kinky" for opportunistic tactics toward reform and presented viewers with a sly pie chart breaking down the new schedule by percentage and explaining that broadcasters were into psychosexual westerns and "family shows," not comedy. "NBC Fall Preview," September 21, 1958, UCLA Film and Television Archive. For records on queer gender in Gobel programming, consult the archives of UCLA and the Writers Guild of America.

86 For these dynamics in a more recent period, see Quinlan Miller, "Masculinity and Male Intimacy."

87 Alan Eichler, "Robert Cummings and Son—Rare 1987 TV Interview [with Skip E. Lowe]," *Skip E. Lowe Looks at Hollywood*, December 17, 2016 (accessed May 14, 2018) https://www.youtube.com/watch?v=45AJWT35u90.

88 On "nonce taxonomies," see Sedgwick, *Epistemology of the Closet*, 23.

89 *The Bob Cummings Show*, "Schultzy's Dream World," CBS, May 15, 1955, UCLA Film and Television Archive.

90 It is difficult to see Coward and company as overcautious and also hard to believe that "ruthless" self-assessment in comparison with gendered sartorial norms is the whole story. Nevertheless, self-gender policing certainly translates to sexual mobility (Faderman and Timmons, *Gay L.A.*, 56). In a *Daily Mail* column based on personal experience, Michael Thornton describes Coward as "reckless in . . . pursuit of . . . lovers . . . skat[ing] on the thinnest of sexual ice, constantly risking scandal and exposure." Thornton also recalls Coward being arrested (on a prostitution charge) while accompanied by a partner, Prince George, Duke of Kent, and dressed in clothes deemed appropriate only for people assigned female. Michael Thornton, "How Predatory Noël Coward Tried to Seduce Me When I Was 19," *Daily Mail*, November 9, 2007. The perfunctory response that Cummings could wear whatever because of the protection of marital status does not negate the significance of clothing choice, and cis-simplifies marriage.

91 *The Bob Cummings Show*, "The Silver-Tongued Orator," written by Paul Henning and Bill Manhoff, June 5, 1955, UCLA Film and Television Archive.

92 *The Bob Cummings Show*, "Schultzy's Dream World." May 15, 1955. In other emblematic exchanges along these lines, Bob relates to Schultzy as a "fella" and also refers to Schultzy as a "guy" through a comic rendition of the phrase "guys like us." See Quinlan Miller, "*Bob Cummings Show*"; and *The Bob Cummings Show*, "Bob and the Bachelor Apartment," March 20, 1955, UCLA Film and Television Archive.

93 See Chen, *Animacies*, 142, and the chapter "Animals, Sex, and Transubstantiation."

94 Horton, *Ernie Kovacs*, xv–xvi, 47.

95 On racist typecasting, intimate partner violence, and the hypersexualization of Latinas in a more recent series, *Sex and the City*, see Hidalgo, "Going Native."

96 DeCamp portrayed many parents, including, in 1942 at the age of thirty-two, the parent of forty-three-year-old James Cagney in *Yankee Doodle Dandy* (and later the parent of Marlo Thomas's Ann Marie in *That Girl*, who appeared alongside Lew Parker as Lew Marie, DeCamp's spouse), but was also a "bad girl of film." See Hannsberry's *Femme Noir*.

97 See Box 60, "My Hero—Publicity Material" folder, Cummings Papers, BYU.

98 On queer anti-urbanism, see Herring, *Another Country*, 12.

3. SEX AND THE SINGLE PERSON

1 Tahmahkera, *Tribal Television*, 104. Villarejo, *Ethereal Queer*, 63.

2 Wojcik, *Apartment Plot*, 4.

3 On Firestone, see KPFK 90.7 FM Los Angeles and Los Angeles Museum of the Holocaust in Pan Pacific Park, "Rene Firestone," *Surviving the Holocaust: Stories of Life*, August 18, 2016 (accessed May 14, 2018), http://survivingtheholocaust.us/2016/08/18/renee-firestone/.

4 Jim Nabors represents a contact point, in this study of camp TV, between LGBTQ+ television production history and the history of queer gender. *Hawaii News Now* reported, during press coverage of Nabors and Stan Cadwallader's 2013 marriage, that while working in Hollywood during the 1960s, "Nabors said he was open about his homosexuality to co-workers and friends." *Hawaii News Now*, "Actor Jim Nabors Marries His Longtime Male Partner," (accessed May 14, 2018), http://www.hawaiinewsnow.com/story/20805642/exclusive-actor-jim-nabors-marries-his-longtime-male-partner. I describe queer gender as a corollary of the epistemology of the closet because the logic of outing around sexuality that generates the binary gender system operates according to instability located in gender. Sedgwick, *Epistemology of the Closet*, 30–31.

5 Ludden was a prominent game show host, including of *Allen Ludden's Gallery* (1969), appeared on *What's My Line?* as a guest panelist and mystery guest, played the part of David Dooley in *Batman*'s "Dizzoner the Penguin" (1966), performed in an episode of the 1966 *Milton Berle Show*, and guest starred as Allen Ludden in *The Odd Couple* ("Password," 1972).

6 "Mental ping-pong" is Ludden's term. "Allen Luden Dies," *New York Times*, June 10, 1981, http://www.nytimes.com/1981/06/10/obituaries/allen-luden-dies.html.

7 Desjardins, *Recycled Stars*.

8 Burch, who peopled *Dick Van Dyke* with queer gender through guest stars, cast Kulp as Peterson in "Passenger Incognito" (*The Gale Storm Show*).

9 For a reading of *Dick Van Dyke* as a Jewish ensemble, see Bill Swislow, "Gentiles in Paradise," Interesting Ideas: Vernacular Culture, Outsider Art and Oddball Ideas (accessed May 14, 2018), https://www.interestingideas.com/ii/rob.htm.

10 Jack Major, "Richard Deacon: He Played the Cards He Was Dealt and Came Out a Winner," *Akron Beacon Journal*, September 6, 1964, http://major-smolinski.com/names/deacon.html.

11 Diller's comic character with the "platinum fright wig" was honed as drag, thanks to an uncredited gay coach. In the words of Bette Midler, the character's situation is "like someone who had been chained to an ironing board for years just said, 'You know what? I'm too smart for this—let me out.'" The coach introduced Diller to drag queens as "great actors" (Kohen, *We Killed*, 15). Working between the Borscht Belt and New York City, especially Greenwich Village and small uptown stages, Diller and Joan Rivers and company moved away from the "titties, and boobs, and dancing girls" apparently required by the Reiner, Caesar, Martin, and Lewis crowd toward the "chic gay guys" (Kohen, *We Killed*, 11). However, already at venues such as the Blue Angel by their time were the likes of Kaye Ballard, Wally Cox, Alice Ghostly, Phil Leeds, and more. "New York City: The Supper Clubs," *Yodelout!*, (accessed May 14, 2018), http://new-york-city.yodelout.com/new-york-city-the-supper-clubs/.

12 Compare their pages at findadeath.com, which archives important details of celebrity lives to the grave and beyond. On the matter of queer gender expression and in trans gender queer camp transposition, Scott Michaels writes of Roger C. Carmel, "How this [person] passed for straight, I will never know." About Deacon, and regarding a fan-submitted photo, Michaels writes, "GHRRL. Look at those stunners. Heh. Thanks ... for the new pic. It is ... breathtaking." Scott Michaels, "Richard Deacon," *FAD: Celebrity Deaths* (accessed May 14, 2018), https://www.findadeath.com/directory/d/Richard_Deacon/index.html and Scott Michaels, "Roger C. Carmel," *FAD* (accessed May 14, 2018), http://www.findadeath.com/directory/c/Roger_Carmel/index.html.

13 The tighter-than-normal pants in "Shall We Dance?"—an embarrassing deviation beyond the pale in the minds of the others onscreen, as indicated by emphatic facial mannerisms performed by the rest of the cast during the reluctant rehearsal sequence in the Finleys's backyard—are uncharacteristic of Deacon's typical role, as an uptight and far from flashy hermit. At the same time, the wardrobe is emblematic of reiterated Finley traits of unselfconscious fixation and self-indulgence, here complementing the extreme devotion to modern dance that the writers script for Deacon to perform. In "Francis Goes to School," Vicki attempts to rescue Francis, a neighborhood dog, from Finley, and witnesses Finley fielding a phone call from Mr. Finley (Burt Mustin), the parent character Roger lives with who has run away from their home, as if the child of the adult pair, after being ignored. After staying up all night testing the pet's intelligence and hearing from Vicki that Mr. Finley slept on the couch at Vicki's place, Deacon's character yells for Mr. Finley to answer the call even though it is Mr. Finley who is on the line, an ineffectual authority figure who in the "Shall We Dance?" episode calls the younger Finley's leggings "stupid

pants" and informs the already reluctant neighbors at the rehearsal that Roger's interests are avant-garde rather than "commercial." Deacon's performances in these examples, as well as throughout the series and in many other substantial recurring roles, consist of contained but expressive eye-and-face acting, a deep, droning, monotone vocal delivery, and precise, effeminate, demonstrative movements. Minute gestures as well as comic contradictions of age and influence convey frustration, focus, absurd commitments, and psychological extremes through straightforwardly fey behavior of the kind continually linked to the production of queer gender in the context of sitcom programming.

14 On this type of television production, rife in *Bob Cummings* and other camp TV of the 1950s, see my "Queer Broadcasts."
15 See Doty, *Making Things Perfectly Queer*, 63; and *The Jack Benny Program*, "How Jack Found Mary," October 31, 1954.
16 See DiAngelo, "White Fragility."
17 *Against Equality, Queer Critiques of Gay Marriage*; Spade, *Normal Life*.
18 For examples of *Get Smart*'s "funhouse-mirror universe" of camp orientalism, see Austerlitz, *Sitcom*, 73.
19 Deborah Schneider, "Selma Diamond," *Jewish Women: A Comprehensive Historical Encyclopedia*, March 1, 2009. Jewish Women's Archive (accessed May 14, 2018), http://jwa.org/encyclopedia/article/diamond-selma.
20 "Dialogue on Film: Carl Reiner," *American Film Magazine* 7, no. 3 (1981): 16, quoted in Waldron, *Official Dick Van Dyke Show Book*, 312.
21 Rose Marie, *Hold the Roses*, 101. "The Love of My Life" is the title of the chapter on Bobby Guy in Rose Marie's autobiography (58–65). See also *Wait for Your Laugh*, by Georgiana Rodrigues and Jason Wise, Forgotten Man Films (2017), with Peter Marshall. Selma Diamond quoted in Deborah Schneider, "Selma Diamond."
22 There are many other episodes like "Br-oom, Br-oom," and, at the same time, there is no other episode quite like "Br-oom, Br-oom" or any of the show's other episodes.
23 For another example of this situation-based queer gender comedy, see "Body and Sol," also written by Carl Kleinschmitt and Dale McRaven, in which Rob fights in boxing matches for the Special Services (Entertainment Unit) of the US Army as Pitter Patter Petrie. Casting contributes to the camp scripting: questions posed by Sally and Buddy frame this flashback episode, and Allan Melvin appears as the eponymous Sol; Ed Peck as Captain Worwick, a choreographer before the war; and Garry Marshall as a referee.
24 On the Disney scene Shore came out of, see Griffin, *Tinker Belles and Evil Queens*, 81.
25 See Randall's interview on *The Mike Douglas Show*, included with the special features on *The Odd Couple* DVD, Paramount Pictures, 2007.
26 R. Becker, *Gay TV and Straight America*.
27 *The Dick Van Dyke Show*, "Baby Fat," April 21, 1965. Erdman is Pete Morrisey

on *Where's Raymond?*, Richard Fairfield III on *The Tab Hunter Show*, Leonard on *Community*, and director of two *Dick Van Dyke* episodes from 1966, "Dear Sally Rogers" and "Buddy Sorrel, Man and Boy." Martin is a waiter in an episode of *I Love Lucy* (1956), Harold Horton in an episode of *Pete and Gladys* (1962), a reverend in *He & She* (1968), and Tyrone Lovey in two episodes of *The Doris Day Show* (1969).

28 The episode's depiction of Rob's task of anonymously improving a respected writer's script goes deep into the mechanics and issues of ghostwriting. A decision about appearing "without hair" (i.e., wigless) to which the Alan character emphatically refers in this episode, opens out, as many threads of and lines of dialogue in this episode do, onto matters of queer gender, with Alan's longtime unspoken and suppressed desire to star in a Broadway show and the question of whether this play, perhaps an only chance, is good enough to merit ditching the toupee as examples.

29 Kenyon is in *The Phil Silvers Show*, *Peter Gunn*, *Gomer Pyle*, *The Donna Reed Show*, *Gidget*, *The Andy Griffith Show*, *That Girl*, *Hogan's Heroes*, *Love on a Rooftop*, and several other *Dick Van Dyke Show* episodes.

30 The setting itself is trans gender queer camp, in that, in the flashback, Rob and Laura meet in Joplin, Missouri, Bob Cummings's birthplace, near the real-life Camp Crowder, meaning that the writers fictionalized an actual stop on the queer United Service Organization performance circuit Steven Cohan analyzes in "Queering the Deal." Terrace, *Sitcom Factfinder, 1948–1984*, 53. The Entertainment National Service Association in the United Kingdom, one corollary to the USO shows in the US, is an example of an intersectional point of interest for future research into a genealogy of the global scale of camp TV.

31 Arquette plays Charley Weaver and Weaver's parent in a *Dale Evans Show* episode, and Mrs. Butterworth in commercials. This series and host Dale Evans are of interest only in part due to naming, but, in terms of naming, queer gender signification, and ethnicity, "Dale" is notably trans gender queer in the context of US cultural production of the 1950s and 1960s. This is the moniker that Dale Messick, the author of the *Brenda Starr* comic strip chose "after . . . encounter[ing] discrimination against women entering the newspaper cartooning business." Richard Severo, "Dale Messick, 98, Creator of 'Brenda Starr' Strip, Dies," *New York Times*, April 8, 2005. "Dale" is also notably in *The Beverly Hillbillies*, in the last name Drysdale, and in the composite story world of Betty White's and Richard Deacon's *Date with the Angels*, in the name of the recurring department store Martindale's. In addition, digital word processing enables me to note Dale McRaven, a writer whose name is not in my mental Rolodex yet appears in chapter four of this work, as an added intertextual association of the kind that might be fruitfully pursued further.

32 *Hollywood Squares* stretches beyond the 1960s into recent years, as does *Match Game* (including in the context of *RuPaul's Drag Race*).

33 Winchell guest stars as Sally's and Buddy's absurdly subpar fallback boss, ventriloquist Claude Wilbur. *Look* magazine named Winchell, who would

later voice Tigger in *Winnie the Pooh*, the most versatile TV actor in 1952 and 1953. Variety Staff, "Paul Winchell: Entertainer," June 26, 2005 (accessed May 14, 2018), https://variety.com/2005/scene/markets-festivals/paul-winchell-1117925081/. According to Adam Bernstein's *Washington Post* obituary for Winchell in 2005, the US Supreme Court ruled in 1989 for Metromedia to pay Winchell $17.8 million "for having destroyed all videotapes of [Winchell's] 1960s children's shows." In *Winchell-Mahoney Time*, NBC, written by Nina Russel, Winchell hosted and played characters that included Bonehead Smiff, Mr. Goody-Goody, and host. Adam Bernstein, "TV Ventriloquist, Cartoon Voice and Inventor Paul Winchell Dies," *Washington Post*, June 27, 2005 (accessed May 14, 2018), http://www.washingtonpost.com/wp-dyn/content/article/2005/06/26/AR2005062601247.html.

34 Firestone appeared in *Peter Gunn, Hennesey, Dobie Gillis, Perry Mason, I Dream of Jeannie, Hogan's Heroes*, and *Here Come the Brides*, as well as other series of interest, such as *Mixed Doubles* and *Telephone Time*.

35 Quinlan Miller, *Dick Van Dyke*.

36 *The Dick Van Dyke Show*, "Where You Been, Fassbinder?" January 29, 1952, CBS, written by John Whedon, guest starring George N. Neise and Barbara Perry. Similar jokes characterize *Will & Grace*'s (1998–2006) Jack (Sean Hayes), who casually announces a need for a new pair of shoes—preferably with a six foot man in them—in "The Truth about Will and Dogs," December 15, 1998, NBC, written by David Kohan and Max Mutchnick, directed by James Burrows, guest starring Gary Grubbs, Tom Gallop, Leigh-Ally, Katie O'Rourke, Michael Lucas, and Anthony Meindl.

37 On "Racy Tracy Rattigan," as camp about sexual harassment, and for audience study of trans gender queer camp signification, see the discussion among fans of Lance Mannion's blog post "Racy Tracy Rattigan Has a Secret," September 21, 2005 (accessed May 14, 2018), http://lancemannion.typepad.com/lance_mannion/2005/09/racy_tracy_rati.html.

38 At the same time, retrospectatorship as theorized by Patricia White remains important to the queer temporalities at play in camp TV critique (*Uninvited*, 15–16).

39 Luckett and Radner, *Swinging Single*, 28, 278; D'Acci, "Nobody's Woman?" 74.

40 Dozier quoted in Torres, "Caped Crusader of Camp," 334.

41 On the industrial configuration of 1960s US TV, see Alvey, "Independents," especially 143–47.

42 Judith Butler, *Undoing Gender*, 1.

43 Craig, in O'Dell, *June Cleaver Was a Feminist!*, 1. As Michael B. Kassel writes in the entry for the programs in the Museum of Broadcast Communications' *Encyclopedia of Television*, *Father Knows Best* "is perhaps more important for what it has come to represent than for what it actually was." What it actually was, in comparison with what it represents, is instructive. Michael B. Kassel, "Father Knows Best: US Domestic Comedy" (accessed May 14, 2018), http://www.museum.tv/eotv/fatherknows.htm.

44 Marc, *Comic Visions*, 60. *Father Knows Best*, "Betty, the Track Star," NBC, April 3, 1957.
45 Marc, *Comic Visions*, 61.
46 Marc, *Comic Visions*, 61.
47 Marc, *Comic Visions*, 60.
48 Trans gender queer representation in *Father Knows Best* includes, among other recurring elements, the vamping of Billy Gray as James Dean – channeling Bud Anderson and the nonconformity of Kathy (Lauren Chapin).
49 Pellegrini, "After Sontag," 178.
50 Alicia Anstead, "A Veteran of TV Gives Storyteller Her 'Gruff' Voice," *Bangor Daily News*, July 4, 2006, archive.bangordailynews.com.
51 Capsuto, *Alternate Channels*, 417.
52 Castiglia and Reed, *If Memory Serves*, 116.
53 Steve Chawkins, "Character Actress was on 'Green Acres,'" *Los Angeles Times*, February 18, 2014, http://articles.latimes.com/2014/feb/18/local/la-me-mary-grace-canfield-20140218.
54 Craig, *Sorry I Don't Dance*, 64.
55 Dance as a component of camp TV is one of many topics raised that deserve more attention, as indicated by the use of jitterbugging in other episodes, such as an episode of *My Hero* featuring Gloria Winters. This is one of many intersections that sets television racism in relief. Fayard and Harold Nicholas danced duets in programs hosted by Ed Wynn in 1951 and 1964 (*The Colgate Comedy Hour*, *The Bell Telephone Hour*) but not much in between. See Hill, *Brotherhood in Rhythm*, 233, 235, 239, 249.
56 Marah Eakin, "RIP Mary Grace Canfield, 'Ralph' of *Green Acres*," *AV Club*, February 18, 2015, https://news.avclub.com/r-i-p-mary-grace-canfield-ralph-of-green-acres-1798266265.
57 The use of the singular pronoun "them" in this instance indicates the queer gender of the set of actors and characters relevant to the rethinking of perception and assignment. In the *Archie* pilot, written by Ray Allen and produced by Ackerman and Winston O'Keefe, Canfield performs a scene spellbound by a love interest. This episode includes notable character actors Jean Vander Pyl, Karen Green, Kathy Bennett, and Harriet E. MacGibbon, who is Martha Drysdale in *The Beverly Hillbillies*.
58 This is a particularly insidious Library of Congress category.
59 M. Williams, "Entertaining 'Difference,'" 30.
60 "Hazel in Hollywood," Box 22, Folder 3, Harry S. Ackerman papers, Collection Number 04876, American Heritage Center, University of Wyoming (hereafter given as Ackerman Papers, AHC). The signature in terms of the authorship of these ideas is industrial. That is, the document lists as writer Screen Gems, the company, rather than Ackerman or any other individuals.
61 Harry Ackerman memo to John Mitchell, February 4, 1965, Box 22, Folder 3, Ackerman Papers, AHC. Tab Hunter and Dwayne Hickman, among other camp TV actors of interest, were considered for this part of Jerry Brigham, who

is as determined to remain unmarried as Hazel is committed to reforming the character's ways. Peter Kortner memo to Harry Ackerman, December 30, 1964, Box 22, Folder 3, Ackerman Papers, AHC.

62 In 1972–73, Ashmont Productions and Screen Gems finally brought Lynde into living rooms weekly in *The Paul Lynde Show* (ABC, 1972–73), as, appropriately enough, a reactionary, after soliciting and considering various scripts for Lynde in the 1950s and 1960s. See H & H Productions, "Leif of the Party," Box 13, Folder 9, Harry Ackerman papers, Rauner Manuscript ML-81, Dartmouth College (hereafter given as Ackerman Papers, Dartmouth); Sidney Sheldon, "Final Script," November 8, 1963, *Paul Lynde Show*, Pilot, Box 14, Folder 79, Ackerman Papers, Dartmouth. See also *Temperatures Rising*, ABC, 1972–74; and Box 41, Folders 1–2, Ackerman Papers, AHC.

63 Box 87, Folder 5, Ackerman Papers, AHC.

64 On sick artists and 1950s and 1960s TV comedy as parody, see Thompson, *Parody and Taste*, 5.

65 "Elly Becomes a Secretary," is also of interest and indicative of camp's feminism in its depiction of Elly evading chronic sexual harassment from Bob Billington (John Ashley) and in its featuring of Joy Harmon as Kitty, who fills in for Jane. The wordplay around "sick" resonates obliquely with "sick" comedy in its more conventional form of stand-up, suggesting a "perverse" current of charged humor in sitcoms, connected to nightclub performance.

66 Howard, *Moe Howard and the 3 Stooges*, 15. See also 10–18.

67 Hogan, *Three Stooges FAQ*, 183.

68 In tracking Besser back through camp TV, I learned of *Hollywood House*, a series from 1949–50 in which Besser appeared as an irate guest at the eponymous hotel managed by a character played by Jim Bakus, reportedly in Bakus's inaugural television role. Dick Wesson, Gale Robbins, and Connie Haines are also credited. Wesson and Robbins both worked on *The Bob Cummings Show*. According to IMDb, Robbins played three parts.

69 *My Sister Eileen*, Harry Ackerman and Dick Wesson, Screen Gems, CBS, 1960–61. Pilot, *Just off Broadway*, written by Rip Von Ronkel, Desilu, UCLA Film and Television Archive. Rose Marie's personal script for this program reads *Girls and Greasepaint*, "Benefit Show." Collection of the author.

70 Wojcik, *Guilty Pleasures*, 149.

71 Rae is Edna Garrett in *Diff'rent Strokes* and the spinoff *The Facts of Life*. See, for example, "The Loves of Sylvia Schnauser." Sylvia's partner Leo, played by Al Lewis of *The Munsters*, is also very camp TV.

72 Smith, *Becoming Belafonte*, 217.

73 Kovacs died in a car accident in 1962 while working on a series of monthly half-hour comedy specials for ABC and developing a Screen Gems sitcom vehicle called *Medicine Man*.

74 Hal Humphrey, "The Wacky World of Ernie Kovacs: A Salute to Ernie Kovacs," *Los Angeles Times*, April 7, 1968.

75 Humphrey, "Wacky World of Ernie Kovacs."

76 Capsuto, *Alternate Channels*, 26.
77 Oscar's persona as performed by Cassidy recalls the character work of Ted Knight, who stayed close to trans gender queer typing in moving from *The Mary Tyler Moore Show* to *Too Close For Comfort* (a show from 1980–86 also about the making of a comic strip featuring Knight's clashes with a neighbor character named Monroe Ficus).
78 *He & She*, "The Old Man and the She," September 6, 1967, written by Leonard Stern and Arne Sultan, UCLA Film and Television Archive. This is the type of role John Amos complained of while making *Good Times*, after Jimmie Walker's J. J. character became primary comic relief, making show-stopping entrances at studio tapings of the kind later associated with the kind of "disruptive" studio audience applause for Michael Richards's Kramer character in *Seinfeld*.
79 *He & She*, "The Old Man and the She."
80 According to Rafkin, Jim Aubrey, via Jack Popkin, rescinded Kuehl's shot at a starring role and canned Rafkin for "directing Ray Walston 'too gay.'" Rafkin, *Cue the Bunny*, 48.
81 Halberstam, *Queer Time and Place*, 57–58.
82 "Advance Information on 1966–67 Programming: Occasional Wife, NBC Television Network," 1966, Box 37, Folder 8, Ackerman Papers, AHC.
83 The major league baseball team had moved from Brooklyn to LA after the 1956 series, in a move coincident with the ongoing relocation of telefilm production.
84 Spigel, *Welcome to the Dreamhouse*, 108. A key pair of episodes here are the "12 Angry Men" parodies "One Angry Man" (*The Dick Van Dyke Show*) and "Eleven Angry Women" (*The Bob Cummings Show*). Bob appears in drag as a nerd photographer uninterested in women and unbiased by looks.
85 See R. Becker, *Gay TV and Straight America*; Joyrich, "Epistemology of the Console."
86 For single studies and writing on the politics of marriage and white privilege, see Cobb, *Single*; Cohen, "Punks, Bulldaggers, and Welfare Queens"; and Against Equality, *Queer Critiques of Gay Marriage*.
87 This is indicative of Cold War era discourse. See Friedman, "The Smearing of Joe McCarthy."
88 On Jorgenson, Kinsey, Liberace, and the ironies of McCarthyism, see Doherty, *Cold War, Cool Medium*, 217–24.
89 See "A Bride's First Meal—Easy!," *Los Angeles Times*, July 19, 1965, which advocated advance planning and awareness of an "ability and time budget" but no notion that a partner might help. The consequences of cooking could be significant. In the 1960 memoir *My Husband, Arthur Murray*, for example, Kathryn Murray describes making "every meal . . . a production" after another item now iconic of period specific consumer culture, a crème de menthe frappé that never froze; under the pressure of throwing a first dinner party and tasked with entertaining and impressing Arthur's friends, a failed attempt to match a cookbook image of a sophisticated host's dessert set the tone for future domestic labor and crystalized anxieties about keeping up appearances

that contributed to an eventual suicide attempt (60–61). In the memoir, Murray recalls a desire to live up to the fancy food service they had on their honeymoon.

90 See Frank, *Conquest of Cool*; and Winnubst, *Way Too Cool*.
91 Austerlitz, *Sitcom*, 82.
92 Kevin Olzak, "First Bonafide Classic Episode," June 4, 2016, http://www.imdb.com/title/tt0832626/reviews?ref_=tt_urv. Austerlitz, *Sitcom*, 83.
93 There are currently several episodes of this series on archive.org thanks to user ArnoldZiffel, someone who has adopted the name of character Arnold Ziffel, Doris and Fred's pig in *Green Acres*, a prime example of trans gender queer representation in camp TV.
94 "Occasional Wife." Box 36, Ackerman Papers, AHC.
95 "Just Married" series proposal, submitted December 30, 1958, Ackerman Papers, AHC.
96 "Just Married" series proposal.
97 "Minutes of Meeting between Harry Ackerman, Alvin Cooperman, and John Wheedon to Discuss Proposed 'Just Married' Series," January 12, 1959, Ackerman Papers, AHC.
98 The moment of deferral introduced through the insertion of the word "like" via Maynard's commercialized beat slang is an example of standard sitcom wordplay doing the work of drag, established as so central to queer studies in Judith Butler's *Gender Trouble*. See Ahmed, *Queer Phenomenology*, 15; as well as Prosser, "Judith Butler."
99 See Miller, *Dick Van Dyke*, for trans gender queer analysis of an episode in which Packer plays Mrs. Huntington, the same character or at least a character with the same name as Packer plays in an episode of *The Bob Cummings Show*.
100 *The Many Loves of Dobie Gillis*, "Zelda, Get Off My Back," February 14, 1961, CBS, written by Maggie Williams and Larry Williams.

4. METHODS FOR *GIRL* HISTORY

1 Jack Smith, "Where Is Wife Once He Wed?," *Los Angeles Times*, October 2, 1967.
2 Ian Crouch, "Dylan TV," *The New Yorker*, November 20, 2013 (accessed May 14, 2018), https://www.newyorker.com/culture/culture-desk/dylan-tv.
3 Conventional treatment evaluates and ranks women based on looks, bodies, and appearance while hypersexualizing and even more stringently appraising, policing, and punishing trans women, women perceived to be trans, and oppositional forms of femininity. In the case of drag scholarship, conventional treatment hinges everything on a fictive notion of readable biological sex.
4 This is an example of using "they" and its conjugations as third-person singular pronouns.
5 Billy Ingram's post about *Girl* on the blog *TVParty!*, a repository of camp TV, describes "a series where the main character was running around in really

bad drag," and misreports that Gene "dressed Timothy up in Hippie chick garb" for the photo shoot. Billy Ingram, "Ugliest Girl in Town," *TVParty!: Classic TV and Pop Culture*, May 22, 2013 (accessed May 14, 2018), https://billyingram.blogspot.com/2013/05/ugliest-girl-in-town.html; Rick Mitz's 1983 reference volume *The Great TV Sitcom Book* groups *Girl* alongside "Felix Unger [Tony Randall's *Odd Couple* character], Charles Nelson Reilly, [and] Paul Lynde" as "sex-change artists," one of sixty-seven stock sitcom characters (13); Joe Saltzman's *Los Angeles Times* article "TV Viewers' Choice: The Pick of the Worst" (February 18, 1979) reports that *Girl* was "the series most frequently mentioned" by television fans. The piece, a follow-up to one that "discussed the worst TV from the vantage point of the creators," highlights the "differing views" and "incredible memories" of audiences. Saltzman allows *Girl* antifan Ferris Kaplan of Van Nuys, California, to proffer the show's premise: "Hollywood talent agent Tim Blair is approached by ... photographer-brother Gene to pose as a girl." Kaplan quoted in Saltzman, "TV Viewers' Choice," N4. To be clear, Tim does not pose as a girl for the pictures; queer gender is not always related to and never reducible to gender transition; your sense of "bad drag" is someone else's lived reality; and not everyone segregates clothing.

6 See Quinlan Miller, "Television," 218.
7 Metz, *Gilligan's Island*, 71.
8 "Mod" is an elusive slang term, as are its sometimes synonyms "camp," "queer," "pop," "kitsch," "cockney," "crazy," and "mad." See Torres, "Caped Crusader of Camp"; and Hebdige, *Subculture*.
9 *Girl* pilot, September 26, 1968, produced by Harry Ackerman, Robert Kaufman, and Jerry Bernstein, UCLA Film and Television Archive.
10 I use Tim as a third term, short for Timmy and Timothy. I feminize and effeminize all three names in order to explicate the composite character's queer gender.
11 This type of camerawork and editing, indicative of new wave aesthetics, reflects a single-camera setup.
12 Ronnie Scheib's May 8, 2006, review in *Variety* of the feature *Keeping Up with the Steins* describes Marshall (*The Joey Bishop Show*, *Make Room for Daddy*) as "a minority goy in the Hollywood Borscht Belt Community" and "a Jew waiting to happen," while Otto Bruno calls Marshall one of the "major Italian American contributor[s]" to *The Dick Van Dyke Show*. Otto Bruno, "The Dick Van Dyke Show, Italian American Style (100th post!)" 2004, *Fra Noi*; repr. ottobruno.org, August 4, 2010.
13 "Beautiful kook" is slang for a free spirit, i.e., one who is appealingly queer.
14 Credited to Helen Miller and Howard Greenfield, with music by George Romanis and music and sound effects by Sunset Editorial, the song is sung by the Will-O-Bees and, according to Wikipedia, also composed by Shorty Rogers. "The Ugliest Girl in Town" (accessed May 14, 2018), https://en.wikipedia.org/wiki/The_Ugliest_Girl_in_Town.
15 Considered talent, Twiggy also worked as an agent, pairing Mary Hopkin

with the Beatles at Apple records after catching one of Hopkin's television appearances.

16 Jack Gould, "TV: Camera on Twiggy," *New York Times*, April 28, 1967.
17 Gail Kelly, "A Great Leap Forward in America's March Toward Fantasyland," *Chicago Tribune*, May 5, 1968, Q4.
18 Whiteside, *Twiggy and Justin*, 16.
19 This US press coverage of Twiggy fixates on accent, vernacular, and the ethnicity marker "cockney," which has been associated with Londoners, vulgarity, and "an immoralist's delight in low sensuality" since the nineteenth century. Cox, "Cockney Cosmopolitanism," 245. See also Jonathan Green, *Vulgar Tongue*, 208–235.
20 Perry, *Screen Gems*. See also Alvey, "Independents."
21 On Cold War discourses of gender and sexual deviance, see Litvak, *The Un-Americans*; D'Emilio, *Sexual Politics, Sexual Communities*; Friedman, "Smearing of Joe McCarthy"; D. Johnson, *Lavender Scare*; Loughery, *Other Side of Silence*; Streitmatter, *Unspeakable*; and Terry, "'Momism' and the Making of Treasonous Homosexuals."
22 Butt, *Between You and Me*, 14–15; Cohan, "Queering the Deal," 41.
23 Meyerowitz, *How Sex Changed*.
24 Prosser, "Judith Butler."
25 Halberstam, *In a Queer Time and Place*, 56.
26 Prosser, "Judith Butler," 258.
27 Serano, *Whipping Girl*, 3.
28 Stone, "*Empire* Strikes Back." See also Currah and Stryker, "Introduction," 3.
29 Interoffice communication from Bernard Slade to Harry Ackerman, "Suggestions for Re-Write," September 26, 1967, Ackerman Papers, AHC.
30 Screen Gems booked a soundstage at Shepperton Studios in Surrey and also shot on location in the streets of London. Other producers include Jackie Cooper, Lloyd Burns, Norman Kurland, Jerry Bernstein, and Chuck Fries; assistants and ASI employees; Jim McGinn at Young & Rubicam; and workers in the Department of Broadcast Standards and Practices for ABC's Western Division, including Leonard Goldbert, Marcia Barrett, and Willis Grant.
31 Interoffice communication from Jerry Davis to Harry Ackerman, May 17, 1968, Ackerman Papers, AHC.
32 Levine, *Wallowing in Sex*, 5.
33 Lynn Lilliston, "Merchandisers of the Mod Look," *Los Angeles Times*, April 23, 1967.
34 Julie Byrne, "How Fashion Twiggy Is Bent to Friend and Foe," *Los Angeles Times*, April 9, 1967; Julie Byrne, "Angeltown Looks at Twiggy, Sees a Mini-Slendered Thing," *Los Angeles Times*, April 25, 1967; Julie Byrne, "ABC Eyes Twiggy Uproar," *Los Angeles Times*, April 28, 1967.
35 Gould, "TV." According to Gould, "Whatever the opinions . . . there's no gainsaying that [Twiggy] is a . . . triumph." On the Beatles, the main invaders, as a trans gender queer pop phenomenon, see Shillinglaw, "Give Us a Kiss." In an

example of the globalized typing sitcoms participated in, Shillinglaw discusses actor Victor Spinetti in the role of an "effeminate TV director" in the first Lester film and an "effeminate mad scientist named Foot" in the second (129).

36 Russell Baker, "Adieu, Old Mr. Muscles," *New York Times*, April 13, 1965, 36. Baker's "Observer" column appeared in syndication nationally.
37 McLuhan quoted in Burt Prelutsky, "McLuhan's Message," *Los Angeles Times*, May 7, 1967. See also John Leo, "McLuhan's Message Leaves New Class Perplexed," *New York Times*, September 19, 1967.
38 Wojcik, *Guilty Pleasures*, 27.
39 Goldman, *American Soul Rush*.
40 Marshall McLuhan and George B. Leonard, "The Future of Sex," In *Look*, July 25, 1967, 56, 61.
41 Cohan, *Incongruous Entertainment*, 18.
42 Santo, "Batman versus The Green Hornet."
43 Brooker, *Batman Unmasked*, 182.
44 See Frank, *Conquest of Cool*.
45 Roxon quoted in Judy Klemesrud, "Rock Fans Play Fashion Game, Too," *New York Times*, December 26, 1969.
46 Cynthia Lowry, "Looking Back," *Los Angeles Times*, January 3, 1968.
47 "ASI In-Depth Test Results, Confidential," American Broadcasting Corporation interdepartment correspondence from Marcia Barrett to Leonard Goldbert, April 18, 1968, Ackerman Papers, AHC. See also Miles Beller, "How Networks Test for Audience Impact," *New York Times*, June 3, 1979, http://www.nytimes.com/1979/06/03/archives/how-networks-test-for-audience-impact-testing-tv-shows-for-audience.html.
48 "ASI In-Depth Test Results," Ackerman Papers, AHC.
49 "ASI In-Depth Test Results," Ackerman Papers, AHC.
50 Bob Kaufman, "Outline: The Ugliest Girl in Town," Received July 26, 1967, Ackerman Papers, AHC.
51 Kaufman, "Outline."
52 Barrett to Goldbert, Ackerman Papers, AHC.
53 "Initial Production Meeting," Ackerman Papers, AHC.
54 "ASI In-Depth Test Results," Ackerman Papers, AHC.
55 Memo from Martin Starger to Donald R. Boyle, August 8, 1968, Ackerman Papers, AHC.
56 Memo from Starger to Boyle, Ackerman Papers, AHC.
57 Interoffice communication from Jerry Hyams to Jackie Cooper, April 22, 1968, Ackerman Papers, AHC.
58 "Girl," March 19, 1968, Ackerman Papers, AHC.
59 "Girl," Ackerman Papers, AHC.
60 Lemke-Santangelo, *Daughters of Aquarius*, 53–54.
61 Bodroghkozy, *Groove Tube*.
62 Straayer, *Deviant Eyes, Deviant Bodies*, 42.
63 Joyrich, "Epistemology of the Console."

64 Sedgwick, *Epistemology of the Closet*, 32.
65 Kaufman, "Ugliest Girl in Town," 5, Ackerman Papers, AHC.
66 Russell Baker, "Adieu, Old Mr. Muscles," *New York Times*, April 13, 1965.
67 Peter Kastner quoted in Bob Tweedell, "Producer Has Three in Row," *The Denver Post*, July 30, 1968.
68 Harry Ackerman quoted in Tweedell, "Producer Has Three in Row."
69 Peter Kastner quoted in Tweedell, "Producer Has Three in Row."
70 Townshend Bryer Associates, news release, May 29, 1968, Ackerman Papers, AHC.
71 Mellencamp, "Situation Comedy, Feminism and Freud"; D'Acci, "Nobody's Woman?"
72 Television tie-in collection, Cornell University, Popular Library 60–2340, ca. 1968 (1st), Cornell University Library Division of Rare and Manuscript Collections, Collection 8001, collection of TV tie-in books, 1945–99. In the decades that followed, Hirschfeld published paperback books with such titles as *Fire Island* (1971), *Provincetown* (1977), *Key West* (1980), and *Return to Fire Island* (1984).
73 "Initial Production Meeting," Ackerman Papers, AHC.
74 Memo from Harry Ackerman to Ted Key, August 13, 1968, Ackerman Papers, AHC.
75 Ackerman quoted in Donnely, "Mod as They Come," *The Washington Daily News*. Undated, Mexico City, Ackerman Papers, Dartmouth.
76 Interoffice communication from Harry Ackerman to Steve Blauner, "Current Projects," June 14, 1967, 7, Ackerman Papers, Dartmouth.
77 Ackerman quoted in Donnely, "Mod as They Come."
78 Memo from Marvin Korman to Don Foley, Vice President Advertising and Promotion, ABC-TV, August 8, 1968, Ackerman Papers, AHC.
79 Memo from Korman to Foley, Ackerman Papers, AHC.
80 Bender, *Beautiful People*, 6.
81 Box 45, folder 2 — Box 47, folder 5, Ackerman Papers, AHC. Timmy also helped plug a limited-edition line of Toyota sports cars with last-minute, whimsical *Girl*-themed detailing.
82 On other uses of nonsynchronous sound and sound effects as industrial "sense making" (Caldwell, *Production Culture*, 20) in camp TV, see Metz, *Bewitched*, 71. On the "heartland" (as camp?), see V. Johnson, *Heartland TV*.

CONCLUSION

1 D. Johnson, *Lavender Scare*.
2 Deutscher, *How to Read Derrida*, 42–43.
3 This brief credit sequence skit in the final *Kovacs Special*, which aired January 23, 1962, ten days after Kovacs's death, represents a camp perspective in that it demonstrates an understanding of script supervisors, or "script girls," as real creators. In the context of the split-second spoof on consensual sexual activity

4   Cresap, *Pop Trickster Fool*, 99. On the Factory as a queer TV counterpublic, see Spigel's *TV by Design*.
5   These are among the many nonsitcoms in which scores of camp actors of note appeared. Take *Ironside*: Wally Cox appeared in the 1967 pilot; Robert Reed (Mr. Brady, *The Brady Bunch*), in "Light at the End of the Journey" (1967); Bill Bixby in four episodes beginning in 1968; Ann Baxter of *All About Eve* (1950) in "An Obvious Case of Guilt" (1968) and "Programmed for Danger" (1969); Ellen Corby in "Why the Tuesday Afternoon Bridge Club Met on Thursday" (1969); and Vito Scotti, another exemplary camp TV actor, in "The Machismo Bag" (1969). *I Spy* and *The Mod Squad* are examples of other hour-long action crime dramas from the 1960s that show crossover with sitcoms in casting shared actors with queer production histories. Outdoor adventure, sci-fi, soaps, and other of the variety of television offerings show their own idiosyncratic overlaps.
6   Benevides also acted in camp TV, in *The Loretta Young Show* ("Power Play," 1957), *The Real McCoys* ("Volunteer Fire Department," 1958), and *The Outer Limits* ("O.B.I.T.," 1963).
7   Lewis and Kovacs are huge camp TV producers. Kovacs repeatedly referred to a hot camera operator while in character as Percy Dovetonsils. Norman Lear intruded onstage in a scripted *Colgate Comedy Hour* routine featured in the documentary *Just Another Version of You* (2016). Another example is Arte Johnson's appearance in an October 2, 1964, episode of *The Jack Benny Program* as "Charlie, a boom-microphone operator who demonstrates to Jack Benny how to tell a joke properly." "Arte Johnson," Wikipedia, accessed May 14, 2018, https://en.wikipedia.org/wiki/Arte_Johnson.
8   Steve Ryfle, "Hiding in Plain Sight: The Secret Life of Raymond Burr—Book Review," *Turner Classic Movies*, accessed May 14, 2018, http://www.tcm.com/this-month/movie-news.html?id=209581.
9   Browne, "Political Economy"; Needham, "Scheduling Normativity," 146; R. Becker, *Gay TV and Straight America*.
10 The people penning *Taxi* half hours use *Car 54* episodes as a starting point, for example. Everitt, *King of the Half Hour*, 110.
11 R. Williams, "Base and Superstructure" and *Television*. "Safe space" here is a reference to Handhardt's historical perspective as an example of the kinds of cultural studies scholarship this book has brought to bear on sitcoms and TV studies. For this use of "misogynous," see Mizejewski, *Pretty/Funny*, 51. As Mizejewski writes, "Notions of 'pretty' are often what women's comedy exploits as funny" (3).
12 Wilchins, "Continuous Nonverbal Communication," 15.
13 K. Warner, *Cultural Politics of Colorblind TV Casting*.

Bibliography

Abrams, Brett L. *Hollywood Bohemians: Transgressive Sexuality and the Selling of the Movieland Dream*. Jefferson, NC: McFarland, 2008.
Against Equality. *Queer Critiques of Gay Marriage*. Edited by Ryan Conrad. Lewiston, ME: Against Equality Publishing, 2010.
Ahmed, Sara. *Queer Phenomenology: Orientations, Objects, Others*. Durham, NC: Duke University Press, 2006.
Allen, Steve. *Bigger Than a Breadbox*. Garden City, NY: Doubleday, 1967.
Alvey, Mark. "The Independents: Rethinking the Television Studio System." In *The Revolution Wasn't Televised: Sixties Television and Social Conflict*, edited by Lynn Spigel and Michael Curtin, 139–60. New York: Routledge, 1997.
Anderson, Christopher. *Hollywood TV: The Studio System in the Fifties*. Austin, TX: University of Texas Press, 1994.
Argadé, Jyoti. *Jungle Boys, Babus, and Camp Orientals*. PhD diss., Northwestern University, 2009.
Attallah, Paul. "The Unworthy Discourse: Situation Comedy in Television." In *Critiquing the Sitcom: A Reader*, edited by Joanne Morreale, 91–115. New York: Syracuse University Press, 2003.
Austerlitz, Saul. *Sitcom: A History in 24 Episodes from "I Love Lucy" to "Community."* Chicago, IL: Chicago Review Press, 2014.
Avila-Saavedra, Guillermo. "Ethnic Otherness versus Cultural Assimilation: U.S. Latino Comedians and the Politics of Identity." *Mass Communication and Society* 14, no. 3 (2011): 271–91.
Baer, Richard. *I Don't Drop Names Like Marilyn Monroe Just to Sell Books*. New York: iUniverse, 2005.
Balcerzak, Scott. *Buffoon Men: Classic Hollywood Comedians and Queered Masculinity*. Detroit, MI: Wayne State University Press, 2013.
Banks, Miranda J. *The Writers: A History of American Screenwriters and Their Guild*. New Brunswick, NJ: Rutgers University Press, 2015.
Barthes, Roland. *The Language of Fashion*. New York: Berg, 2006.
Bashi Treitler, Vilna. *The Ethnic Project: Transforming Racial Fiction into Ethnic Factions*. Stanford, CA: Stanford University Press, 2013.

Bayless, Martha. "Danny Kaye and the 'Fairy Tale' of Queerness in *The Court Jester*." In *Queer Movie Medievalisms*, edited by Kathleen Coyne Kelly and Tison Pugh, 185–200. Farnham, UK: Ashgate Publishing, 2009.

Becker, Christine. *It's the Pictures That Got Small: Hollywood Film Stars on 1950s Television*. Middletown, CT: Wesleyan University Press, 2009.

Becker, Ron. *Gay TV and Straight America*. New Brunswick, NJ: Rutgers University Press, 2006.

Bender, Marylin. *The Beautiful People*. New York: Dell, 1968.

Berke, Annie. "Bad Feminists: The Secret History of TV's *How to Marry a Millionaire*." *Feminist Media Histories* 3, no. 2 (2017): 166–74.

Bhabha, Homi K. *The Location of Culture*. 1994; repr., New York: Routledge Classics, 2004.

Boddy, William. *Fifties Television: The Industry and Its Critics*. Urbana: University of Illinois Press, 1990.

Bodroghkozy, Aniko. *Groove Tube: Sixties Television and the Youth Rebellion*. Durham, NC: Duke University Press, 2001.

Booth, Mark. "*Campe-toi!*: On the Origins and Definitions of Camp." In *Camp: Queer Aesthetics and the Performing Subject: A Reader*, edited by Fabio Cleto, 66–79. Ann Arbor: University of Michigan Press, 1999.

Bratten, Lola Clare. "Nothin' Could Be Finah: The Dinah Shore Chevy Show." In *Small Screens, Big Ideas: Television in the 1950s*, edited by Janet Thumin, 88–104. New York: I. B. Taurus, 2002.

Brettschneider, Marla. "Critical Attention to Race: Race Segregation and Jewish Feminism." *Bridges: A Jewish Feminist Journal* 15, no. 2 (2010): 20–33.

Bronski, Michael. *Culture Clash: The Making of Gay Sensibility*. Boston, MA: South End Press, 1984.

Brook, Vincent. *Something Ain't Kosher Here: The Rise of the "Jewish" Sitcom*. New Brunswick, NJ: Rutgers University Press, 2003.

Brooker, Will. *Batman Unmasked: Analyzing a Cultural Icon*. New York: Continuum, 2000.

Browne, Nick. "The Political Economy of the Television (Super) Text." *Quarterly Review of Film Studies* 9, no. 3 (1984): 174–82.

Butler, Jeremy. *Television: Critical Methods and Applications*. 4th ed. New York: Routledge, 2012.

Butler, Judith. *Gender Trouble: Feminism and the Subversion of Identity*. New York: Routledge, 1999.

Butler, Judith. "Politics, Power and Ethics: A Discussion between Judith Butler and William Conolly." *Theory and Event* 4, no. 2 (2000). https://muse.jhu.edu/. (accessed May 14, 2018).

Butler, Judith. *The Psychic Life of Power: Theories in Subjection*. Stanford, CA: Stanford University Press, 1997.

Butler, Judith. *Undoing Gender*. New York: Routledge, 2004.

Butt, Gavin. *Between You and Me: Queer Disclosures in the New York Art World, 1948–1963*. Durham, NC: Duke University Press, 2005.

Caldwell, John Thornton. *Production Culture: Industrial Reflexivity and Critical Practice in Film and Television*. Durham, NC: Duke University Press, 2008.

Capsuto, Steven. *Alternate Channels: The Uncensored Story of Gay and Lesbian Images on Radio and Television 1930s to the Present*. New York: Ballantine Books, 2000.

Cassidy, Marsha. "Touch, Taste, Breath: Synaesthesia, Sense Memory, and the Selling of Cigarettes on Television, 1948–1971." In *Convergence Media History*, edited by Janet Staiger and Sabine Hake, 34–45. New York: Taylor and Francis, 2009.

Cassidy, Marsha. *What Women Watched: Daytime Television in the 1950s*. Austin: University of Texas Press, 2005.

Castiglia, Christopher, and Christopher Reed. *If Memory Serves: Gay Men, AIDS, and the Promise of the Queer Past*. Minneapolis: University of Minnesota Press, 2011.

Chen, Mel Y. *Animacies: Biopolitics, Racial Mattering, and Queer Affect*. Durham, NC: Duke University Press, 2012.

Chude-Sokei, Louis. *The Last "Darky": Bert Williams, Black-on-Black Minstrelsy, and the African Diaspora*. Durham, NC: Duke University Press, 2006.

Clare, Eli. "Gawking, Gaping, Staring." GLQ 9, no. 1–2 (2003): 257–61.

Cobb, Michael. *Single: Arguments for the Uncoupled*. New York: New York University Press, 2012.

Cohan, Steven. *Incongruous Entertainment: Camp, Cultural Value, and the MGM Musical*. Durham, NC: Duke University Press, 2005.

Cohan, Steven. "The Manic Bodies of Danny Kaye." *Cinema Journal* 56, no. 3 (2017): 1–23.

Cohan, Steven. "Queering the Deal: On the Road with Hope and Crosby." In *Outtakes: Essays on Queer Theory and Film*, edited by Ellis Hanson, 23–45. Durham, NC: Duke University Press, 1999.

Cohen, Cathy. "Punks, Bulldaggers, and Welfare Queens: The Radical Potential of Queer Politics." In *Black Queer Studies: A Critical Anthology*, edited by E. Patrick Johnson and Mae G. Henderson, 21–51. Durham, NC: Duke University Press, 2005.

Cole, Shaun. *"Don We Now Our Gay Apparel": Gay Men's Dress in the Twentieth Century*. New York: Berg, 2000.

Conner, Robin, and Paul Johnson. "Starlit Screens: Preserving Place and Public at Drive-in Theaters." *Southern Spaces*. October 10, 2008. https://southernspaces.org/2008/starlit-screens-preserving-place-and-public-drive-theaters.

Cox, Jeffrey N. "Cockney Cosmopolitanism." *Nineteenth-Century Contexts* 32, no. 3 (2010): 245–59.

Craig, Maxine Leeds. *Sorry I Don't Dance: Why Men Refuse to Move*. New York: Oxford University Press, 2014.

Cresap, Kelly M. *Pop Trickster Fool: Warhol Performs Naivete*. Chicago, IL: University of Illinois Press, 2004.

Critchlow, Donald T. *When Hollywood Was Right: How Movie Stars, Studio Moguls, and Big Business Remade American Politics*. New York: Cambridge University Press, 2013.

Currah, Paisley, and Susan Stryker. Introduction to *Transgender Studies Quarterly* 1, no. 1–2 (2014): 1–18.

D'Acci, Julie. "Nobody's Woman? *Honey West* and the New Sexuality." In *The Revolution Wasn't Televised: Sixties Television and Social Conflict*, edited by Lynn Spigel and Michael Curtin, 73–94. New York: Routledge, 1997.

D'Amore, Laura Mattoon. Introduction to *Smart Chicks on Screen: Representing Women's Intellect in Film and Television*, edited by D'Amore, 1–6. Lanham, MD: Rowman & Littlefield, 2014.

D'Emilio, John. *Sexual Politics, Sexual Communities: The Making of a Homosexual Minority in the United States, 1940–1970*. 1983; repr., Chicago, IL: University of Chicago Press, 1998.

Desjardins, Mary R. *Recycled Stars: Female Film Stardom in the Age of Television and Video*. Durham, NC: Duke University Press, 2015.

Deutscher, Penelope. *How to Read Derrida*. London: Granta Books, 2005.

de Villiers, Nicholas. *Opacity and the Closet*. Minneapolis: University of Minnesota Press, 2012.

DiAngelo, Robin. "White Fragility." *International Journal of Critical Pedagogy* 3, no. 3 (2011): 54–70.

Doherty, Thomas Patrick. *Cold War, Cool Medium: Television, McCarthyism, and American Culture*. New York: Columbia University Press, 2005.

Doty, Alexander. *Flaming Classics: Queering the Film Canon*. New York: Routledge, 2000.

Doty, Alexander. "I Love Shari: My Queer Feminist Life with TV." *Flow*. July 2, 2010. https://www.flowjournal.org/2010/07/i-love-shari/.

Doty, Alexander. *Making Things Perfectly Queer: Interpreting Mass Culture*. Minneapolis: University of Minnesota Press, 1993.

Douglas, Susan. *Listening In: Radio and the American Imagination*. New York: Random House, 1999.

Edwards, Anne. *Katherine Hepburn: A Remarkable Woman*. 1985; repr., New York: St. Martin's Griffin, 2000.

Enfant Terrible! Jerry Lewis in American Film, edited by Murray Pomerance. New York: New York University Press, 2002.

Everitt, David. *King of the Half Hour: Nat Hiken and the Golden Age of Comedy*. Syracuse, NY: Syracuse University Press, 2001.

Faderman, Lillian, and Stuart Timmons. *Gay L.A.: A History of Sexual Outlaws, Power Politics, and Lipstick Lesbians*. New York: Basic Books, 2006.

Feinberg, Leslie. *Transgender Warriors: Making History from Joan of Arc to Dennis Rodman*. Boston, MA: Beacon Press, 1996.

Ferguson, Roderick A. "Sissies at the Picnic: The Subjugated History of a Black Rural Queer." In *Feminist Waves, Feminist Generations: Life Stories of Three Generations in the Academy, 1968–1998*, edited by Hokulani Aikau, Karla Erickson, and Jennifer Pierce, 188–96. Minneapolis: University of Minnesota Press, 2007.

Feuer, Jane. "Genre Study and Television." In *Channels of Discourse, Reassembled*, ed-

ited by Robert C. Allen, 138–60. Chapel Hill: University of North Carolina Press, 1992.
Fordin, Hugh. *MGM's Greatest Musicals: The Arthur Freed Unit*. 1975; repr., New York: Da Capo Press, 1996.
Frank, Thomas. *The Conquest of Cool: Business Culture, Counterculture, and the Rise of Hip Consumerism*. Chicago, IL: University of Chicago Press, 1997.
Freeman, Elizabeth. "Introduction." *GLQ: A Journal of Lesbian and Gay Studies* 13, no. 2–3 (2007): 159–76.
Friedman, Andrea. "The Smearing of Joe McCarthy: The Lavender Scare, Gossip, and Cold War Politics." *American Quarterly* 57, no. 4 (2005): 1105–29.
Frost, Jennifer. *Hedda Hopper's Hollywood: Celebrity Gossip and American Conservatism*. New York: New York University Press, 2011.
Gitlan, Todd. *Inside Prime Time*. 1983; repr., Berkeley: University of California Press, 1994.
Glick, Elisa. "Harlem's Queer Dandy: African-American Modernism and the Artifice of Blackness." *Modern Fiction Studies* 49, no. 3 (2003): 414–42.
Goldman, Marion. *The American Soul Rush: Esalen and the Rise of Spiritual Privilege*. New York: New York University Press, 2012.
Gray, Jonathan. *Watching with the Simpsons: Television, Parody, and Intertextuality*. New York: Routledge, 2006.
Green, Jamison. *Becoming a Visible Man*. Nashville, TN: Vanderbilt University Press, 2004.
Green, Jonathon. *The Vulgar Tongue: Green's History of Slang*. New York: Oxford University Press, 2015.
Griffin, Sean. *Tinker Belles and Evil Queens: The Walt Disney Company from the Inside Out*. New York: New York University Press, 2000.
Hainley, Bruce. "How to Proceed in Everything I Can Think Of." PhD diss., Yale University, 1993.
Halberstam, Jack. *Female Masculinity*. Durham, NC: Duke University Press, 1998.
Halberstam, Jack. *In a Queer Time and Place: Transgender Bodies, Subcultural Lives*. New York: New York University Press, 2005.
Hall, Stuart. "Encoding, Decoding." In *The Cultural Studies Reader*, edited by Simon During, 90–103. New York: Routledge, 1993.
Halperin, David. *How to Be Gay*. Cambridge, MA: Belknap Press of Harvard University, 2012.
Handhardt, Christina. *Safe Space: Gay Neighborhood History and the Politics of Violence*. Durham, NC: Duke University Press, 2013.
Hannsberry, Karen Burroughs. *Femme Noir: Bad Girls of Film*. Jefferson, NC: McFarland, 1998.
Hayes, Joy Elizabeth. "White Noise: Performing the White, Middle-Class Family on 1930s Radio." *Cinema Journal* 51.3 (2012): 97–118.
Hebdige, Dick. *Subculture: The Meaning of Style*. 1979; repr., New York: Routledge, 2002.

Herring, Scott. *Another Country: Queer Anti-Urbanism*. New York: New York University Press, 2010.

Herring, Scott. *Queering the Underworld: Slumming, Literature, and the Undoing of Gay and Lesbian History*. Chicago, IL: University of Chicago Press, 2009.

Hidalgo, Melissa M. M. "Going Native on Wonder Woman's Island: The Exoticization of Lesbian Sexuality." In *Televising Queer Women: A Reader*, edited by Rebecca Beirne, 121–33. New York: Palgrave Macmillan, 2007.

Higham, Charles. *Kate: The Life of Katherine Hepburn*. 1975; repr., New York: W. W. Norton, 1981.

Hill, Constance Valis. *Brotherhood in Rhythm: The Jazz Tap Dancing of the Nicholas Brothers*. New York: Oxford University Press, 2000.

Hill, Erin. *Never Done: A History of Women's Work in Media Production*. New Brunswick, NJ: Rutgers University Press, 2016.

Hogan, David J. *Three Stooges FAQ: Everything Left to Know about the Eye-Poking, Face-Slapping, Head-Thumping Geniuses*. Milwaukee, WI: Applause Theater and Cinema Books, 2011.

Horn, Katrin. *Women, Camp, and Popular Culture: Serious Excess*. Cham, Switzerland: Springer Nature, 2017.

Horton, Andrew. *Ernie Kovacs and Early TV Comedy: Nothing in Moderation*. Austin: University of Texas Press, 2010.

Howard, Moe. *Moe Howard and the 3 Stooges: The Pictorial Biography of the Wildest Trio in the History of American Entertainment*. 1977; repr., Secaucus, NJ: Carol Publishing Group, 1996.

Hunter, Tab, with Eddie Muller. *Tab Hunter Confidential: The Making of a Movie Star*. Chapel Hill, NC: Algonquin Books, 2006.

Irvin, Richard. *George Burns Television Productions: The Series and Pilots, 1950–1981*. Jefferson, NC: McFarland, 2014.

Jacobs, Will, and Gerard Jones. *The Beaver Papers: The Story of the "Lost Season."* New York: Crown Publishers, 1983.

Johnson, David K. *The Lavender Scare: The Cold War Persecution of Gays and Lesbians in the Federal Government*. Chicago, IL: University of Chicago Press, 2004.

Johnson, Victoria E. *Heartland TV: Prime Time Television and the Struggle for U.S. Identity*. New York: New York University Press, 2008.

Joyrich, Lynne. "Epistemology of the Console." *Critical Inquiry* 27, no. 3 (2001): 439–67.

Karlyn, Kathleen. *The Unruly Woman: Gender and the Genres of Laughter*. Austin: University of Texas Press, 1995.

Keefe, Maryellen V. *Casual Affairs: The Life and Fiction of Sally Benson*. Albany, NY: State University Press, 2014.

Kendall, Elizabeth. *The Runaway Bride: Hollywood Romantic Comedy of the 1930s*. 1990; repr., New York: Cooper Square Press, 2002.

Kent, Kathryn R. "People Are Different." *GLQ* 19, no. 2 (2013): 267–69.

Klugman, Jack, with Burton Rocks. Foreword by Garry Marshall. *Tony and Me: A Story of Friendship*. West Linn, OR: Good Hill Press, 2005.

Kodat, Catherine Gunther. "Making Camp: *Go Down, Moses*." *American Literary History* 19, no. 4 (2007): 997–1029.

Koestenbaum, Wayne. *The Anatomy of Harpo Marx*. Berkeley: University of California Press, 2012.

Kohen, Yael. *We Killed: The Rise of Women in American Comedy*. New York: Farrar, Straus and Giroux, 2012.

Krefting, Rebecca. *All Joking Aside: American Humor and Its Discontents*. Baltimore, MD: Johns Hopkins University Press, 2014.

Kruse, Kevin M. *White Flight: Atlanta and the Making of Modern Conservatism*. Princeton, NJ: Princeton University Press, 2005.

Lear, Norman. *Even This I Get to Experience*. New York: Penguin, 2014.

Leff, Leonard. "Becoming Clifton Webb: A Queer Star in Mid-Century Hollywood." *Cinema Journal* 47, no. 3 (2008): 3–28.

Leibman, Nina C. *Living Room Lectures: The Fifties Family in Film and Television*. Austin: University of Texas Press, 1995.

Lemke-Santangelo, Gretchen. *Daughters of Aquarius: Women of the Sixties Counterculture*. Lawrence: University of Kansas Press, 2009.

Levine, Elana. *Wallowing in Sex: The New Sexual Culture of 1970s American Television*. Durham, NC: Duke University Press, 2007.

Lipsitz, George. *Time Passages: Collective Memory and American Popular Culture*. Minneapolis: University of Minnesota Press, 1990.

Litvak, Joseph. *Strange Gourmets: Sophistication, Theory, and the Novel*. Durham, NC: Duke University Press, 1997.

Litvak, Joseph. *The Un-Americans: Jews, the Blacklist, and Stoolpigeon Culture*. Durham, NC: Duke University Press, 2009.

Lott, Eric. *Love and Theft: Blackface Minstrelsy and the American Working Class*. New York: Oxford University Press, 1993.

Loughery, John. *The Other Side of Silence: Men's Lives and Gay Identities: A Twentieth-Century History*. New York: Henry Holt, 1998.

Luckett, Moya, and Hilary Radner. *Swinging Single: Representing Sexuality in the 1960s*. Minneapolis: University of Minnesota Press, 1999.

Marc, David. *Comic Visions: Television Comedy and American Culture*. Boston, MA: Unwin Hyman, 1989.

Marc, David. "Bob Cummings." *American National Biography*. Oxford University Press. Collection of the author.

Marc, David. *Demographic Vistas: Television in American Culture*. Philadelphia: University of Pennsylvania Press, 1996.

Martínez, Ernesto Javier. *On Making Sense: Queer Race Narratives of Intelligibility*. Stanford, CA: Stanford University Press, 2012.

May, Elaine Tyler. *Homeward Bound: American Families in the Cold War Era*. New York: Basic Books, 1999.

McCarthy, Anna. "Ellen: Making Queer Television History." *GLQ* 7, no. 4 (2001): 593–620.

McDonald, Boyd. *Cruising the Movies: A Sexual Guide to Oldies on TV*. 1985; repr., South Pasadena, CA: Semiotext(e), 2015.

McHugh, Dominic, ed. *Alan Jay Lerner: A Lyricist's Letters*. New York: Oxford University Press, 2014.

Mellen, Joan. *Big Bad Wolves*. New York: Pantheon Books, 1977.

Mellencamp, Patricia. *Logics of Television: Essays in Cultural Criticism*. Bloomington: Indiana University Press, 1990.

Mellencamp, Patricia. "Situation Comedy, Feminism and Freud: Discourses of Gracie and Lucy." In *Feminist Television Criticism: A Reader*, edited by Charlotte Brundson, Julie D'Acci, and Lynn Spigel, 60–73. New York: Oxford University Press, 1997.

Metz, Walter. *Bewitched*. Detroit, MI: Wayne State University Press, 2007.

Metz, Walter. *Gilligan's Island*. Detroit, MI: Wayne State University Press, 2012.

Meyerowitz, Joanne. *How Sex Changed: A History of Transsexuality in the United States*. Cambridge, MA: Harvard University Press, 2002.

Miller, D. A. "Sontag's Urbanity." In *The Lesbian and Gay Studies Reader*, edited by Henry Abelove, Michele Aina Barale, and David M. Halperin, 212–20. New York: Routledge, 1993.

Miller, Monica. *Slaves to Fashion: Black Dandyism and the Styling of Black Diasporic Identity*. Durham, NC: Duke University Press, 2009.

Miller, Quinlan. "*The Bob Cummings Show*'s 'Artists at "Work"': Gender Transitive Programming and Counterpublicity." *Spectator* 28 (2008): 10–28.

Miller, Quinlan. "*Dick Van Dyke*: Queer Meanings." In *How to Watch TV*, edited by Ethan Thompson and Jason Mittell, 112–20. New York: New York University Press, 2013.

Miller, Quinlan. "Masculinity and Male Intimacy in Nineties Sitcoms: *Seinfeld* and the Ironic Dismissal." In *The New Queer Aesthetic on Television: Essays on Recent Programming*, edited by James Keller and Leslie Stratyner, 147–59. Jefferson, NC: McFarland Press, 2007.

Miller, Quinlan. "Television." *TSQ* 1, no. 1–2 (2014): 216–19.

Miller, Quinlan. "Queer Broadcasts: Backstage Television, Insider Material, and Media Producers." In *The International Encyclopedia of Media Studies: Media Production*, edited by Angharad N. Valdivia and Vicki Mayer, 445–65. Malden, MA: Blackwell, 2013.

Miller, Quinlan, and Erica Rand. "Hot for TV, Hot for Ann B: Ann B. Davis, Queer Attractions, and Trans Media." *Spectator* 37, no. 2 (2017): 30–39.

Miller-Young, Mireille. *A Taste for Brown Sugar: Black Women in Pornography*. Durham, NC: Duke University Press, 2014.

Minturn, Henry L. *Departing from Deviance: A History of Homosexual Rights and Emancipatory Science in America*. Chicago, IL: University of Chicago, 2002.

Mitz, Rick. *The Great TV Sitcom Book*. New York: Perigee Books, 1983.

Mizejewski, Linda. *Pretty/Funny: Women Comedians and Body Politics*. Austin: University of Texas Press, 2014.

Mizejewski, Linda. *Ziegfeld Girl: Image and Icon in Culture and Cinema*. Durham, NC: Duke University Press, 1999.

Morreale, Joanne. "Dreams and Disruption in the Fifties Sitcom." *Journal of e-Media Studies* 4, no. 1 (2015).

Muñoz, José Esteban. *Disidentifications: Queers of Color and the Performance of Politics*. Minneapolis: University of Minnesota Press, 1999.

Murray, Kathryn, with Betty Hannah Hoffman. *My Husband, Arthur Murray*. New York: Avon, 1960.

Murray, Susan. *Hitch Your Antenna to the Stars: Early Television and Broadcast Stardom*. New York: Routledge, 2005.

Nash, Jennifer. *The Black Body in Ecstasy: Reading Race, Reading Pornography*. Durham, NC: Duke University Press, 2014.

Nealon, Christopher. *Foundlings: Lesbian and Gay Historical Emotion before Stonewall*. Durham, NC: Duke University Press, 2001.

Needham, Gary. "Scheduling Normativity: Television, the Family, and Queer Temporality." In *Queer TV: Theories, Histories, Politics*, edited by Glyn Davis and Gary Needham, 143–58. New York: Routledge, 2009.

Newcomb, Horace. *TV: The Most Popular Art*. Garden City, NY: Anchor Press, 1974.

Newitz, Annalee. *Pretend We're Dead: Capitalist Monsters in American Pop Culture*. Durham, NC: Duke University Press, 2006.

O'Dell, Cary. *June Cleaver Was a Feminist: Reconsidering the Female Characters of Early Television*. Jefferson, NC: McFarland, 2013.

O'Reilly, Julie D. *Bewitched Again: Supernaturally Powerful Women on Television, 1996–2011*. Jefferson, NC: McFarland, 2013.

Ovalle, Priscilla Peña. *Dance and the Hollywood Latina: Race, Sex, and Stardom*. New Brunswick, NJ: Rutgers University Press, 2010.

Parks, Lisa. "Watching the 'Working Gals': Fifties Sitcoms and the Repositioning of Women in Postwar American Culture." *Critical Matrix* 11, no. 2 (1999): 43–66.

Pellegrini, Ann. "After Sontag: Future Notes on Camp." In *A Companion to Lesbian, Gay, Bisexual, Transgender, and Queer Studies*, edited by George E. Haggerty and Molly McGarry, 168–193. Malden, MA: Blackwell, 2007.

Perry, Jeb H. *Screen Gems: A History of Columbia Pictures Television from Cohn to Coke, 1948–1983*. Metuchen, NJ: Scarecrow Press, 1991.

Prosser, Jay. "Judith Butler: Queer Feminism, Transgender, and the Transubstantiation of Sex." In *The Transgender Studies Reader*, edited by Susan Stryker and Stephen Whittle, 257–80. New York: Routledge, 2006.

Rafkin, Alan. *Cue the Bunny on the Rainbow: Tales from TV's Most Prolific Sitcom Director*. Syracuse, NY: Syracuse University Press, 1998.

Red Channels: The Report of Communist Influence in Radio and Television. New York: American Business Consultants, 1950.

Reid-Pharr, Robert F. *Archives of Flesh: African America, Spain, and Post-Humanist Critique*. New York: New York University Press, 2016.

Reumann, Miriam G. *American Sexual Character: Sex, Gender, and National Identity in the Kinsey Reports*. Berkeley: University of California Press, 2005.

Rogin, Michael. *Blackface, White Noise: Jewish Immigrants in the Hollywood Melting Pot*. Berkeley: University of California Press, 1996.

Roof, Judith. *All about Thelma and Eve: Sidekicks and Third Wheels*. Chicago, IL: University of Illinois Press, 2002.

Rose Marie. *Hold the Roses*. Lexington: University Press of Kentucky, 2002.

Rosenthal, Phil. *You're Lucky You're Funny: How Life Becomes a Sitcom*. New York: Viking, 2006.

Ross, Andrew. *No Respect: Intellectuals and Popular Culture*. New York: Routledge, 1989.

Ross, Steven J. *Hollywood Left and Right: How Movie Stars Shaped American Politics*. New York: Oxford University Press, 2011.

Salamon, Gayle. *Assuming a Body: Transgender and Rhetorics of Materiality*. New York: Columbia University Press, 2010.

Santo, Avi. "*Batman* versus *The Green Hornet*: The Merchandisable TV Text and the Paradox of Licensing in the Classical Network Era." *Cinema Journal* 49, no. 2 (2010): 63–85.

Schneider, Deborah. "Selma Diamond." *Jewish Women: A Comprehensive Historical Encyclopedia*. March 1, 2009, Jewish Women's Archive (accessed May 14, 2018), http://jwa.org/encyclopedia/article/diamond-selma.

Schwoch, James. *Global TV: New Media and the Cold War, 1946–69*. Chicago, IL: University of Illinois Press, 2009.

Sconce, Jeff. "What If?: Charting Television's New Textual Boundaries." In *Television after TV: Essays on a Medium in Transition*, edited by Lynn Spigel and Jan Olson, 93–112. Durham, NC: Duke University Press, 2004.

Scott, Mack. "From Blackface to *Beulah*: Subtle Subversion in Early Black Sitcoms." *Journal of Contemporary History* 49, no. 4 (2014): 743–69.

Sedgwick, Eve K. *Epistemology of the Closet*. Berkeley: University of California Press, 1990.

Seldes, Gilbert. *Writing for Television*. Garden City, NY: Doubleday, 1952.

Serano, Julia. *Whipping Girl: A Transsexual Woman on Sexism and the Scapegoating of Femininity*. Emeryville, CA: Seal Press, 2007.

Shandley, Robert R. *Hogan's Heroes*. Detroit, MI: Wayne State University Press, 2011.

Shillinglaw, Ann. "Give Us a Kiss: Queer Codes, Male Partnering, and the Beatles." In *The Queer Sixties*, edited by Patricia Juliana Smith, 127–44. New York: Routledge, 1999.

Shimizu, Celine Parreñas. *The Hypersexuality of Race: Performing Asian/American Woman on Screen and Scene*. Durham, NC: Duke University Press, 2007.

Smith, Judith E. *Becoming Belafonte: Black Artist, Public Radical*. Austin: University of Texas Press, 2014.

Snorton, C. Riley. *Black on Both Sides: A Racial History of Trans Identity*. Minneapolis: University of Minnesota Press, 2017.
Sontag, Susan. "Notes on Camp." In *Camp: Queer Aesthetics and the Performing Subject: A Reader*, edited by Fabio Cleto, 53–65. 1964; repr., Ann Arbor: University of Michigan Press, 1999.
Spade, Dean. *Normal Life: Administrative Violence, Critical Trans Politics, and the Limits of the Law*. Durham, NC: Duke University Press, 2015.
Spigel, Lynn. *Make Room for TV: Television and the Family Ideal in Postwar America*. Chicago, IL: University of Chicago Press, 1992.
Spigel, Lynn. *TV by Design: Modern Art and the Rise of Network Television*. Chicago, IL: University of Chicago Press, 2009.
Spigel, Lynn. *Welcome to the Dreamhouse: Popular Media and Postwar Suburbs*. Durham, NC: Duke University Press, 2001.
Spigel, Lynn, and Michael Curtin. *The Revolution Wasn't Televised: Sixties Television and Social Conflict*. New York: Routledge, 1997.
Staiger, Janet. *Blockbuster TV: Must-See Sitcoms in the Network Era*. New York: New York University Press, 2000.
Stark, Seymour. *Men in Blackface: True Stories of the Minstrel Show*. Bloomington, IN: Xlibris, 2000.
Sterritt, David. *The Honeymooners*. Detroit, MI: Wayne State University Press, 2009.
Stone, Sandy. "The *Empire* Strikes Back: A Posttranssexual Manifesto." In *Bodyguards: The Cultural Politics of Gender Ambiguity*, edited by Julia Epstein and Kristina Sraub, 280–304. New York: Routledge, 1991.
Stone, Sandy. "Guerrilla." *TSQ* 1, no. 1–2 (2014): 92–96.
Straayer, Chris. *Deviant Eyes, Deviant Bodies: Sexual Re-orientation in Film and Video*. New York: Columbia University Press, 1996.
Streitmatter, Rodger. *Unspeakable: The Rise of the Gay and Lesbian Press in America*. Boston, MA: Faber and Faber, 1995.
Stryker, Susan, Paisley Currah, and Lisa Jean Moore. "Trans-, Trans, or Transgender." *WSQ* 36, no. 3–4 (2008): 11–22.
Swislow, Bill. "*The Dick Van Dyke Show*: Gentiles in Paradise." Interesting Ideas: Vernacular Culture, Outsider Art and Oddball Ideas (accessed May 14, 2018), https://www.interestingideas.com/ii/rob.htm.
Tahmahkera, Dustin. *Tribal Television: Viewing Native People in Sitcoms*. Chapel Hill: The University of North Carolina Press, 2014.
Tartaglia, Jerry. "The Perfect Queer Appositeness of Jack Smith." *Quarterly Review of Film and Video* 18, no. 1 (2001): 39–52.
The Television Genre Book. Edited by Glen Creeber. London: BFI, 2001.
Terrace, Vincent. *Sitcom Factfinder, 1948–1984*. Jefferson, NC: McFarland, 2002.
Terry, Jennifer. "'Momism' and the Making of Treasonous Homosexuals." In *"Bad" Mothers: The Politics of Blame in Twentieth-Century America*, edited by Molly Ladd-Taylor and Lauri Umansky, 169–90. New York: New York University Press, 1998.

Thompson, Ethan. *Parody and Taste in Postwar American Television Culture*. New York: Taylor and Francis, 2011.

Tinkcom, Matthew. "Labor Camp: Brett Farmer Interviews Matthew Tinkcom about His New Book, *Working Like a Homosexual: Camp, Capital, Cinema.*" *Genders* 36 (2002) (accessed May 14, 2018). https://web.archive.org/web/20140704055026/http://www.genders.org/g36/g36_farmer.html.

Tinkcom, Matthew. *Working Like a Homosexual: Camp, Capital, and Cinema*. Durham, NC: Duke University Press, 2002.

Toll, Robert C. *Blacking Up: The Minstrel Show in Nineteenth-Century America*. New York: Oxford University Press, 1974.

Tongson, Karen. *Relocations: Queer Suburban Imaginaries*. New York: New York University Press, 2011.

Torres, Sasha. "The Caped Crusader of Camp: Pop, Camp, and the Batman Television Series." In *Camp: Queer Aesthetics and the Performing Subject*, edited by Fabio Cleto, 330–43. Ann Arbor: University of Michigan Press, 1999.

Torres, Sasha. *Living Color: Race and Television in the United States*. Durham, NC: Duke University Press, 1998.

Tuck, Eve and C. Ree. "A Glossary of Haunting." In *Handbook of Autoethnography*, edited by Stacey Holman Jones, Tony E. Adams, and Carolyn Ellis, 639–658. 2013; repr., New York: Routledge, 2016.

Twomey, Alfred E., and Arthur F. McClure. *The Versatiles: Supporting Character Players in the Cinema, 1930–1955*. New York: A. S. Barnes, 1969.

Valerio, Max Wolf. *The Testosterone Files: My Hormonal and Social Transformation from Female to Male*. Emeryville, CA: Seal Press, 2006.

Van Doren, Mamie, with Art Aveilhe. *Playing the Field: My Story*. New York: G. P. Putnam's Sons, 1987.

Villarejo, Amy. *Ethereal Queer: Television, Historicity, Desire*. Durham, NC: Duke University Press, 2014.

Villarejo, Amy. *Lesbian Rule: Cultural Criticism and the Value of Desire*. Durham, NC: Duke University Press, 2003.

Waldron, Vince. *The Official Dick Van Dyke Show Book: The Definitive History and Ultimate Viewer's Guide*. New York: Applause Theatre Books, 1994.

Warhol, Andy, and Pat Hackett. *POPism: The Warhol Sixties*. 1980; repr., San Diego, CA: Harvest, 1990.

Warhol, Robyn R. *Having a Good Cry: Effeminate Feelings and Pop-Culture Forms*. Columbus: Ohio State University Press, 2003.

Warner, Kristen J. *The Cultural Politics of Colorblind TV Casting*. New York: Routledge, 2015.

Warner, Michael. *Publics and Counterpublics*. New York: Zone Books, 2002.

Warner, Michael. *The Trouble with Normal: Sex, Politics, and the Ethics of Queer Life*. New York: The Free Press, 1999.

Weinstein, David. *The Forgotten Network: DuMont and the Birth of American Television*. Philadelphia, PA: Temple University Press, 2004.

White, Mimi. "Crossing Wavelengths: The Diegetic and Referential Imaginary of American Commercial Television." *Cinema Journal* 25, no. 2 (1986): 51–64.

White, Patricia. *Uninvited: Classical Hollywood Cinema and Lesbian Representability*. Bloomington: Indiana University Press, 1999.

Whiteside, Thomas. *Twiggy and Justin*. New York: Farrar, Straus and Giroux, 1968.

Wilchins, Riki. "A Continuous Nonverbal Communication." In *Genderqueer: Voices from beyond the Sexual Binary*, edited by Joan Nestle, Clare Howell, and Wilchins, 11–17. Los Angeles, CA: Alyson Press, 2002.

Williams, Mark. "Entertaining 'Difference': Strains of Orientalism in Early Los Angeles Television." In *Living Color: Race and Television in the United States*, edited by Sasha Torres, 12–34. Durham, NC: Duke University Press, 1998.

Williams, Raymond. "Base and Superstructure in Marxist Cultural Theory." *New Left Review* 82 (1973): 3–16.

Williams, Raymond. *Television: Technology and Cultural Form*. 1974; repr., New York: Routledge, 2003.

Wilson, John C. with Thomas S. Hischak and Jack Macauley. *Noel, Tallulah, Cole, and Me: A Memoir of Broadway's Golden Age*. London: Rowman & Littlefield, 2015.

Winnubst, Shannon. *Way Too Cool: Selling Out Race and Ethics*. New York: Columbia University Press, 2015.

Wlodarz, Joe. "'We're Not All So Obvious': Masculinity and Queer (In)visibility in American Network Television of the 1970s." In *Queer TV: Theories, Histories, Politics*, edited by Glyn Davis and Gary Needham, 88–107. New York: Routledge, 2009.

Wojcik, Pamela Robertson. *The Apartment Plot: Urban Living in American Film and Popular Culture, 1945–1975*. Durham, NC: Duke University Press, 2010.

Wojcik, Pamela Robertson. *Guilty Pleasures: Feminist Camp from Mae West to Madonna*. Durham, NC: Duke University Press, 1996.

Wojcik, Pamela Robertson. "Mae West's Maids: Race, 'Authenticity,' and the Discourse of Camp." In *Hop on Pop: The Politics and Pleasures of Popular Culture*, edited by Henry Jenkins, Tara McPherson, and Jane Shattuc, 287–99. Durham, NC: Duke University Press, 2002.

Wojcik, Pamela Robertson. "Typecasting." *Criticism* 45, no. 2 (2003): 223–49.

Index

Accidental Family, 162
Ace, Goodman, 170n6
Ackerman, Harry: *Hazel*, 110; *Love on a Rooftop*, 127; *The Paul Lynde Show*, 111; schlocky projects of, 125; *The Ugliest Girl in Town*, 133, 137–39, 145, 147, 151, 152
Adams, Don, 13
Addams Family, The, 104, 123, 161
advertising, 22, 28, 40–41, 160–61
Albright, Lola, 56
Aldrich, Henry, 63–64
Aldrich Family, The, 63–64, 176n38
Alice in Wonderland, 47
Allen, Steve, 166n10
All in the Family, 175n10
All-Star Revue, 169n50
Amateau, Rod, 69
Ames, Walter, 169n50
Amos, John, 189n78
Anderson, Robert, 77
Andy Griffith Show, The, 109
Arden, Eve, 6, 12, 166n6
Arno, Sig, 34, 190n1
Arquette, Cliff, 101, 185n31
Arthur Freed's Hollywood Melody, 77
Astin, John, 104, 122
astrology, 39, 52, 58, 89, 174n1
Attallah, Paul, 72–73, 179n54
Aubrey, Jim, 189n80
authorship, collective or dispersed: advertising format and, 23; *The Bob Cummings Show*, 69; *Ed Wynn Show*, 47; *My Friend Irma*, 34; names and, 3; queer gender and,

29; "speaking back" and, 46; *The Ugliest Girl in Town*, 137
Avila-Saavedra, Guillermo, 14–15

Bachelor Father, 161
Backus, Jim, 140
Baer, Max, Jr., 153–54
Baer, Richard, 77
Bailey, Raymond, 149*f*
Baker, Russell, 139
Bakus, Jim, 188n68
Ballard, Kaye, 6–8, 7*f*, 93, 167n25, 167nn24–26, 183n11
Bankhead, Tallulah, 50–51
Barty, Billy, 171n35
Batman, 104–5, 140
Baxter, Ann, 195n5
Beaton, Cecil, 176n24
Beatty, Warren, 129
Becker, Chris, 46, 70
Becker, Ron, 14
Belafonte, Harry, 176n24
Bell Telephone Hour, The, 187n55
Beloin, Eddie, 178n52
Bender, Marylin, 153
Benevides, Bob, 159, 160, 195n6
Benjamin, Richard, 115
Bennett, Kathy, 187n57
Bennett, Marjorie, 85
Benny, Jack, 53, 172n38
Berg, Gertrude, 29–30
Berke, Annie, 174n2
Berle, Milton, 19–20, 30, 32–33*f*

Besser, Joe, 113, 188n68
Betty Hutton Show, The, 138
Beverly Hillbillies, The: as backdrop of camp TV, 161; "The Clampetts Entertain," 112; costumes and props, use of, 123; Drysdale as name in, 185n31; "Elly Becomes a Secretary," 112, 188n65; employee disparagement in, 115; "Hedda Hopper's Hollywood," 148, 149–50f; Henning and, 58, 73, 87; Jethrine Bodine, 153–54; Kulp's Jane Hathaway, 9, 72, 87, 90–91, 111–12, 115, 148, 149–50f, 178n54; singleness in, 111–12; "speaking back" and, 172n43
Bewitched, 93, 108–9, 116, 138, 140, 151, 153, 161
Bill Dana Show, The, 13
Bishop, Julie, 174n3
Bixby, Bill, 161
blackface performance, 2, 36, 168n44
blacklisting, 37–38, 117
Blanc, Mel, 53
Blondie, 140
Bob Cummings Show, The (Love That Bob): about, 56; animal costumes, 83–85; as backdrop of camp TV, 161; "'The Bob Cummings Show' (Emergency Script)" (parody script), 74–76; "Bob Falls in Love," 82–83; "Bob Meets Mamie Van Doren," 78, 180n84; "Bob Meets the Mortons," 78–81; *Burns and Allen* and, 78–79, 177n45; cancellation of, 37; character representations, 71–73; critics on, 69–71; Davis as Brando, 99; Davis as character actor on, 81–84; *The Gale Storm Show* and, 65; Grünwald fan letter, 86; guest-star system and, 78, 81–85; Henning and, 58; *He & She* compared to, 117; Messinger fan letter, 76–77; *Occasional Wife* compared to, 123; "The Sheikh," 69; "The Silver-Tongued Orator," 85; syndication and reruns, 86–87, 177n44; teen viewers and Chuck as naive outsider, 86
Bob Newhart Show, The, 138
Bodine, Max, Jr., 111
Bodroghkozy, Aniko, 145
Bolger, Ray, 113

Booth, Mark, 4–5
Booth, Shirley, 110
Bostock, Barbara, 126
Brady Bunch, The, 9
Brake, Patricia, 133, 146, 152
Brando, Marlon, 31, 32–33f, 99
Bratten, Lola Clare, 169n46
Bronski, Michael, 18
Brooks, Mel, 98
Browne, Nick, 40
Bruno, Otto, 191n12
Bryar, Paul, 66–68f
Buick-Berle Show, 20, 30–31, 32–33f
Bullock, Jim J., 99
Burch, Ruth, 92
Burns, George, 13, 74–75, 86
Burns, Willie, 74–75
Burns and Allen, 58, 78–79, 166n6, 177n45
Burr, Raymond, 159, 160
Butler, Jeremy, 5
Butler, Judith, 4, 17, 105, 137, 190n98
Butt, Gavin, 136
Button, John, 60
Byrne, Julie, 138

Cadwallader, Stan, 182n4
Caesar, Jimmy, 81
Caesar, Sid, 100
Caesar's Hour, 97–98
Caldwell, Donn, 62
Callen, Michael, 118
camp: characterization elements, 167n26; couple camp, 52; function of, 18; as gay subcultural knowledge, 61; gender as site of camp production, 4–5; guest-star system and, 5–8; identity-based understanding of, 61; intertextual landscape of camp TV, 58–62; as mode of production, 14–15; performativity, the everyday, and, 115–16; sitcom characterization as camp drag, 8–13; Sontag's "Notes on Camp," 60, 175n21; as status quo in television, 3; trans-gay overlap and, 15; Warhol's "probably even gayer" quip, 156, 159; whitening and clampdowns on, 35. *See also* specific shows and actors

Canfield, Mary Grace, 12, 45, 108–9, 187n57
Cantor, Eddie, 166n6
Capsuto, Steven, 109, 116
Car 54, Where Are You?, 113–14, 116
Carmel, Roger C., 93, 183n12
Carson, Jack, 49
Carter, Jack, 103
Cassidy, Jack, 115, 116–17
Cassidy, Marsha, 38, 173n47
Castiglia, Christopher, 109
censorship, 39, 104–5, 112–13, 116, 125, 152
character actors and the guest-star system, 5–8, 167n19
Chawkins, Steve, 109
Chevillat, Dick, 13
cissexism: exclusion and, 162; feminist television historiography and, 106; guest-star system and, 39; production process and, 142, 144; queer gender and, 24–25; violent context of, 20; "working women" classification and, 110
Clare, Eli, 165n4
Cleese, John, 56
Coca, Imogene, 12, 45, 100, 173n49
Code of Practices for Television Broadcasters, 38–40, 116
Cohan, Steven, 136, 140
Cohane, Mary Ellen, 20
Cole, Shaun, 60–61
Colgate Comedy Hour, The, 171n35, 187n55, 195n7
"college boy" trope, 58, 174n7
Collins, Jack, 120
colors, 79, 140, 180n85
Comedy Cameos, 173n49
Community, 185n26
Conn, Carol, 69
Conried, Hans, 122, 190n1
continuity experts, 30, 96, 195n3
Cooper, Tamar, 106–7
Cooperman, Alvin, 127
Corby, Ellen, 195n5
counterculture: *Love on a Rooftop*, 126, 128–29; *Occasional Wife*, 122; *The Ugliest Girl in Town*, 132, 139–40, 141, 145, 153
Coward, Noël, 60, 83, 175–76nn23–24, 181n90

Cowley, William, 69
Cox, Wally, 27–28, 44, 99, 111, 183n11, 195n5
Craig, Maxine Leeds, 109
Craig, Yvonne, 105
Cresap, Kelly, 156, 159
Crunch and Des, 171n28
Crystal, Billy, 99
Cucamonga, 52–53
Cummings, Mary Elliot (MEC): about, 57; camp amplified by, 64; character development, uncredited, 87; as independent television executive, 55–56; press descriptions of, 62–65; syndication and, 86. See also *Bob Cummings Show, The*
Cummings, Robert (Bob), ix; about, 57–58; *The Bob Cummings Show*, 71–73; as goodwill ambassador for Holiday Magic, 177n44; *My Hero*, 57; *My Living Doll*, 57; press descriptions of, 62–65; *The Steve Allen Show*, 180n85; "12 Angry Men," 174n5. See also *Bob Cummings Show, The*
Currah, Paisley, 166n11

D'Acci, Julie, 104, 151
Dale Evans Show, 185n31
Damone, Vic, 99, 102, 111
Dana, Bill, 13
"dandyism," 2, 60, 165n6
Daniel Boone, 140
Darden, Severn, 120
Date with Angels, 93, 94–95f, 183n13, 185n31
Davis, Ann B.: *The Bob Cummings Show*, 69, 70, 71, 81–84, 174n2; *The Brady Bunch*, 9; as Marlon Brando, 99; Mary Elliot Cummings and, 87
Davis, Jerry, 138
Dawson, Richard, 103
Deacon, Richard: as character actor, 5–6; "closet" and, 160; *Date with Angels*, 93, 94–95f, 185n31; *The Dick Van Dyke Show*, 93, 115; *The Gnome Mobile*, 50; Michaels on, 183n12; *The Pruitts of Southampton*, 93
DeCamp, Rosemary, 56, 69, 70, 71, 74, 85
Denver, Bob, 123, 129, 178n50
Desjardins, Mary, 46, 92, 172n43
de Villeneuve, Justin, 135, 152

Diamond, Selma, 97–98, 104
Dick Van Dyke Show, The: "Anthony Stone," 96–97; "Baby Fat," 100–101, 113; as backdrop of camp TV, 161; "Body and Sol," 184n23; "Br-ooom, Br-ooom," 99; employee disparagement in, 115; episode names, 102–3; "A Farewell to Writing," 178n50; "Fifty-Two, Forty-Five, or Work," 42; "Honeymoons Are for the Lucky," 101; Margie Mullen character, 96; marriage, dismissal of, 92–93; Moore's Laura, 96–97; "The Pen Is Mightier Than the Mouth" and "Dear Sally Rogers," 9, 10-*f*; Rose Marie's Sal, 9, 10-*f*, 42, 54, 97–100, 101–4, 168n31; "Sally and the Lab Technician," 102; "Talk to the Snail," 102; Whedon and, 127
Diff'rent Strokes, 188n71
Diller, Phyllis, 93, 148, 183n11
Dinah Shore Chevy Show, The, 41
Donahue, Elinor, 22, 106
Donna Reed Show, The, 127
Donovan, King, 56
Doris Day Show, The, 167n25, 185n26
Doty, Alexander, 19, 44, 172n38
Douglas, Donna, 111
Dozier, Bill, 104–5
drag: Berle and, 19–20; forms of, 13; made televisual, 49; sitcom characterization as camp drag, 8–13. *See also* specific shows and actors
dream sequence device, 123
Duff, Howard, 52–54
Duke, Patty, 167n26
Durante, Jimmy, 41–43, 49
Dylan, Bob, 131

Easton, Bob, 178n54
eccentricity: binary discourse and, 143; *The Bob Cummings Show*, 57–58, 84, 85; character actors and, 5–6; as classed and raced, 163–64; *Ed Wynn Show*, 48, 51; *The George Jessel Show*, 44; *Love on a Rooftop*, 126, 128; *The Many Loves of Dobie Gillis*, 129; *My Friend Irma*, 34; *Occasional Wife*, 122, 123–24; variety conventions and, 45

Ed Sullivan Show, The, 131, 167n19
Ed Wynn Show, 45–51
Ellerman, Al, 74–75
Ellis, Havelock, 63
Emerson, Faye, 176n24
Epstein, Brian, 139
Erdman, Richard, 100, 184n26
Ernie Kovacs Specials, 156, 157–58*f*, 194n3
ethnicity. *See* nonethnic-ethnic representation
Evans, Dale, 185n31
Everybody Loves Raymond, 170n9

Facts of Life, The, 188n71
Family Matters, 74
Farr, Jamie, 101
Father Knows Best, 22, 105–8, 186n43, 187n48
Federal Communications Commission (FCC), 38
Feinberg, Leslie, 19–20
"fellas," 52–53, 98, 102, 181n92
Felony Squad, 159
Ferguson, Roderick, 169n48
Feuer, Jane, 12, 22
Fibber McGee and Molly, 58
Field, Sally, 119–20, 140
Firestone, Eddie, 102, 186n34
Firestone, Renee, 89
Flicker, Theodore J., 13
Flintstones, 140
Flying Nun, The, 140, 151
Fonda, Paul, 56
Fordin, Hugh, 180n80
Franken, Steve, 129
Freed, Arthur, 77, 180n80
Fromm, Sam, 62

Gabor, Zsa Zsa, 53
Gale Storm Show, The, 65, 66–68*f*, 177n47, 182n8
Garry Moore Show, The, 116
Gay Caballero, The, 180n85
Gay Deceivers, The, 101
gay male type, white, 1, 61, 99–100, 115, 160
gender as site of camp production, 4–5
gender nonconformity: Halberstam on

characterization of, 118; insult vs. gender rebellion, 163; jokes about, as part of trans history, 2; Marc on, 106; partnering and, 109; *Password* and, 90; "shocking pink," 79; singleness and, 103, 125; sitcom irony, 6; white-centric gay stereotype and, 117–18. *See also* specific shows
genderqueer representation: *The Bob Cummings Show* and, 81; 1960s subcultures and, 136, 138; nonbinary, trans, and, 8, 15–16; *Occasional Wife* and, 120; *Password* and, 90; prevalence of, 1; as term, 3, 166n11; trans gender queer and, 3, 16; Twiggy and, 141; *The Ugliest Girl in Town* and, 134–35, 142, 148, 151; white fragility and, 97; Wynn and, 47–48
George Burns and Gracie Allen Show, The. See *Burns and Allen*
George Jessel Show, The, 43–44
Get Smart, 98
Ghostly, Alice, 183n11
Gibson, Henry, 102
Gidget, 138
Gilbert, Ruth, 30, 170n6
Gilligan's Island, 122–23, 178n50
Ginsberg, Allen, 132
Gleason, Jackie, 173n49
Glen or Glenda (Wood), 60
Gnome Mobile, The, 50
Gobel, George, 180n85
Goldbergs, The, 29
Golden Girls, The, 22
Gomer Pyle, U.S.M.C., 90
Good Times, 74, 175n10, 189n78
Gordon, Shirl, 69
Gorgeous George, 17
Gould, Jack, 192n35
Grant, Cary, 176n35
Great Gildersleeve, The, 127
Green, Jamison, 19–20
Green, Karen, 187n57
Green Acres, 58, 108–9, 123, 190n93
Green Hornet, 105
Grossman, Bud, 177n38
Grünwald, Grizelda E., 86
guest-star system, 5–8, 12, 39, 41, 78, 128–29
Gunsmoke, 123, 178n50

Guy, Bobby, 98
Gwynne, Fred, 113

Hail, Caesar, 110
Haines, Connie, 188n68
Halberstam, Jack, 3, 118, 137
Hale, Alan, 178n50
Handhardt, Christina, 195n11
Hardy, Patricia, 118
Harris, Jonathan, 109
Hathaways, The, 108
Hayes, Joy Elizabeth, 170n5
Hayes, Sean, 186n36
Hazel, 109–11, 161
Henning, Linda, 153–54
Henning, Paul, 58; *The Beverly Hillbillies*, 58, 73, 87, 90, 91; *The Bob Cummings Show*, 69, 70, 86
Henry, Buck, 98
Hepburn, Katherine, 77
He & She, 89, 115–17, 185n26
Hickman, Dwayne, 56, 69, 70–73, 76, 111, 129, 187n61
Hilmes, Michelle, 170n5
Hines, Hal, 91
Hirschfeld, Burt, 151, 194n72
Hogan, David, 113
Hollywood House, 188n68
Hollywood Squares, 8, 101, 185n32
homosexuality: censorship and, 39; Marc on *Father Knows Best* and, 107; subculture and, 61, 62; *The Ugliest Girl in Town* and, 136, 147; white gay male type, 1, 61, 99–100, 115, 160
Honeymoon Suite, 41
Hooker, Evelyn, 62
Hope, Bob, 79, 180n85
Horn, Hal, 69
Horn, Katrin, 166n11
Horton, Edward Everett, 100
House Un-American Activities Committee, 37
Howard, Moe, 112–13
Hudson, Rock, 62
Humphrey, Hal, 116, 166n10
Hunter, Tab, 187n61
Hyams, Jerry, 144

I Love Lucy, 116, 138, 162, 185n26
impersonation, 13, 41–44, 51, 163
Ingram, Billy, 190n5
In Name Only, 122
intertextuality: *The Bob Cummings Show*, 79; camp TV, intertextual landscape of, 58–62; camp TV archive and, 108; *The Dick Van Dyke Show*, 103, 168n31; *Ed Wynn Show*, 173n48; *Hazel*, 110–11; *He & She*, 116; names as ambigous intertextual references, 173n48; *The Patty Duke Show*, 167n26; Rose Marie's Liberace parody (*The George Jessel Show*) and, 44; sitcom production and, 23; *The Ugliest Girl in Town*, 136, 143, 148
Ironside, 159
Irvin, Richard, 177n45
I Spy, 195n5

Jack Benny Program, The, 162, 172n38, 195n7
Jacobs, Seaman, 50, 173n45
Jeffersons, The, 175n10
Jessel, George, 44
Jimmy Durante Show, The, 41–43
Joey Bishop Show, The, 113
Johnson, Arte, 195n7
Johnson, Russell, 178n50
Jones, Carolyn, 104
Joyrich, Lynne, 14, 146
Jurist, Ed, 177n38
Just off Broadway, 113

Kallen, Lucille, 97
"Kansas City Mo," 52–53
Kassel, Michael B., 186n43
Kastner, Peter, 133, 144, 145, 147–48
Kaufman, Robert, 138, 142–43, 145
Keating, Larry, 78
Kelly, Gail, 135
Ken Murray Show, The, 47
Kenyon, Sandy, 101, 185n29
Kleinschmitt, Carl, 184n23
Knight, Ted, 189n77
Korman, Marvin, 151, 152
Kovacs, Ernie, 85, 90, 104–5, 116, 159, 188n73, 195n7

Kuehl, Sheila, 117, 129, 189n80
Kulp, Nancy: *The Beverly Hillbillies*, 9, 72, 87, 90–91, 111–12, 115, 148, 149–50f, 178n54; *The Bob Cummings Show*, 56, 70, 71–73, 81, 85, 174n2; as character actor, 168n31; circumscribed by gender, 127; *The Gale Storm Show*, 65, 66–68f, 177n47, 182n8; on *Password*, 90–92

Landecker, Amy, 8
Landers, Hal, 69
Lansing, Joi, 56, 69, 74, 75–76
Laugh-In, 102
lavender scare, 18, 155–56
Lear, Norman, 175n10, 195n7
Leave It to Beaver, 93, 127
Lee, Bruce, 105
Leeds, Phil, 6, 183n11
Lemke-Santangelo, Gretchen, 145
Leonard, George B., 139–40
Levy, David, 76
Lewis, Jerry, 159, 169n50, 195n7
Lewis, Sylvia, 69
Liberace, 43–44, 171n35
Litel, John, 69
Little, Rich, 126, 128
Loretta Young Show, The, 195n6
Lost in Space, 109
Love on a Rooftop, 89, 125–30
Love That Bob. See Bob Cummings Show, The
Lowry, Cynthia, 141
Luckett, Moya, 104
Lucy-Desi Comedy Hour, The, 30
Ludden, Allen, 90–92, 182n5
Lupino, Ida, 52–54, 122
Lynde, Paul, 27–28, 100, 109, 111, 127, 188n62, 191n5

MacGibbon, Harriet E., 187n57
Many Loves of Dobie Gillis, The, 71, 73, 76, 123, 129, 174n7
Marc, David, 58, 72, 106–7
Margolin, Stuart, 122
Marks, Guy, 36, 102
marriage: *The Bob Cummings Show*, 82–83; "Bride's First Meal" genre, 120–21, 189n89;

Deacon's married characters, 93; *The Dick Van Dyke Show*, 96–98; dismissal of, 92–93; *He & She*, 115–17; Kulp on *Password* and, 90–92; *Love on a Rooftop*, 125–30; matchmaking tropes, 81, 178n54; *Occasional Wife*, 118–25; "Where Is Wife Once He Wed?" (Smith), 131–32. See also singleness and unmarried characters
Marsac, Maurice, 66–68f
Marshal, Gary, 134
Marshall, Garry, 184n23, 191n12
Martell, Donna, 85, 86
Martha Raye Show, The, 27–28
Martin, Mary, 19
Martin, Strother, 100, 185n26
Mary Poppins, 51
Mary Tyler Moore Show, The, 31, 96, 189n77
M*A*S*H, 101
Match Game, 185n32
Mayer, Louis B., 77, 180n80
Maynard, John, 64
McCarthy, Anna, 22
McCarthy, Joseph, 37
McLuhan, Marshall, 132, 139–40
McRaven, Dale, 184n23, 185n31
Medicine Man, 188n73
Mellencamp, Patricia, 37, 151
Mel Tormé, 8
Melvin, Allan, 184n23
Messick, Dale, 185n31
Messinger, Lillie, 76–77, 180n80
Meyerowitz, Joanne, 137
Meyler, Fintan, 107–8
Michaels, Scott, 183n12
Midler, Bette, 183n11
Mikolas, Joe, 157–58f
Miller, D. A., 175n21
Milton Berle Show, The, 182n5. See also *Buick-Berle Show*
Minow, Newton, 125
Mister Peepers, 44, 172n38
mod, 133, 141, 142–45, 147, 191n8
Mod Squad, The, 195n5
Monkees, The, 138, 162
Montgomery, Elizabeth, 140
Moore, Gary, 48, 51, 173n47
Moore, Lisa Jean, 166n11

Moore, Mary Tyler, 10–11f, 96–97
Morey Amsterdam Show, The, 45, 47
Morton, Maurice, 74, 75
Mothers-in-Law, The, 6, 93
Movie Maniacs, 49, 113
Mr. Adams and Eve, 52–54, 122, 174n55
Mr. Ed, 123, 161
Mrs. G Goes to College (The Gertrude Berg Show), 29
Mullally, Megan, 56
Mullen, Marjorie, 96
Muñoz, José Esteban, 61
Murphy, Michael, 139
Murray, Kathryn, 189n89
Murray, Susan, 35
Mustin, Burt, 94f, 183n13
My Fair Lady, 136
My Favorite Martian, 123, 161
My Friend Irma, 31–35
My Hero, 57, 69, 86, 87, 187n55
My Living Doll, 57, 152
My Sister Eileen, 113

Nabors, Jim, 90, 92, 109, 160, 182n4
Naked City, 116
National Association of Broadcasters, 38, 116
Nealon, Christopher, 63–64
New Bob Cummings Show, The, 57, 76
Newitz, Annalee, 61
Newmar, Julie, 57
Nicholas, Fayard, 187n55
Nicholas, Harold, 187n55
Nicolaides, John, 74
Noel, Chris, 120
nonethnic-ethnic representation: *The Bob Cummings Show*, 85; Chitlin' Circuit and Borscht Belt, 36, 183n11; Liberace parody (*The George Jessel Show*), 43–44; *My Friend Irma*, 34–35; as term, 170n9, 170n70; Three Stooges, 112–13; variety format and, 35–36; white "cultural forum" and, 39
"Notes on Camp" (Sontag), 60, 175n21

O'Byrne, Bryan, 140
Occasional Wife, 89, 118–25

O'Connor, Donald, 111
Odd Couple, The, 138, 191n5
O'Hara, Frank, 59–60
O.K. Crackerby, 29
Olzak, Kevin, 123
O'Reilly, Julie D., 18–19
Our Miss Brooks, 138, 162
Outer Limits, The, 195n6
Ovalle, Priscilla Peña, 99, 169n46

Paar, Jack, 71
Packer, Doris, 129, 190n99
Panama Hattie, 77
Parsons, Louella, 63–64
Partridge Family, The, 138
Password, 90–92
Patty Duke Show, The, 6–8, 7f, 167n26
Paul Lynde Show, 111, 188n62
Peck, Ed, 184n23
Pellegrini, Ann, 108
Perry Mason, 159
Pete and Gladys, 185n26
Peter Pan (Producers' Showcase), 19
Petticoat Junction, 58
Phil Silvers Show, The, 37
Pinza, Ezio, 169n50
Pitts, ZaSu, 66–68f, 177n47
Popkin, Jack, 189n80
Porter, Cole, 61
Prentiss, Paula, 89, 115
Presley, Elvis, 178n50
Prickett, Maudie, 94f
Prosser, Jay, 137
Pruitts of Southampton, The, 93

queer gender: as already there in television, 3; coercive assignment and, 169n48; as corollary of closet epistemology, 90, 182n4; guest-star system and, 5–8; industry production and, 160; as mode of erotic difference, 63; movement across, 15; 1960s network economics and, 105; trans agency and, 137. *See also* genderqueer representation; *and specific sitcoms and actors*
queer semiotics and self presentation, 60–62
quiz show scandals (1958), 24, 37–38

racism and racialization: blackface performance, 2, 36, 168n44; *The Bob Cummings Show*, 85; camp production and, 14–15; civil rights and white privilege, 160; Dinah Shore and, 169n46; eccentricity and, 164; economics, censorship, and, 36–40; Jewish representation, 29–36; "(white) Man/(black) animal binary," 70; *The Many Loves of Dobie Gillis*, 129; "TV's Snow White Land," 114; white gay male type, 1, 61, 99–100, 115, 160; whitening of schedules, 35, 37; "working women" classification and, 110. *See also* nonethnic-ethnic representation; whiteness and whitening
Rae, Charlotte, 27–28, 114, 188n71
Rafkin, Alan, 117, 189n80
Randall, Tony, 99, 191n5
Rango, 36
Raye, Martha, 27–28, 169n50
Real McCoys, The, 50, 195n6
Red Channels, 21, 52
Reed, Christopher, 109
Reed, Robert, 195n5
Reeves, Richard, 94f
Reid-Pharr, Robert F., 70
Reilly, Charles Nelson, 17, 191n5
Reiner, Carl, 97–98, 100–101
Ritter, John, 99
Rivers, Joan, 183n11
Robbins, Gale, 188n68
Rodney, Eugene B., 106
Romero, Caesar, 180n85
Rose Marie: *The Bob Cummings Show*, 56; as character actor, 9, 168n31; *The Dick Van Dyke Show*, 9, 10f, 42, 54, 97–100, 101–4, 168n31; *The Dinah Shore Chevy Show*, 41; *Honeymoon Suite*, 41; *The Jimmy Durante Show*, 41–43; *Just off Broadway* pilot, 113; Liberace parody (*The George Jessel Show*), 43–44, 90; marriage to Bobby Guy, 98; Mary Elliot Cummings and, 87; *My Sister Eileen*, 113; *Occasional Wife*, 89; unmarried characters of, 41
Rosenthal, Phil, 170n9, 170n70
Ross, Andrew, 18

218   Index

Ross, Joe E., 113
Roxon, Lillian, 141
Rubin, Eddie, 69
RuPaul's Drag Race, 185n32
Russell, Nipsey, 114
Ruthie on the Telephone, 170n6
Ryan, Irene, 149f
Ryfle, Steve, 159

Saks, Sol, 174n55
Saltzman, Joe, 191n5
Sargent, Dick, 93
Scheib, Ronnie, 191n12
Schneider, Deborah, 98
Scorpio Rising, 99
Scott, Randolph, 176n35
Scotti, Vito, 195n5
"script girls," 30, 194n3
Scully, Vin, 119
Sedgwick, Eve, 19, 20, 146
Seinfield, 189n78
Seldes, Gilbert, 12, 14
self-reflexive production: advertising and, 22, 28; *Buick-Berle Show*, 30; camp TV archive and, 108; *Car 54*, 114; *The Dick Van Dyke Show*, 92–93, 100; *Ed Wynn Show*, 46–47; *Hazel*, 111; *Jessel Show*, 44; *The Mothers-in-Law*, 6; *Occasional Wife*, 121
Serano, Julia, 137
Shandley, Robert, 49
Sharpe, Don, 86
Shillinglaw, Ann, 193n35
Shore, Dinah, 41, 169n46
Silvers, Phil, 35
Simon, Neil, 97–98
Singer, Ray, 13
singleness and unmarried characters: *The Beverly Hillbillies*, 111; marriage investment assumption, 103; *Occasional Wife*, 118–25; Rose Marie's characters, 41; Rose Marie's Sal and, 97–100, 101–4. *See also* marriage
sitcom auteurs, notion of, 58, 175n10
sitcoms: characterization as camp drag, 8–13; charged content of, 22, 35, 188n65; commercialized sphere of, 22; historicizing as queer and trans, 14–17; as industrial production, 12; as new product, 37; shift from live variety to prerecorded comedy series, 40–41. *See also* specific shows and persons
Slade, Bernard, 138
slapstick, 111
Smith, Jack, 131–32
Smith, Judith, 114
Some Like It Hot, 123
Sontag, Susan, 60, 175n21
"speaking back," 46, 172n43
Spigel, Lynn, 38
Spigelgass, Leonard, 61
Spinetti, Victor, 193n35
"spinster" category, 4, 103, 109, 162
Stang, Arnold, 30
Starger, Martin, 144
Starr, Eve, 58, 160
Starr, Michael Seth, 159
Steve Allen Show, The, 178n50, 180n85
Stone, Sandy, 137
Storm, Gale, 66–68f, 177n47
Straayer, Chris, 4, 146
Stryker, Susan, 166n11
Styne, Margaret, 157–58f
Sutton, Frank, 90, 92
Swanson, Gloria, 172n43
Sylvester, Harold, 96

Tab Hunter Show, The, 185n26
Tanin, Eleanore, 81–82
Tea and Sympathy (Anderson), 77
Tebet, David, 76
Tenny, Margie, 69
Texaco Star Theater, 20, 30
That Girl, 126, 134, 138
The Phyllis Diller Show, 93
"There's No Business Like Show Business" (Berlin), 41
Thomas, Danny, 49, 50
Thompson, Hunter S., 139
Three's Company, 99
Three Stooges, 48, 49, 112–13
Till Death Us Do Part, 175n10
Tinkcom, Matthew, 12, 61

Tokar, Norman, 177n38
Tolkin, Mel, 97–98
Too Close for Comfort, 99, 189n77
trans: gender nonconformity jokes and, 2; genderqueer as, 15–16; intertextual landscape and, 60; minoritizing of trans identity, 163; trans agency, 137
trans gender queer: anachronistic framing of, 162; concept of, 3–4, 166n11; movement across queer gender and, 15
Transparent, 8
transphobia, 16, 20, 28, 142, 144, 164
Tuttle, Mark, 90
"12 Angry Men," 174n5
Twiggy, 132, 135–36, 138–39, 141, 152, 191n15, 192n19, 192n35

Ugliest Girl in Town, The: about, 132–33; mod vs. hippie wardrobe and, 142–45; trans camp, 152–54; trans history and development of, 133–40; trans-testing the television market, 140–45; trans textuality, 145–52
"unattractive" characters, 56, 73, 92, 107, 133, 135. See also *Ugliest Girl in Town, The*

Valerio, Max Wolf, 166n14
Vander Pyl, Jean, 187n57
Van Doren, Mamie, 62, 78
Van Dyke, Dick, 10–11*f*, 97, 100. See also *Dick Van Dyke Show, The*
Van Horne, Harriet, 70–71, 84
Vast Wasteland rhetoric, 125, 175n15
Vaudeville, 35–36, 168n44
Villarejo, Amy, 166n6
von Zell, Harry, 166n6

Walker, Jimmie, 74, 189n78
Walker, Nancy, 31, 32–33*f*
Walston, Ray, 161, 189n80

Warhol, Andy, 156, 159
Warhol, Robyn, 166n12
Warner, Michael, 18, 65
Webb, Clifton, 167n19
Weinrib, Lennie, 96
Wesson, Dick, 56, 188n68
West, Mae, 139
West, Paul, 106
western spoofs, 69, 178n50
"What TV Is Doing to the Movie Industry" (*US News and World Report*), 59
Whedon, John, 126–27
Where's Raymond?, 58, 113, 185n26
White, Betty, 92, 93, 95*f*, 185n31
White, Jaleel, 74
White, Mimi, 12
White, Patricia, 186n38
white fragility, 59, 96–97
white gay male type, 1, 61, 99–100, 115, 160
whiteness and whitening, 35, 37, 111, 169n46
Wilchins, Riki, 163
Wilde, Oscar, 63
Will & Grace, 56, 186n36
Williams, Bill, 94*f*
Williams, Raymond, 12
Williams, Van, 105
Wilson, Marie, 31–35
Winchell, Paul, 102, 185n33
Wojcik, Pamela Robertson, 115, 139
Wood, Audrey, 76
Wood, Ed, 60
wordplay: beat slang, 190n98; *The Bill Dana Show* and, 13; "fellas," 52–53, 98, 102, 181n92; Kansas City Mo character, 52–54; *Password*, 92; "sick," 188n65; "where you has been," 46, 172n42
Wylie, Philip, 171n28
Wynn, Ed, 45–51

York, Dick, 93, 160

www.ingramcontent.com/pod-product-compliance
Lightning Source LLC
Chambersburg PA
CBHW071818230426
43670CB00013B/2489